How Nations See Each Other

A
study
in
public
opinion

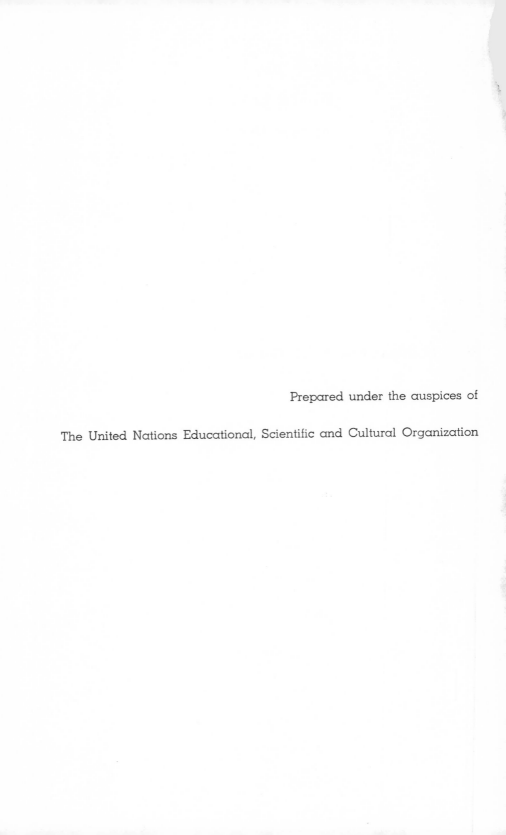

Prepared under the auspices of

The United Nations Educational, Scientific and Cultural Organization

William Buchanan and Hadley Cantril

with the assistance of

Virginia Van S. Zerega, Henry Durant, James R. White

HOW NATIONS SEE EACH OTHER

a study in public opinion

GREENWOOD PRESS, PUBLISHERS
WESTPORT, CONNECTICUT

The Library of Congress has catalogued this publication as follows:

Library of Congress Cataloging in Publication Data

Buchanan, William, 1918–
    How nations see each other.

        Prepared under the auspices of the United Nations
    Educational, Scientific and Cultural Organization.
        Reprint of the 1953 ed.
        Includes bibliographical references.
        1. Public opinion. 2. Public opinion polls.
    3. International relations. I. Cantril, Hadley,
    1906–1969, joint author. II. United Nations Edu-
    cational, Scientific and Cultural Organization.
    III. Title.
    [HM261.B8 1972]   301.15'4   70–138210
    ISBN 0–8371–5565–7

Originally published in 1953
by University of Illinois Press, Urbana

This reprint has been authorized by Unesco

First Greenwood Reprinting 1972

Library of Congress Catalogue Card Number 70-138210

ISBN 0-8371-5565-7

Printed in the United States of America

Foreword

It has now been nearly six years since the Unesco General Assembly, meeting in Mexico City, 1947, authorized a study of "Tensions Affecting International Understanding." As the first director of the Tensions Project, it was my assignment to translate the series of resolutions which constituted the project into an action program which might help bring some of the knowledge and techniques of social scientists to bear on an understanding of problems with which men and women everywhere are concerned. When I arrived in the Paris headquarters of Unesco on March 4, 1948, a huge desk in a mirrored room was supplied with a copy of the Unesco resolutions, sharpened pencils, and some pads of paper.

With the encouragement of Julian Huxley and Walter Laves, then Director-General and Deputy Director-General, respectively, a start was made, active help being given by Arvid Brodersen, Otto Klineberg, P. W. Martin, and others who were my colleagues in the Social Science Department. Recalling these days, I find it gratifying to see a number of the projects initiated then coming to a head now in published form.

Among the resolutions which constituted the original Tensions Project was one that read: "Inquiries into the conceptions which the people of one nation entertain of their own and of other nations." Among several other studies that were initiated to carry out this resolution, we felt that surveys in different countries, utilizing modern sampling techniques and asking the same questions of people in different nations at approximately the same time, might be revealing. Accordingly a modest sum was set aside for this undertaking, and plans were drawn up to get it under way.

These plans were then discussed at some length with Alfred Max, Jean Stoetzel, and Helene Riffault of the Institut Français d'Opinion Publique and with Dr. Henry Durant of the British Institute of Public Opinion. Our major problem was, of course, to decide what might prove to be the most significant problems for inquiry and then to decide, with due regard for geographical spread, on the countries in which the studies might be conducted, and the organizations that could cooperate with us.

A list of countries in which polls were taken, together with the organization making the surveys, their directors, the dates during which the survey was made, and the size of the sample of people interviewed follows:

AUSTRALIA: Australian Public Opinion Polls, Roy Morgan, July, 1948, sample—945.

BRITAIN: British Institute of Public Opinion, Henry Durant, July, 1948, sample—1,195.

FRANCE: Institut Français d'Opinion Publique, Alfred Max and Jean Stoetzel, June, 1948, sample—1,000.

GERMANY: Public Opinion Research Office, Political Division, British Military Government, James R. White, August, 1948, sample —Berlin, 644; sample—British Zone of Occupation, 3,371. The survey was repeated in Berlin in October, 1949, sample—430.

ITALY: DOXA (Istituto per le Ricerche Statistiche e l'Analisi dell' Opinione Pubblica), P. Luzzatto-Fegiz, July, 1948, sample—1,078.

THE NETHERLANDS: Nederlands Instituut voor de Publieke Opinie, Jan Stapel and W. de Jonge, July, 1948, sample—942.

NORWAY: Norsk Gallup Institutt A/S, Bj. Balstad, August, 1948, sample —1,030.

MEXICO: International Public Opinion Research, Inc., Elmo C. Wilson, December, 1948–January, 1949, sample—1,125. (Interviews only in cities of 10,000 or more population.)

UNITED STATES OF AMERICA: Benson & Benson, Inc., Lawrence E. Benson, September–October, 1948, sample—1,015.

Thus the "Germans" sampled—and referred to as such in the text—are the population of the British Zone of Occupation, while the Mexicans are an entirely urban sample. Further information on sampling and interviewing methods are given in Appendices C and D.

It should be noted here that for one reason or another, other organizations invited to participate were unable to join in the undertaking. These were: Professor G. Jacquemyns of the Institut Universitaire d'Information Sociale et Économique (INSOC) of Brussels; Mr. Wallace Johnson of the American

Institute of Chinese Public Opinion; Mr. Elmo Wilson of International Public Opinion Research, for some major South American country; and the National Opinion Research Center which was initially approached to do the survey in the United States. We also unofficially approached persons in contact with a Hungarian survey organization and the Czech Institute of Public Opinion, which were operating at that time; but we did not find it possible to arrange for surveys in either of those countries. After preliminary field tests and several revisions of the questionnaire, the form of the questionnaire used in this study was sent to all cooperating organizations together with a set of instructions for tabulations and translation. The sample was set at 1,000 for each country.

All results were returned to Paris headquarters of Unesco, and a preliminary analysis of the results was made by Dr. Durant. Because of the pressure of other duties, Dr. Durant was unable to complete the final synthesis and report, and arrangements were made with the Office of Public Opinion Research at Princeton University for Mr. William Buchanan to complete the analysis, interpret the findings, and write the report. While Mr. Buchanan's report can speak for itself, I should like to add a note of gratitude to him and to Miss Virginia Zerega, as well as to Dr. Durant, for the patience and skill with which they have gone over a really tremendous mass of data and have brought together the results of the first international survey made under the auspices of an arm of the United Nations. Acknowledgment is also due Dr. F. P. Kilpatrick, Elizabeth Deyo, and Esther Alford for their most helpful editorial suggestions. It is to be hoped that the survey tool, which becomes more refined each year, may be put to frequent use in the service of international understanding.

Articles in learned journals have discussed the various difficulties encountered in international surveys.[1] Many of the problems pointed to in these articles were largely overcome because of the competence and reliability of the organizations that collaborated with us in this undertaking.

In addition to the semantic problem involved when one is trying to convey the same meaning in different languages, a major problem in international surveying is that of drawing valid comparisons and accurate explanations of the various and varying results, while bearing in mind how the backgrounds of the people in different countries differ from each other. The difficulty is, of course, not a new one for those who deal with surveys. But the difficulty is present to a greater degree when surveys are on an international scale. There is no easy solution to the problem, which involves chiefly an exchange of knowledge of the backgrounds and opinion contexts to be found in different areas of the world. Increased experience in inter-

[1] See p. 105.

national surveys and, wherever possible, some face-to-face communion with those responsible for the surveys should in time increase the accuracy with which we can interpret results.

One final comment: when this survey was planned, we were quite conscious of the possible dangers of publishing results which indicated what people in one nation thought of people in another nation. We recalled that people often do not like to see themselves as others see them. But obviously the findings of research must be made available to all who can utilize them to increase our understanding of each other, even at the risk that some might misuse them and try to exacerbate existing prejudices.

Hadley Cantril

Princeton University

Contents

—— **Chapter** 1

Maps in Our Heads

Walter Lippmann gave currency to the word "stereotypes," defining it thirty years ago as "pictures in our heads." The general semanticists lean heavily on the analogy of words to "maps," which represent reality but are not themselves "reality." In somewhat the same sense, the Unesco survey was an endeavor to bring out into the open for examination the "pictures" of foreign peoples and the "maps of the world" in the heads of the citizens of nine nations.

Hayakawa says:

There is a sense in which we all live in two worlds. First, we live in the world of the happenings about us which we know at first hand. But this is an extremely small world, consisting only of that continuum of the things that we have actually seen, felt or heard—the flow of events constantly passing before our senses. As far as this world of personal experience is concerned, Africa, South America, Asia, Washington, New York, or Los Angeles do not exist if we have never been to these places. . . .

Most of our knowledge, acquired from parents, friends, schools, newspapers, books, conversations, speeches, and radio is received *verbally*. . . . These reports are not given us by people who saw it happen, but are based on other reports: reports of reports of reports. . . .

Let us call this world that comes to us through words the *verbal world*, as opposed to the world we know or are capable of knowing through our own experience, which we shall call the *extensional world*.

Now this verbal world ought to stand in relation to the extensional world as a *map* does to the *territory* it is supposed to represent. If the child grows to adulthood with a verbal world in his head which corresponds fairly closely to the extensional world that he finds around him in his widening experience, he is in relatively small danger of being shocked or hurt by what he finds, because his verbal world has told him what, more or less, to expect. He is prepared for life.

1

If, however, he grows up with a false map in his head—that is, with a head crammed with false knowledge and superstition—he will constantly be running into trouble, wasting his efforts, and acting like a fool. He will not be adjusted to the world as it is; he may, if the lack of adjustment is serious, end up in an insane asylum.[1]

Stuart Chase elaborates this statement somewhat:

General semantics uses the analogy of a map in three basic premises:

1. A map is not a territory. Words are not the things they represent.

2. A map does not represent all of a territory. Words cannot say *all* there is to be known about anything.

3. A map is self-reflexive. An ideal map of its own territory would include a map of a map of a map. We can speak words about words, etc.

Inside each of us lies a picture of the world. It stands for the whole realm of material objects, happenings, relationships, out there. Into our picture has gone everything we know, or think we know. It is our *map* of reality, without which we could not find our way through life at all. We are well adjusted in proportion to its correctness and in proportion as we remember its limitations.[2]

Without diverging too far into a discussion of what constitutes "reality," it should be pointed out that Hayakawa's implication that what we see and hear and touch is "real" and what we perceive second hand is not, has been modified by psychologists and others experimenting with illusory effects. One example is the so-called "distorted room," so constructed that the walls are not where they appear to be. The viewer is frustrated when he attempts to touch the walls because he brings to his perception the assumption, based on his experience with other rooms, that *all rooms are rectangular*. Only by acting, i.e., moving about in the room, or watching someone else act in it, is he able to correct his impression. Our perceptions of things close at hand are also "maps," subject to distortion by other-than-verbal misapprehensions but better "maps" because they are based on personal experience and have generally proved effective in use. This has involved bringing into account another important factor that shapes these "maps"—the *purposes* for which they are used. These "maps" vary with the individual purposes of each person, as well as with his own unique experience.[3]

It is not possible to draw the individual "map" of the world which every man carries around in his head and to which he refers when he has to pass judgment on the possibility of, say, peace or the nature of "Russian na-

[1] S. I. Hayakawa, *Language in Action* (New York: Harcourt, Brace & Co., 1939), pp. 21-24.

[2] Stuart Chase, *The Proper Study of Mankind* (New York: Harper and Bros., 1948), p. 252.

[3] F. P. Kilpatrick, *Human Behavior from the Transactional Point of View* (Hanover, N. H.: Institute for Associated Research, 1952), Pt. I, Ch. 3.

tional character." Each of these "maps" is somewhat different because of different experiences, exposure to different cultures, and different purposes. On the other hand, the "maps" are similar because certain peoples have had similar experiences, have read the same newspapers, and have the same purposes.

The Unesco survey attempts to discover the similarities and differences in these "maps" that go with similarities and differences of nationality, of culture, of class, and of income. By asking questions and treating the results statistically, one can achieve a sort of composite "map" for a nation or a class—one whose differences from that of another nation or class will, it is hoped, reveal a little of why these people act as they do. Perhaps two nations collide with each other in war because they are following different "maps," both of which show clear channels ahead.

Maps on Paper

These "maps" of the semanticists are figurative in that they exist "in our heads." In the field of international affairs, maps which exist on paper may have caused almost as much trouble. Each of them is at fault in some respect because it attempts the impossible task of representing a three-dimensional world on a two-dimensional piece of paper. The Mercator projection of the world with its center at 0°—the longitude of Greenwich, England—is the principal offender; but only because it has been the most frequently used. It is most accurate along the Equator; thus the sea route between New York and London lies in a rather distorted area. "The earlier perplexities of Anglo-American relations," the underestimation of cross-polar distances between northern countries, and certain distorted notions of power relations have been blamed on the inappropriate use of a map designed for nineteenth-century British ship masters to "indicate political relationships of the states of the world" in the twentieth century. "American complacency" has been attributed to the traditional map of the "Western Hemisphere," which has its center and most of its periphery in mid-ocean and "embraces almost the maximum area of ocean," whereas a hemisphere centered in the middle of the United States would contain all of Europe and parts of Africa, Turkey, Russia, Manchuria, and Japan.[4]

Thus we must use different maps for different purposes. For this reason, a good atlas will have a variety of maps—one showing natural barriers, one rainfall and temperature, one natural resources, and one showing political

[4] From "Maps, Strategy and World Politics," by R. E. Harrison and R. Strausz-Hupé; "The Geography of the Peace," by N. J. Spykman; and "This Hemisphere," by S. W. Boggs; reprinted in *Foundations of National Power*, H. and M. Sprout, editors (Princeton, N. J.: Princeton University Press, 1945).

divisions. Another variety is the demographic map with the area of each political division proportionate to its population. This helps us to take into account the relative political importance of sheer manpower, expressed as votes in an area with representative government or as military potential in the world as a whole.

All of these maps are "in proportion" in one sense. All of them are "out of proportion" in another. This depends on the purpose for which they will be used. No one can say that another's map is "wrong" or "does not conform to reality" merely because it does not agree with his own.

In the charts and graphs used for illustrative matter here and in the descriptive passages in the text, an attempt will be made to construct an "atlas and gazeteer" of part of the world. The distances between peoples will be more akin to the "social distance" of the sociologist than the actual distance of the geographer. The boundaries on these "maps" will include the "boundaries" between economic and status groups as well as national groups. Among the "natural resources" to be listed will be the national level of "security" and "satisfaction." These nations will be peopled with "stereotypes" that exist only in the minds of the beholder.

These "maps" of the ideas of groups, it may be recalled, are no more "inaccurate" than the flat Mercator map of a round globe. They are simply used for a different purpose. Moreover, in Stuart Chase's words, they do not "represent all of the territory" but only certain aspects that may be discovered by the questionnaire technique. And, since they are composite "maps" of individual "maps" in the heads of individual people, they are in a sense "self-reflexive." They are important because they are the "maps" that are used to guide people in their relationships to other people at home and across borders.

Subject Matter of the Survey

Implementing the Unesco directive,[5] a questionnaire was designed which would elicit statements that (1) describe how respondents in one country

---

[5] "5.1.1. The Director-General is instructed to promote enquiries into:
   i. the distinctive character of the various national cultures, ideals, and legal systems;
   ii. the ideas which the people of one nation hold concerning their own and other nations;
   iii. modern methods developed in education, political science, philosophy and psychology for changing mental attitudes, and into the social and political circumstances that favour the employment of particular techniques;
   iv. the influences which make for international understanding or for aggressive nationalism."
The wording of the Tensions Project directive is taken from Otto Klineberg's *Tensions Affecting International Understanding*, Social Science Research Council Bulletin 62 (New York, 1950), p. 1, which discusses the various Tensions Projects and relates them to a large body of research in allied fields.

react to people in another, and (2) reveal causative factors behind their reaction, so far as this tool of research permits.

Out of the thousands of pertinent questions that might have been asked, fourteen [6] were selected to probe the five general areas of opinion considered most important and, at the same time, most amenable to the interviewing process.

These areas are:

1. The individual's estimate of his own position in the class structure of his country, and its relation to his view of other people at home and abroad (Q.9–10).

2. His feeling of personal security in matters unrelated to international affairs, and his satisfaction with life in his own country (Q.5–8).

3. The peoples toward whom he feels friendly or unfriendly (Q.11–12).

4. The stereotypes he carries in his head of his own and certain foreign peoples (Q.13).

5. His ideas about human nature, peace, world government, and national character (Q.1–4).

It will be noted that these questions (1–13) include enough material on his opinions about his own countrymen to provide a standard of comparison. Q.14 was used to get at the political views of the respondent. The interviewer also noted the respondent's sex, estimated his socio-economic status, and asked his age, education, and occupation. These background factors were later utilized in tabulating the answers.

The Questionnaire

The questions were rearranged on the ballot in the order that would facilitate interviewing, so that early questions would not "give away" later ones or otherwise prejudice the answers the respondent might make. The English-language, master version of the questionnaire, which was sent to the survey agencies, is given below.[7]

Q.1a: *Do you believe that human nature can be changed?*
                Can   Cannot   Don't know

Q.1b: If can: *Do you think that this is likely to happen?*
                Likely   Unlikely   Don't know

---

[6] Actually 21, if "a," "b," and "c" divisions of some questions are counted separately.

[7] Copies of the questionnaires used in each country, showing translations into the six languages other than English, are given in Appendix D, along with pertinent data about sampling, survey agency comments, and the percentaged results for each individual country.

Q.2: *Do you think that our* (British) *characteristics are mainly born in us, or are they due to the way we are brought up?*

Born in us   Way brought up   Don't know

Q.3a: *Do you believe that it will be possible for all countries to live together at peace with each other?*

Possible   Not possible   Don't know

Q.3b: *Do you think that this is likely to happen?*

Likely   Unlikely   Don't know

Q.4: *Some people say that there should be a world government able to control the laws made by each country. Do you agree or disagree?*

Agree   Disagree   Don't know

Q.5: *When the war ended, did you expect you would be getting along better, worse, or about the same as you actually are getting along at the present time?*

Better   Worse   About the same   Don't know

Q.6a: *Do you feel that from the point of view of your (husband's) job you are more secure, or less secure, than the average* (Britisher)?

More   Less   About the same   Don't know

Q.6b: *In general do you feel that you are sufficiently secure to be able to plan ahead?*

Yes   No   Don't know

Q.7: *How satisfied are you with the way you are getting on now?*

Very   All right   Dissatisfied   Don't know

Q.8: *Which country in the world gives the best chance of leading the kind of life you would like to lead?*_____

(NOTE TO INTERVIEWER: This question includes respondent's own country if he asks the question.)

Q.9: *If you were asked to use a name for your social class, would you say you belonged in the middle class, working class, or upper class?*

Middle   Working   Upper   Don't know

Q.10a: *Do feel that you have anything in common with* (own) *class people abroad?*

Yes   No   Don't know

Q.10b: *Do you feel that you have anything in common with* (British) *people who are not* (own) *class?*

Yes   No   Don't know

Q.10c: (Ask only if Yes on both or No on both a and b.) *Which of these two would you say that you have more in common with?*

Abroad   British   Don't know

Q.11: *Which foreign people do you feel most friendly toward?*_____

Q.12: *Which foreign people do you feel least friendly toward?*_____

Q.13a: *From the list of words on this card, which seem to you to describe the American people best? Select as many as you wish and call off the letters and the words that go with them. If you have no particular feelings one way or the other, just say so.*

1. HARDWORKING
2. INTELLIGENT
3. PRACTICAL
4. CONCEITED
5. GENEROUS
6. CRUEL

7. BACKWARD
8. BRAVE
9. SELF-CONTROLLED
10. DOMINEERING
11. PROGRESSIVE
12. PEACE-LOVING

13. IMPOSSIBLE TO CHARACTERIZE

Q.13b: *Now go over the list again and select the words you think best describe the Russian people.*

Q.13c: *Now select the words that best describe* (own countrymen).

Q.14: *Do you think our present government is too much to the right, too much to the left, or about where you would like it to be?*

Too right   Too left   All right   Don't know

Plan of Analysis

All the percentages giving the various responses to the fourteen questions in the survey, when cross-tabulated by the various classifications of respondents, give a table for each country with something over 2,000 cells in it. These percentages for a single country may be compared to each other, a process that is the customary basis for analysis of a national survey. In addition, any percentage for one country may be compared to the equivalent figure for any or all of the other eight countries, a total of some 16,000 possible comparisons.

Two complementary systems of analysis are employed to reduce this mass of data, not all of which is equally valuable, to workable dimensions:

1. Percentages on a single question or group of questions in all nine nations are juxtaposed, and *similarities* between all or most of the nations examined.

2. Each national survey is treated as a unit, and examined in the light of what was known about that country, with *differences* and possible explanations of these differences receiving major attention.

Each of the five areas of opinion is treated as a unit. The information which the survey elicited on the class structure of the various countries, as seen from the individual's viewpoint, is summarized in Chapter 2, and the relative strength of class and national identification appraised. In Chapter 3 personal security—that is, the extent to which respondents are confident of holding their jobs or are satisfied in their expectations and feel able to plan ahead—is summarized for each country as a whole as an index to the tensions in that country. Then, in Chapter 4, the selections of the foreign people that each national group feels most and least friendly toward are analyzed in an attempt to discover what the common characteristics of these "liked" and "disliked" peoples are. Some of the "pictures in our heads" of certain foreigners, and the relation of these stereotypes to friendliness, are examined in Chapter 5 through the use of the "word-list" technique and are compared with earlier studies using this technique. The prevalence of confidence in world peace and approval of world government, and the relation of these ideas to views on human nature and to background factors, are explored in Chapter 6.

Chapter 7 is a country-by-country treatment of the highlights of each separate survey, considering the opinions in the country as a unit, and examining trends peculiar to that country. Chapter 8 is a report on an experiment in Western Berlin, where the Unesco questionnaire was repeated under the direction of Dr. James White some fourteen months after the original survey, in order to gauge its effectiveness as a measure of changing conditions.

All the findings are drawn together and summarized in Chapter 9, with some suggestions as to how these findings may be acted upon by those who are interested in international amity. Methodological matter and raw data are to be found in Appendices A-D.

Techniques of Analysis

The procedures used for examining the results of surveys in these nine countries are really combinations of the usual techniques utilized in national surveys. Since the surveys are generally treated separately, which makes the results sound more complex than they actually are, it may be helpful to summarize the procedures as they would apply to a hypothetical question: Do you believe in transmutationism?

1. The percentage saying "Yes" may be compared to the percentage saying "No" in a single country: "In France there are more believers (70%) than non-believers (30%)."

2. One national result may be compared to another: "In England there are fewer believers (60%) than in France (70%)." Thus all nine countries may be ranked in the order of the percentage of believers.

3. Within one country an opinion may be found to be related to some other variable: "In France belief is related to wealth (75% of wealthy say 'Yes,' but only 65% of poor)."

4. This may be done for all nine countries, according to some standard —usually the "significant" difference (see p. 111): "In five countries believers were 'significantly' likely to be wealthy, in three there was no 'significant' relationship, and in one they were 'significantly' likely to be poor." The calculations behind these generalizations are not always given in the text, since complete tables are available in Appendix D.

5. An index may be constructed from answers to one or more questions, and countries then ranked by indices. Two such indices may be compared with each other, or an index may be compared with an independent set of national statistics, such as population.

6. Percentages, indices, or differences for the nine countries may be added or averaged, but this is avoided where possible, since it serves to obscure national variations from the pattern.

Qualifications

Detailed examination of the perplexing methodological matters that confront international opinion surveyors is impossible, but a brief treatment of them is inevitable. The statisticians, to whom we are indebted for the tools we use, insist that the reader be informed of drawbacks, both measurable and implicit, in the data, so he may make proper reservations about the conclusions drawn.

It should be pointed out first that, while this investigation sheds light on cross-national thought patterns, the interpretations cannot be proved conclusively. There are biases in the data, the extent of which is often unknown and unknowable. The reader must bear this fact in mind while he reviews the comparisons which have been made among results from different countries.

A discussion of the problems of methodology, unique to international surveying, will be found in Appendix A. The reader who is more interested in substantive results than in technique may wish to ignore these complications. At the same time, he may, remembering the 1948 pre-election polls in the United States, feel uncertain about how much credence he may place in any of these findings.

The cautious reader may place himself on safe ground, statistically and semantically by

1. Recalling that the terms "significant" and "consistent" are used in a special sense here, as explained on page 112.

2. Considering any derivation of data in the text, such as: "The wealthier group was more likely than the poorer one to expect peace," as a sort of shorthand abbreviation for an expanded statement that would run about as follows:

Among those respondents whom interviewers in a particular country considered "above average" or "well-to-do" by the standards of that country, there was a higher percentage which responded "Yes" to the question "Do you believe it will be possible for all countries to live together at peace with each other?" as translated into their native language by the personnel of the agency conducting the survey after consulting both French and English texts of the original questionnaire, than among those whom the interviewers classified, also according to their own fallible judgment, and with what motives we may never know, as "below average" or "very poor," but this is no guarantee that all the respondents understood the question completely, that all interpreted it in the same way, that "peace," "possible," "countries," "together," and certain other words mean precisely the same in all seven languages, and that the grammatical processes necessary to joining these concepts in an interrogatory fashion did not produce further distortion, that the respondents were answering truthfully, that the interviewer did not misunderstand them, or err in recording the responses in a number of possible ways, that some of the respondents he classified as "poor" might not have been otherwise classified in another country or by another interviewer in that country, or that another group of "poor" respondents selected by different sampling methods would not have responded in different proportions.

The cautious reader may be further assured that wherever reasonable grounds exist for believing that some finding may be accounted for by the translation difficulty, it will be specifically called to his attention in the text. If he should wonder why anyone would use a lens so cloudy and refractory to examine relations between people, he will find comfort in the following observations:

1. Despite these biases, national surveys in many countries have consistently managed to predict the total vote of candidates for election within reasonable margins of error—less than 5%.[8] They have provided, and con-

---

[8] The average error of Gallup affiliates in eleven countries in 500-odd national and local elections is within four percentage points.

tinue to provide, information of sufficient accuracy for businessmen and government agencies to continue to support their activities. These tests are unrelated to opinions about other nations; but there is no reliable evidence that surveys are either more, or less, accurate in this realm.

2. For any particular use to which it is put, a tool must be evaluated not against an absolute standard of efficiency but against the efficiency of alternative tools that are available. If one postulates, as Unesco does, that "wars begin in the minds of men" and seeks to explore the content of these minds, he must make some provisions for quantitative as well as qualitative analysis. No other technique reaches down through all strata in a nation to disclose in terms that may be aggregated, even imprecisely, the nature and extent of the impact of the real and fancied characteristics of other peoples on the daily lives and purposes of the mass of the population. These are the people who, though they may exert little *active* pressure on the foreign policy of a country, do set very real *limits* beyond which the policy maker dares not tread.

The Scope of the Survey

This is a pilot study. It does not attempt to develop a theory or demonstrate a hypothesis; it is, rather, descriptive and suggestive. It maps out in broad outlines a few of the attitudes which underlie reactions between peoples; it explores the relationships between views on human nature, heredity, peace, and world government; it tests the comparative impermeability of class and national boundaries; it sketches in rough outline a few of the "pictures in our heads" of other peoples; it investigates the effect of tensions resulting from threatened unemployment or disappointed expectations; it finds some apparent similarities between strata that run through all nine countries, and some that do not.

Hopefully, these observations may lead students in various nations to develop theories that can be tested in small, specific, intensive surveys in single countries; and methodologists may be led to improve the procedures for comparing the views of people who live in different countries and speak different languages.

The text explores a few avenues, but the meat of the survey is in the tables, given in full in Appendix D. They are a unique and challenging body of data from which students of specific problems may derive valuable interpretations that are not covered in the generalized treatment here.

National Patterns
of Class Consciousness

—————— **Chapter** 2

The connection between class affiliation and nationalism has been the subject of speculation, not only by Marxists but by scholars concerned with international relations.[1]

Subjective class identification—that is, the class that an individual *thinks* he belongs to, as opposed to the class in which some observer, such as a student of sociology, might place him—was empirically explored through the polling technique in 1943.[2] Richard Centers developed this further in *The Psychology of Social Classes*,[3] a detailed study based on an extensive questionnaire. Klineberg has lamented the lack of comparable data for cross-national and cross-cultural studies.[4]

Since the concept of class is important both to sociologists and social psychologists and since comparable international studies are rare, the results are presented here in somewhat greater detail than is immediately pertinent to the problem of international tensions.

Three questions were asked. The first (Q.9) was to uncover the individual's class identification so that it might be compared to his "objective" class position, as revealed by his education, his occupation, and the interviewer's judgment of his socio-economic status. Then two questions (Q.10a

---

[1] For example: ". . . the identification of the individual with the power and the international policies of the nation proceeds largely in terms of the typical frustration and insecurities of the middle class." Hans J. Morgenthau, *Politics Among Nations* (New York: Alfred A. Knopf, 1948), p. 79.

[2] Hadley Cantril, "Identification with Social and Economic Class," *Journal of Abnormal and Social Psychology*, 38, No. 1 (1943), 74-80.

[3] Richard Centers, *The Psychology of Social Classes* (Princeton, N. J.: Princeton University Press, 1949). A recent review of his position is found in: Centers, "Toward an Articulation of Two Approaches to Social Class Phenomena," *International Journal of Opinion and Attitude Research*, 4, No. 4 (1950-51), 499-514.

[4] Klineberg, *op. cit.*, pp. 70-71.

and 10b) gauged the effect, if any, that his position in the class hierarchy exerted on his perception of other people, those of his own country and those of other countries, as well as his relations to these people.

Analysis of the replies to these questions in the nine national societies surveyed will shed some light on the extent to which the phenomenon of "class" is a universal one and on its variability from nation to nation in definiteness and structure; on the class to which members of various occupational groups assign themselves and on the standardization of this occupational-class relationship in various countries; on the comparative strength of class allegiance as opposed to national allegiance and on a few of the factors that seem to determine the individual's loyalty pattern.

Class and Nation

Q.9: *If you were asked to use a name for your social class, would you say you belong to the middle class, working class, or upper class?*
Following are the national totals:

	Austral.	Brit.	Fr.	Ger.	Ital.	Mex.	Neth.	Nor.	U.S.
Middle	50	35	44	52	54	45	33	43	42
Working	47	60	46	41	42	51	60	45	51
Upper	2	2	6	3	4	2	4	1	4
Don't know	1	3	4	4	0	2	3	11	3

The Unesco results for the United States conform closely to those found on earlier surveys. In other countries they do not contradict the results of similarly worded questions. However, translation is a particularly difficult problem; changing the word "working" to "laboring" could have diminished sharply the percentage in the United States identifying with that class. Similar semantic difficulties may apply to other languages.[5]

In view of the differences caused by the alteration of one word in a question under identical survey conditions, these totals should be interpreted with caution. However, some consolation is afforded by the fact that one of the lowest percentages saying "middle" occurs in Britain and one of the highest in Australia, both of which speak the King's English.[6]

Americans have been widely interpreted as the psychological products of a "middle-class-oriented" society; the British as a "nation of shopkeepers." In the light of the statements about their class identification made by the

---

[5] Discussion of semantic aspects of the question will be found in Appendix A, and comparable results from several countries in Appendix B.
[6] Translations into the other six languages, in the order in which they are given in Table 1, of the terms "middle," "working," and "upper" are: Moyenne, ouvrière, aisée; Mittelstand, Arbeiterstand, Oberschicht; media, operaia, superiore; media, trabajadora, alta; middenklasse, werkende klasse, hoogste klasse; middelstanden, arbeiderklassen, høyere sosiale klasse.

TABLE 1   HOW OCCUPATIONAL GROUPS STRATIFY THEMSELVES IN NINE COUNTRIES

Rank	Australia			Britain			France			Germany			Italy			Mexico			Netherlands			Norway			United States		
	Occ.	Index	D.K.	Occ.	Index	D.K.	Occ.	Index	D.K.	Occ.	Index	D.K.	Occ.	Index	D.K.	Occ.	Index	D.K.	Occ.	Index	D.K.	Occ.	Index	D.K.	Occ.	Index	D.K.
1	B.Own	89		Prof	63		B.Own	124		S.Own	99		Prof	133		F.Own	115		B.Own	121		Sal	72	4	Prof	83	4
2	Sal	85		Sal	57		Prof	106		B.Own	90		B.Own	94		B.Own	71		Prof	114		B.Own	57	7	Sal	75	7
3	Ret	71	4	B.Own	53	12	F.Own	53		Prof	89		Sal	76		Prof	71		Sal	83		Prof	48	12	B.Own	57	12
4	Prof	51	5	S.Own	9	5	Sal	42		Sal	58		Ret	73		Sal	65		S.Own	19	4	S.Own	26	14	Ret	39	11
5	F.Own	43		Ret	−9		S.Own	39	7	F.Own	53		House	56		Ret	24	5	Ret	4	11	F.Own	10	10	F.Own	37	
6	S.Own	10		F.Own	−14		House	37	9	Cler	49		Cler	44		House	11		Cler	1	4	House	8	8	S.Own	−6	
7	House	9		Cler	−18		Ret	25		House	12		F.Own	36		Cler	1		F.Own	−42		Cler	0	12	House	−8	4
8	Cler	7		House	−32		Cler	−3		Ret	9	11	S.Own	−6		S.Own	−21		F.Wor	−73		Ret	−5	25	Cler	−16	
9	Man	−61		Man	−76		F.Wor	−65	5	F.Wor	−52		Man	−75		Man	−42		Man	−89		F.Wor	−39	15	Man	−57	
10	F.Wor	−84		F.Wor	−80		Man	−78		Man	−55		F.Wor	−82		F.Wor	−63	38	House*			Man	−40	6	F.Wor	−66	
	Nat. Tot.	5		*Nat. Tot.*	−21		*Nat. Tot.*	10		*Nat. Tot.*	17		*Nat. Tot.*	20		*Nat. Tot.*	−2		*Nat. Tot.*	−19		*Nat. Tot.*	0		*Nat. Tot.*	−1	

* Housewives were not listed as a separate category in the Netherlands.

OCCUPATIONS (See Appendices for full details.)

Prof	Professional workers
B. Own	Owners of businesses
S. Own	Workers on own account
Sal	Salaried-managerial
Cler	Other clerical workers
Man	Manual workers
F. Wor	Farm workers, fishermen, etc.
F. Own	Farm owners
House	Housewives
Ret	Retired, independent

INDEX

This index reduces to a single figure the percentage of respondents in an occupation selecting all three class designations, by the following arbitrary method: Percentage of respondents in an occupation saying "middle" minus percentage saying "working" plus double the percentage saying "upper." Possible maximum is 200 (if everyone said "upper"); possible minimum is −100 (if everyone said "working").

DON'T KNOW'S

Figures are given only where 4% or more said "Don't know."

CAUTION

Lest too much quantitative significance be attached to differences among the indices and rankings in this table, it should be noted that the Centers survey among American men in 1945, if indexed in this manner, gives the following results for occupational groups that are comparable:

Rank	Unesco survey		Centers' survey	
1	Prof	83	Large business	97
2	B. Own	57	Professional	81
3	F. Own	37	Small business	52
4	S. Own	−6	White collar	31
5	Cler	−16	Farm owners and managers	−3
6	Man	−57	Farm tenants and laborers	−53
7	F. Wor	−66	All manual workers	−57

The differences are probably due largely to the difference in composition of the occupational groups in the two surveys.

Unesco respondents, which indicate that fewer people consider themselves members of the "middle" class in America and Britain than in any of the other nine countries except the Netherlands, this sort of glib generality and the interpretations based on it are shown to be in need of revision, or at least careful re-examination.

Occupation and Class Identification

Richard Centers found occupation to be most obviously related to class identification, with education and economic status also closely related. In order to see how far the occupational effect he found in the United States was characteristic of other countries, an index was computed that reduced the percentages in an occupation claiming the three classes to one representative figure which gave a large positive value to those occupations whose members claimed "middle"- and "upper"-class status and a negative value to those whose members claimed "working"-class status. Table 1 gives these figures for each occupational group in each country.

Farm workers and manual workers consistently fall at the bottom of the list. At the top there is more variation from country to country: owners of businesses are among the top three groups in every country; professionals and salaried managers are among the top four. Farm owners range from first to seventh place (depending probably on the size of holdings and nature of agricultural economy in the various countries).

Norway, by its large percentage of "Don't know's," the small range of its index figures in Table 1, and the fairly equal gradations between occupations, indicates a relative lack of class consciousness.[7] The higher proportion of "Don't know's" among business owners in Britain, professional workers and farm owners in Germany, farm workers in Mexico, and retired persons everywhere may be symptomatic of uncertainty resulting from shifting of class lines due to local economic developments. By contrast, salaried managers among the top groups seem least doubtful of their high position in the class structure.

Few persons had difficulty in fitting themselves into one of the three categories. "Don't know's" did not run higher than 4% in any country except

---

[7] An appendix to the Norwegian report (written by a staff member of the Norwegian Gallup Institute before comparison with the other national studies) commented: "Only 1% say they belong in the upper class, a finding which is certainly due to the fact that there is no very distinct upper class in Norway. . . . In the 'very poor' group 31% term themselves 'middle class.' They are independent fishermen, small farmers, apprentices, pensioners, etc., with very low incomes, but who will not say they are 'workmen.' On the other hand, many of the manual workers term themselves 'middle class' no doubt because their incomes are comparatively high at present. Thus it may safely be said that class distinctions are not very definite in Norway now."

Norway (11%). On no other question in the Unesco survey were refusals to answer and "Don't know" responses consistently this small. The national totals indicate a general tendency for Italians and Germans as a whole to rate themselves high, and for the British and Dutch to rate themselves low.

Other Factors in Class Identification

Class lines conformed rather closely to the level of education as stated by the respondents and to socio-economic status as judged by the interviewers; in no country was there an exception to the tendency for those with the least education and the lowest socio-economic status to consider themselves predominantly in the "working" class, and those with higher education and status to place themselves in the "middle" or "upper" class.

In four of the countries women were "significantly" [8] more likely than men to place themselves in the higher classes. However, in one, the United States, there was a "significant" tendency in the opposite direction.

Very few respondents designated themselves members of the "upper" class—in no country more than 6% of the total. There was no occupational group in any country more than half of whose members considered themselves "upper" class.

There was a tendency for class identification to "rise" with increasing age. Subject to occasional minor irregularities, there was a decreasing percentage of "workers" with advancing age, and a slight increase in the percentage saying "upper class." There was an increase in "middle"-class identification directly as age went up in some countries, in others this increase went through the two, middle-age groups and dropped back in the eldest group. This relationship could be caused by actual mobility—i.e., those who start as workers feel their class status has increased when, with advancing years, they attain a higher income bracket and more responsibility in their jobs. Or it might be that more elderly respondents have a different outlook—they attach more prestige to status and consequently tend to inflate it. In either case, there is no evidence that elderly respondents, even in those countries where class lines are sharp, are more "content with their stations" than younger ones.

Mexico, where age brought a steady decline in subjective status, and Norway, where classes were not at all clearly defined, are exceptions to these tendencies.

"Objective" vs. "Subjective" Status

The correlation between "subjective" class lines, as measured by Q.9,

---

[8] For an explanation of the special sense in which this term is used in this study, see p. 111.

and "objective" ones, as measured by interviewers' judgment of respondents' socio-economic status, were computed to determine which countries have the most distinct class lines.[9]

The following tabulation gives the index for each country in the final column. Those with a high index are the ones in which there is a large area of agreement between interviewer and respondent on the latter's status. It is a reasonable supposition that these are countries in which class lines are "distinct" or "rigid"—that is, where the respondent acquiesces in the judgment of the community (represented in this case by the interviewer) as to what his position should be. In those countries with low indices, the interviewer is less able to make a judgment (on the basis of clothes, speech, neighborhood, or apparent affluence) which corresponds with the respondent's own estimate of his position.

Country	r	$r^2 \times 100$
GERMANY	.77 ± .01	59[a]
NETHERLANDS	.71 ± .02	50
MEXICO	.70 ± .02	49
BRITAIN	.57 ± .02	32
ITALY	.56 ± .02	31
AUSTRALIA	.50 ± .02	25
FRANCE	.47 ± .03	22
UNITED STATES	.38 ± .03	14
NORWAY	.31 ± .03	10

[a] The German correlation may be higher than it should because interviewers classified socio-economic status in almost the same terms as respondents on Q.9. See pp. 152-53.

According to these indices, the countries appear to fall into three groups. In Germany, the Netherlands, and Mexico, one would say that class boundaries are quite distinct; in the United States and Norway, they are not at all distinct; other countries fall into a middle group.

National vs. Class Loyalty

The purpose of the class question (Q.9) was to provide a background for the analysis of the succeeding questions:

Q.10a: *Do you feel that you have anything in common with* (own) *class people abroad?*

[9] The measure of correlation here was the product-moment coefficient, squared and multiplied by 100 to give the "coefficient of determination." This latter measure may be used in a linear scale for comparison with other indices. The data used here do not meet all the requirements for a product-moment r since they are to some extent qualitative (i.e., "middle" class cannot be said to be numerically "greater" than "working" class), and the socio-economic status involves an interviewer judgment that takes into account factors other than income. The measure was used in spite of these objections because it is a familiar one and because the purpose here was not to demonstrate a significant relationship between the two factors but rather to find an approximate index of the extent to which the two sets of data correspond.

Q.10b: *Do you feel that you have anything in common with* (own nationality) *people who are not* (own) *class?*

Q.10c (If "Yes" on both or "No" on both a and b [10]): *Which of these two would you say that you have more in common with?*

Abroad   Own nation   Don't know

The drafters assumed that class and nation might be conflicting attractions to the individual. In the words of Henry Durant, one of the drafters, "We wanted to discover, if possible, the respective strengths of social self-identification and of national self-identification. In brief, it might be expressed as social class-feeling versus nationalism, although this would be inexact phraseology." [11]

The results, when finally tabulated, did not bear out this expectation. Those who answered "Yes" to both questions, plus those who answered "No" to both (a much smaller group) comprised roughly half the respondents.

In every country except the Netherlands, a higher percentage say they have something in common with their compatriots than say they have something in common with their class members abroad. (Figures are given in

TABLE 2   NATIONAL VS. CLASS ALLEGIANCE[a]

	Percentage of respondents saying they have something in common with:			
	Own Class Abroad		Countrymen Not of Own Class	
	"Yes" on Q.10a	"Abroad" on Q.10c	"Yes" on Q.10b	"Own nation" on Q.10c
Australia	67	6	78	51
Britain	58	7	67	34
France	48	12	63	34
Germany	30	5	64	20
Italy	41	9	50	24
Mexico	40	*b	56	*b
Netherlands	61	9	56	24
Norway	41	7	64	22
United States	42	7	77	32

[a]Figures are percentages of all respondents.
[b]Figures not available.

[10] For example, if an Australian had just told the interviewer he considered himself "middle" class, the questions would have read: "Do you feel that you have anything in common with middle-class people abroad?" and "Do you feel that you have anything in common with Australians who are not middle class?" Q.10c would not have been asked unless he had given the same answer to both.

[11] Their instructions to the survey agencies for Q.10c read: "Sample here may be very small; if so, give only absolute figures."

the "Yes" columns in Table 2.) Those who did not see the pair of questions as a dichotomy were forced to accept it as one on Q.10c. In this case they plumped heavily in the direction of patriotism. Taking countries as units, there seems to be neither a positive nor a negative relation between class loyalty and national loyalty, nor do either of them show a clear relationship to the index of class discreteness above.

Factors in National Loyalty

In every country those who considered themselves "middle" class were more likely than the "working" class to feel they had something in common with their compatriots of other classes. Differences in eight of nine countries were "significant," ranging from 9% to 16%; the exception, Norway, had only a 2% difference. (These differences are conservative: Either percentage of "middle" class minus percentage of "working" class saying "Yes" to Q.10b, or percentage of "working" class minus percentage of "middle" class saying "No", whichever is *smaller*.)

Similar differences were also found between the categories of the population which overlap with the "middle" and the "working" classes, respectively. Those with secondary education were more likely than those with primary or less education to feel common ties with their countrymen— "consistent" [12] for the nine countries, "significant" in eight of the nine, differences from 6% to 13%. The "B" socio-economic group [13] was more likely than the "C" group to express this sentiment—"consistent" for all nine countries, "significant" for three of the nine, differences from 3% to 11%.[14]

---

[12] For an explanation of the special sense in which the word "consistent" is used in this connection, see p. 112.

[13] The socio-economic breakdown called for four categories. As given in the instructions to interviewers in various countries, these were:

"A": Well-to-do, average +, aisée, Oberschicht.

"B": Middle class, average, better off, moyenne plutôt aisée, Mittelstand.

"C": Working class, average −, artisans, etc., moyenne plutôt pauvre, Arbeiterschicht.

"D": Very poor, Group D, lowest income, pauvre.

Some of the agencies set up criteria, such as possession of radio, telephone, automobile, etc. (for details, see notes on each national survey, Appendix D.) The proportion of respondents falling in each category was not the same in every country. Because the terms "middle class" and "working class" may be confused with the subjective-class identification in Q.9 and because the terms "average" and "below average" imply a threefold division, the terms "A," "B," "C," and "D" will be used in the text. Although different interviewers within a country might disagree as to the classification of a particular respondent, it is safe to say that the bulk of "A" respondents are better off than the bulk of "B" respondents, and so on down the line.

[14] The extreme groups—"upper" class, university-educated, socio-economic groups "A" and "D"—were not computed because their numbers are small and hence less reliable, and because the tables revealed that their differences were, with occasional exceptions, in the same direction as those cited and even more pronounced.

The tabulations available did not permit testing to see which of the three—high socio-economic status, high educational level, or "upper" and "middle" class identification—was the strongest factor predisposing toward national identification.

Age and sex did not have a pronounced effect although there was a slight but not "consistent" tendency for men and the older groups to feel more than women and younger groups that they had something in common with countrymen not of their own class.

Factors in Class Loyalty

"Workers," though they were less likely to feel attached to other classes in their own country, did not "consistently" transfer this allegiance to foreign workers, as might be expected by believers in the ideal of the "international brotherhood of working men." The "middle" class was more likely than the "working" class to feel they had something in common with others of their class abroad, but this was "consistent" for only five countries, "significant" for only one, and had one important exception—France. In France there was a "significant" difference of 9% in the opposite direction— that is, "workers" were more likely to feel common cause with non-French "workers" than were "middle"-class Frenchmen with foreigners of their own class. There may be a large overlap within this 9% and the 9% of the French "workers" who believe the U.S.S.R. offers them the kind of life they would like to lead. Only 1% of the "middle" class so believe.

Examining the other categories—primary education and below-average income—that overlap with "working" class, one finds the same pattern. The uneducated were less likely than those with secondary education to "have anything in common" with their class abroad—"consistent" for seven of nine, "significant" for four; and the "C" socio-economic groups were less likely than the "B"—"consistent" for five of nine, "significant" for one.

All this can be schematically illustrated as follows:

Respondents having a higher:	Education	Subjective Status	Objective Status
Are more likely to "have something in common" with			
(1) Countrymen of other classes:	"Consistent" for 9	"Consistent" for 9	"Consistent" for 9
	"Significant" for 8	"Significant" for 8	"Significant" for 3
(2) Own class abroad:	"Consistent" for 7	"Consistent" for 5	"Consistent" for 5
	"Significant" for 4	"Significant" for 1	"Significant" for 1

It is not too surprising that those who are more privileged in respect to education and income, and who feel themselves a cut above the "working man," are more likely to feel that they have something in common with others of their nation and class.

The Office of Public Opinion Research (OPOR) found in its wartime studies in the United States that one criterion of high morale was a "Yes" response to the question: "Do you think most people can be trusted?" The national total for one survey was: "Yes," 66%; "No," 25%; Qualified and "Don't know," 9%. The "Yes" response among the well-to-do was 74%, among those on pensions or relief, 57%. Better educated respondents in all economic categories were also more likely to say "Yes."

This suggests that a sense of security governs the responses to the Unesco survey question as well—the more privileged respondent sees no threat from other groups at home or abroad.

Education seems to separate the two groups more than socio-economic status. This may be due entirely to differences in the method of categorizing respondents (*respondent's* avowal of level of education vs. *interviewer's* judgment on socio-economic status), but it is also consistent with earlier findings in the United States [15] that education is more important than economic status in supporting "allegiance to certain general social stereotypes" while economic status determines opinion relative to matters of "financial return." The notion of international class bonds appears to be one of these "social stereotypes"—one which at the present time is too abstract to arise without prompting by teachers.

A question which deals with the same issue but slices it somewhat more sharply, putting it in an exclusively economic context, was recently asked by the Institut Français d'Opinion Publique (IFOP).[16]

Pensez-vous que votre condition économique dépend davantage de la richesse relative de la France parmi les autres nations, ou davantage du sort qui est réservé à votre classe sociale à l'intérieur de la nation française?

davantage du sort de la classe sociale	42%
davantage de la richesse relative de la France	33
des deux à la fois	4
autres réponses	3
ne répondent pas	15
	100%

There is a striking economic effect on the answers, as may be seen in the following tabulation, which is approximately equivalent to the socio-economic breakdown in the Unesco survey:

	Leur classe sociale	La richesse de la France
riche	32%	46%
aisée	38	39
modeste	46	28
pauvre	43	24

[15] Hadley Cantril, editor, *Gauging Public Opinion* (Princeton, N. J.: Princeton University Press, 1944), Ch. XIV.

[16] "Revue Française de l'Opinion Publique" (Service de Sondages et Statisques, 1951), No. 3, pp. 14-15.

The editors comment that while the two responses are not logically exclusive, people lean to one or the other; and the choice they make gives a clue to their ideology. Generalizations about class and national identification from this particular question should take into account the atypical reaction of French "workers" to the Unesco questions. The large proportion of respondents in all countries who had to be asked Q.10c indicates that some of these IFOP respondents may have been forced into a choice which they would not spontaneously have made.

Nevertheless, it is interesting that class identification when positively and internationally expressed, as in the Unesco questions, seems to be less appealing than when it is placed in a national, competitive, economic context, as in the IFOP question.

Summary

Class and nation are not opposite poles of affiliation but are complementary to the extent that the more fortunate people are more likely than others to feel they have something in common with both reference groups. International class bonds (at least those touched on by these questions) and national unity are not mutually exclusive.

Comparatively low wealth, low education, and lack of subjective "social superiority" discourage sentiments of commonality abroad and at home. Lack of education may be a more important factor than the other two; presumably the narrower horizons of the uneducated man keep him from seeing the manifold important interrelationships he has with his compatriots and fellow world citizens. "The uninformed usually believe that no political event can greatly affect their personal fortunes. While foreign policy issues agitate the informed, the world of the uninformed is circumscribed by the daily cares of a child's cough, a boss's gripe, an unexpected frost." [17]

The term "social class," then, has a real meaning to people in all these countries. The individual places himself in a class. Though he may be cognizant that there are similar class hierarchies elsewhere (the survey does not bear on this point), this bit of information seems to be of relatively little importance to him. His own countrymen are more frequently his "reference group," but he is not likely to see this spontaneously in terms of making a choice. If he is willing to identify with both groups or refuses to identify with either, you may confront him with the choice. In this case, the chances are three or four to one that he will pick his countrymen.

These figures point to a sense of isolation felt by the less privileged

---

[17] Martin Kriesberg, "Dark Areas of Ignorance," *Public Opinion and Foreign Policy,* Lester Markel, ed. (New York: Harper & Bros., 1949), p. 62.

everywhere. This lack of fellow-feeling is probably related to their apathy toward national and international affairs, which seem irrelevant to them and to their lives and purposes, which they see no opportunity to influence, and which involve people whose concerns are not their concerns, whom they have never seen in person, and whom they seldom have brushed against in business, study, or recreation.

Almond, following Mannheim, points out that "there is a cultural impairment of the capacity for moral autonomy and intellectual independence implicit in the socio-economic system. Persons who tend to be objects of remote decision and manipulation in their private lives are unlikely to approach problems of public policy with a sense of mastery and independence." [18]

The "map of the world" in the heads of these people would show boundaries that seal them off from members of other groups in their homeland just as effectively as their national boundaries seal them off from other nations.

[18] Gabriel A. Almond, *The American People and Foreign Policy* (New York: Harcourt, Brace & Co., 1950), p. 130.

Security and
Satisfaction
with Opportunities

—————— Chapter 3

Five questions (Q.5, 6, 7, 8, and 14) dealt with the individual's personal security, his attitude toward the regime then in power, and his satisfaction with life in his country.

The problem of international tension has frequently been posed in terms of individual security. Standard-of-living and population pressures have been cited to "explain" war as the classic struggle between the "have's" and the "have-not's." Personal insecurity and frustration are believed to lead to aggression, which may be directed against one's compatriots in the form of revolution and class warfare, or against other nations in aggressive war.[1] If this is the case and if "all other things are equal," it is those countries with a high level of insecurity that should be kept under surveillance as potential trouble spots.

[1] For example: "The greater the stability of society and the sense of security of its members, the smaller are the chances for collective emotions to seek an outlet in aggressive nationalism and vice versa. These collective emotions may, of course, seek an outlet in aggressiveness within the nation as well, that is, in the form of class struggle, revolution and civil war." (Morgenthau, op. cit., p. 76.)

"The question of the relationship of stress and suffering to a nation's potential for aggression . . . is a critical matter. . . . [When certain stresses] exceed the threshold that can be tolerated, one common result is active hostility, and that the potential for this action is increased as other modes of seeking relief fail. If this sequence constitutes a universal principle of human behavior, then the reduction of stress throughout the world becomes one of the essential steps toward peace. It opens as a major problem for social science, the estimation of stresses and the devising of ways and means for their reduction." (Alexander H. Leighton, Human Relations in a Changing World (New York: E. P. Dutton, 1949), p. 106.)

24

Satisfaction with National Government

Q.14: Do you think our present government is too much to the right, too much to the left, or about where you would like it to be?

While this question was designed to reveal the *individual's* views and is used for that purpose throughout the analysis, it is inevitably affected by the actual color of the regime in power in his country in the fall of 1948.

This is evidenced by the order in which the countries fall when ranked according to degree of "leftness." The figure for each country was obtained by subtracting the percentage of respondents who replied that their government was "Too right" from the percentage replying "Too left." Thus a high positive index signifies a regime generally considered leftist and a high negative index signifies one considered rightist. The results are:

Australia	46
Britain	29
United States	21
Norway	10
Netherlands	6
Mexico	2
Germany	−2
France	−11
Italy	−25

This probably does not differ in more than one or two instances from the order in which the governments might have been ranked by a panel of informed judges, if such a panel could have been able to agree on what political, economic, social, and religious factors are connoted by the terms "Right" and "Left" which are used with such abandon. However, this ranking does not actually "compare" the governments with each other since in each case it depends on a standard *internal* to the country involved—presumably a standard expressing what the people in that country were accustomed to expect of their government on the basis of their previous national experience.

Hereafter, the answers to this question will be used to separate respondents into "Rightists" (those who said "Too left") and "Leftists" (those who said "Too right"). The preceding tabulation may be used for reference in estimating the extent to which, in any country, the actual complexion of the government has caused displacement in the lines between groups. For example, in Australia it is reasonable to suppose that the "Rightist" group includes a great many middle-of-the-roaders while the "Leftist" group consists mostly of extremists; whereas in Italy the "Rightist" group would be extreme, and the "Leftist" would include a good many moderates.

Individual Security: A National Index

Four questions were asked to gain a measure of the individual respondent's security in respects not immediately related to international affairs. These questions and the check boxes provided for interviewers, were:

Q.5: *When the war ended, did you expect you would be getting along better, worse, or about the same as you actually are getting along at the present time?*

Better   Worse   About the same   Don't know

Q.6a: *Do you feel that from the point of view of your (husband's) job you are more secure, or less secure, than the average* (Australian, Britisher, Frenchman, etc.)?

More   Less   About the same   Don't know

Q.6b: *In general do you feel that you are sufficiently secure to be able to plan ahead?*

Yes   No   Don't know

Q.7: *How satisfied are you with the way you are getting on now?*

Very   All right   Dissatisfied   Don't know

From these questions a national "security index" was compiled as follows:

1. For each question the percentage of respondents in the country as a whole giving the most pessimistic answer to each question was subtracted from the percentage giving the most optimistic answer. The resulting figure for any question may be compared from country to country to determine how that particular component of security varies.

2. These percentage differences for the four questions were added in each country. Since the resulting totals ranged from -205 to $+24$, they were divided by 10 and a constant, 40, was added to give "indices" ranging from 20 to 42 on a scale that runs from a possible low of 0 to a possible high of 80. (These adjustments do not change the relationship of the countries, they merely remove the misleading appearance of negativeness and accuracy.)[2]

---

[2] The formula for this index in any country may be expressed as follows:

$$\frac{\overset{(Q.5)}{\text{Worse} - \text{Better}} + \overset{(Q.6a)}{\text{More} - \text{Less}} + \overset{(Q.6b)}{\text{Yes} - \text{No}} + \overset{(Q.7)}{\text{Very} - \text{Dissat.}}}{10} + 40$$

It should be noted that this index is not the Security Score used elsewhere for measuring an individual respondent's security and placing him in the "most-," "medium-," or "least-secure" class. These individual Security Scores, summed for the nation, would rank the nations in about the same order as the above "index" since both are based on the same data. However, scores were tabulated at the time the cards were punched and, because of misleading survey instructions, were not available for France and Australia. (See p. 123.)

Two or more countries may be compared by juxtaposing either their national indices or the figures for a particular "component of security" in the tabulation below (e.g., total security and job security for Australia are both higher than for Britain), but comparisons may not be made for components within a country (e.g., it is not safe to say that job security is higher than general satisfaction in Australia) except with reference to some outside standard (e.g., British insecurity is due more to disappointment than to job security than is the case in Australia). The "security index" may also be computed for a group (socio-economic, occupational, etc.) within a country to provide for comparison with the national index or with groups in other countries. It is, of course, less reliable because of the smaller sample.

The national index for each country and the percentage differences for each question are given in the following tabulation:

	Austral.	Brit.	Fr.	Ger.	Ital.	Mex.	Neth.	Nor.	U.S.
National security index	42	35	20	26	32	39	33	39	39
Components of security:									
Q.5: Postwar expectations	−38	−47	−76	−25	−15	−8	−44	−39	−29
Q.6a: Job security	39	16	−15	−7	0	18	2	7	19
Q.6b: Ability to plan	21	2	−60	−67	−26	23	−6	9	10
Q.7: General satisfaction	2	−21	−54	−42	−41	−41	−26	11	−11

This index, being based on several questions, smooths out some of the variations that might be caused by translations, since they would be more likely to apply to one question than to all four. The questions were composed by the drafters to touch four areas: the broad one of "general satisfaction" (Q.7); and three particular aspects of security—comparison of current reality with one's previous expectations (Q.5), present economic security as compared with that of others to whom one has immediate reference (Q.6a), and expectation of continued stability (Q.6b).

No one supposes that these items and only these items compose "personal security," or that they should all be given equal weight, or that the weighting system must be the same for every country. It is entirely possible that the components of total security vary from culture to culture; actually the variations between the answers to the four questions within the same country suggest that this is the case. The index, then, is a shotgun approach: if one question does not hit, another may. Questions 5 and 7 are deliberately "projective"—that is, they can be expected to tap different sources of worry with different respondents. Italians and Germans rate comparatively high on Q.5 because at the war's end they expected little; Frenchmen and Britons rate low because they expected a great deal. The contexts in which these questions were answered may also vary between countries as well as between individuals, with some nationalities dwelling on political disappointments, others on social or economic ones.

For purposes of analysis, however, it is assumed that the index *does* measure security *everywhere,* at least to a degree that comparison of nations is possible. This is the starting point for examining other variables. The opposite might be assumed, from which point psychologists, by further intensive interviewing to account for the differences in response to the four questions, might use them to determine more exactly what "individual security" does consist of, and how it varies. Thus a better index may be derived and adjusted to account for national differences. This is an equally important area of research but beyond the scope of the present analysis.

To these questions, which touch on matters much more important to the individual than such abstractions as "human nature" and "world peace," there were few "Don't know" responses. Only on the question regarding ability to plan ahead (Q.6b) were the "Don't know's" appreciable in number; and even here it may be argued that "I don't know whether I am secure enough to plan ahead" is the equivalent of "I am not sure enough. . . ."

"Security Index" as Measuring Device

The figures above suggest that France, with an index of 20, in 1948 was closest of the nine nations to a condition of pathological tension. Although Frenchmen did not feel appreciably less secure in their jobs (Q.6a) than people in the other countries surveyed, their hopes for the postwar period (Q.5) had been more severely dashed, and their expectations, for the future (Q.6b) were gloomier. In 1947 the Institut Français d'Opinion Publique asked: "In your opinion which is the country where things are worst now?" Greece came first, picked by 19% of respondents; and *France second,* picked by 16%. Spain, Germany, Italy, Britain, Indo-China, and Palestine followed in that order.[3] Yet, when asked, "If you had your choice, would you rather stay in France or go to live in another country?" 75% of respondents preferred to stay.[4]

Although there are no recent questions which are comparable, one would surmise that the tension in France was not appreciably relieved in the years of continued crisis that followed the survey. Yet no explosions have taken place in France, and none appear imminent. Tentatively, then, the danger level of tensions may be set at some point below 20 as measured by the Unesco scale.

The survey in West Berlin gave a "security index" of 16 during the "blockade" in 1948. A repetition of the questions in 1949 showed that the index had risen to 23 after the "blockade" was lifted. (See pp. 86-87.)

[3] The countries in which "things were best" according to Frenchmen were Switzerland, the United States, U.S.S.R., Belgium, and Sweden.

[4] These figures from the brochure *World Opinion,* June, 1947, published by the American Institute of Public Opinion.

This sensitivity suggests that the Unesco index will serve as a discriminating tool for measuring the stress caused by economic deprivations and political instability.

Factors in Security

Men were found to be more secure than women in Australia, Britain, Norway, and the United States. In other countries there was no clear-cut difference. All the former are countries with high security indices in the preceding tabulation. In them, the main sources of difference between men and women are on the questions of postwar expectations (Q.5) and ability to plan ahead (Q.6b). Apparently in these nations—all of which were victorious and all of which could be said in 1948 to be better off than most others on the list—women had demanded more of the future in 1945 and continued to demand more of it in 1948.

The age breakdown produces nothing unexpected. Older people are somewhat less optimistic than younger ones on all four questions. But those over sixty-five could hardly have answered the questions on job security (Q.6a) and ability to plan ahead (Q.6b) in quite the same context as younger respondents.

In every country, respondents with higher socio-economic status feel more secure than the lower groups. The differences are large, "consistent," and "significant." Those with higher education also feel more secure, but this is apparently a by-product of economic status since the greatest differences between the educated and the uneducated are on the question about job security (Q.6a) and the corollary one on ability to plan ahead (Q.6b). Everywhere, but varying in extent from country to country, there is a tendency for the better educated, especially those with university training, to reply that the 1948 world was about what they had expected at the war's end (Q.5). This could reflect either a better adjustment, or a better understanding of the course that economic and political events were expected to take and did in fact take.[5]

There is less difference between the educated and the uneducated on the question regarding general satisfaction (Q.7) than on the other three. Apparently those with primary education do not set their standards so high. They are conditioned to expect instability of employment.

To these generalizations about education, Germany is an exception. There, the secondary educated have a slightly higher margin of total security than do either their more educated or less educated countrymen.

---

[5] Americans with limited education, in their attitudes on foreign policy, tend to fluctuate between extremes of despair and optimism as they are confronted by events they feel unable either to control or understand. See Almond, *op. cit.*, p. 58.

Satisfaction with Opportunities at Home

Q.8: *Which country in the world gives you the best chance of leading the kind of life you would like to lead?*

The principal purpose of this question was to get a rating from the respondent, in as personal terms as possible, of his own country as against other countries. Therefore a note to interviewers printed on the ballot beneath the question read, "This question includes respondent's own country if he asks the question." This technique was employed to set the question in an unstructured context, so that those respondents who were not satisfied could so indicate naturally, without fighting qualms of patriotism. Presumably, the respondent who had pondered the possibility of emigration would be likely to name the country he had concluded was the most practicable for him to go to. This injects a strain of *feasibility* into the question for these unidentified respondents, but not for others. Consequently, in considering the results, one cannot be certain to what extent they reflect an academic, theoretical, all-other-things-being-equal approach, and to what extent certain countries have been eliminated in the minds of the respondents because of their impracticability for emigration. This tendency will be more evident as the breakdowns are examined.

The percentages naming their own country as offering them the kind of life they would like to lead are as follows:

Austral.	Brit.	Fr.	Ger.	Ital.	Mex.	Neth.	Nor.	U.S.
83	51	43	30	36	45	31	50	96

Women were more likely to name their own country than men, and older people were more likely than younger ones, with few exceptions. These differences were generally small, and seldom "significant," but their importance lies in their consistency. They suggest that a number of respondents did translate the question into very personal terms and that women and elderly people, whose prospects for emigration were slimmer, were quicker to accept the existing situation.

Factors in Satisfaction

If satisfaction with life in one's own country is related to individual economic conditions, one would expect a difference between the socio-economic strata. There is a regular decrease in the number selecting their own country from the "A" group down through the "D" group in the United States, Netherlands, and Italy; and in Norway and Britain this trend held for three of the four groups. The tendency of the lower groups to answer "Don't know" may account for part of this effect. Only in Italy was there a "significant" difference between the "B" and "C" groups that make up the bulk of the sample.

The self-styled "upper" class deviated sharply from the others, but with no consistency in its direction: in Australia, Britain, and Germany it was less satisfied; in France, Italy, and Mexico more satisfied. These countries may be at different points in the cyclical swing between conservatism and populism. There was no "consistent" or "significant" difference between "workers" and the "middle" class. The question was not tabulated by education.

Generally those who said this government was "about where they would like it" were more likely to pick their own country as offering them the life they wanted to lead than were either those who thought it "too left" or "too right." The latter—"Leftists"—were "significantly" less likely to name their homeland in Britain, Norway, the Netherlands, Italy, and France. "Rightists" differed "significantly" only in Australia. But comparison with the percentage picking Russia as the nation offering the life they would like to lead for the first five countries mentioned above indicates that Communists (who fall into the "Leftist" category along with less intransigent advocates of change) probably account for the difference. If one excludes them from consideration, there is little evidence that approval of the regime in office is related to one's satisfaction with life in one's own country.

Where 4% or more of all respondents selected a particular country or continent, the results were tabulated by background factors. Only the United States was picked by this many respondents in the other eight countries.

In five of the eight ("significant" for two), "Rightists" were more likely than "Leftists" to pick the United States; in six of the eight ("significant" for two), the "middle" class was more likely than the "working" class; in five of the eight, the "upper" class was more likely (by margins of more than 10% in three, but nowhere "significant" because of the small number in the sample).

There was no obvious tendency for a particular income group to pick the United States. Of the four groups, the very poor were least likely, but this could be accounted for by a higher proportion of "Don't know's" and "No answers" in this group.

Comparative National Satisfaction

The countries or continents selected by 0.5% or more of all respondents are given in Table 3.

Inspection of this list suggests criteria which are likely to have been in the minds of various respondents while making their selections. Though

TABLE 3 PERCENTAGES PICKING A NATION OTHER THAN THEIR OWN ON Q.8[a]

Countries selected	Austral.	Brit.	Fr.	Ger.	Ital.	Mex.	Neth.	Nor.	U.S.	Total
United States	5	9	12	25	27(8)[b]	31	21	21		151(132)[b]
Switzerland	1		9	8	5			1		24
South Africa	1	6		1	1		8	1		18
Canada	1	4	2	2			6			15
Russia	1		4	1	2		2	1		11
Argentina			1	2	5	3				11
Australia		8		1				1		10
Britain	4		3	1	1					9
New Zealand	1	6		1						8
South America			1		3		3	1		8
Sweden	1		1	2	1			2		7
Belgium			4	1			1			6
Denmark				2						2
France					2					2
Netherlands Indies							2			2
Spain						1				1
Netherlands				1						1

[a] Countries mentioned by less than 0.5% were not tabulated. This accounts for the blank column under "U. S."

[b] See p. 176.

incapable of mathematical demonstration, they might be arrayed roughly in the following order of importance:

1. Standard of living (especially United States, Switzerland, Canada, Argentina).

2. Availability for immigration (especially British Commonwealth countries).

3. Familiarity with language.

4. Neutrality and hope for peace (especially Switzerland, Argentina, Sweden).

5. Ideology (Russia and Argentina).

6. Proximity and familiarity to respondents.

The answers to this question (Q.8) point up the devastation wrought by the war on the individual through displacement of his national economy. *The people in the overcrowded and war-shattered parts of Europe in 1948 looked with envy on countries that could offer them space and an opportunity to improve their level of living. People of the extra-Continental countries, having escaped the brunt of the war damage, indicated a higher degree of satisfaction with their way of life.*

The percentage of respondents picking their own country varies considerably from nation to nation, but not so obviously from group to group within a nation, indicating that this sort of satisfaction is more a national than a class phenomenon.

Economic Conditions and National Morale

A man who does not have enough to feed and clothe himself and his family and to look into the future with a certain amount of confidence may be a dangerous man to his society. Groups of people denied benefits they see other people enjoying may cause trouble. A "have-not" nation endangers the security of its more fortunate neighbors.

These are all rather gross oversimplifications—they need to be qualified and clarified. Exceptions are almost as easy to think of as examples. One way of qualifying them is to say that tensions result when economic hardships exist and people do not "accept" them. This suggests *the intervening factor of human reaction* that enters between demonstrably difficult conditions and the behavior "caused" by them.

The economic level of a group (and the group this study deals with is the nation) can be summarized with tolerable accuracy in various national index numbers that are used to represent the "standard of living" or "population density." These provide a single figure to make possible comparisons between nations differing in size, location, population, and economic system.

The Unesco survey provides index figures in another area: the realm of human reaction. The "security index" is a single figure roughly indicative of how contented the citizens of a nation are with the benefits which the economic and social system throws their way. The percentage registering satisfaction with the opportunities offered them in their own country is a similar measure, but with a standard external rather than internal to the country. The index for rigidity of the class system approximates the degree of acceptance by the people of the mechanism employed to distribute the store of goods available within the country.

Table 4 brings together the national figures for three of the opinion or "reaction" variables: (1) "satisfaction," i.e., the percentage naming their own country as offering them the kind of life they would like to lead (see p. 30); (2) "security" as indicated by the national index (see p. 27); and (3) "class rigidity," as measured by the correlation between the interviewer's and the respondent's judgment (see p. 17). High levels of "satisfaction" and "security" and a "loose" class structure appear in the same countries, subject to certain irregularities and exceptions.[6] Since all three of these qualities are gauged by measurements internal to the survey, the relationship could be accounted for by the survey mechanism.

***

[6] A fourth variable—whether governments are considered "Too right" or "Too left" (see p. 25) also seems to be related. "Too left" countries are higher in "satisfaction" and the other qualities. However, the inclusion of "All right" as a response to this question introduces another dimension of approval into the answers, making its use in this sort of comparison questionable.

TABLE 4 RELATION OF UNESCO SURVEY RESPONSES TO CERTAIN ECONOMIC VARIABLES

	Response (national totals)			Economic Variables			
	Percent picking own country (Q.8)	"Security index" (see p. 27)	Class "rigidity" (see p. 17)	Per cap. income (U.S. $), '49[a]	Real per cap. income, '47[b] (1938=100)	Per cap. calorie supply '48/49[c]	Pop. per sq. km. '48[d]
United States	96	39	14	1453	150	3130	19
Australia	83	42	25	679[e]	[f]	3210	1
Great Britain	51	35	32	773	110	3045	205
Norway	50	39	10	587	103	2970	10
Mexico	45	39	49	121	[f]	2054	12
France	43	20	22	482	92	2695	74
Italy	36	32	31	235	66	2355	152
Netherlands	31	33	50	502	96	2880	291
West Germany	30	26	59	320	[f]	2525	191

[a] Statistical Office of the United Nations, Statistical Papers E-1, *National and Per Capita Income of Seventy Countries—1949* (New York: Lake Success, 1950), p. 14-16.

[b] Statistical Office of the United Nations, *National Income Statistics, 1938-48* (New York: Lake Success, 1950), p. 245.

[c] Food and Agriculture Organization of the United Nations, *The State of Food and Agriculture, Review and Outlook, 1951* (Rome, 1951), table on p. 89 giving "Estimated Energy and Protein Content of National Average Food Supplies per Caput in 1950-51 Compared With 1949-50 and 1948-49."

[d] *United Nations Statistical Yearbook* (New York, 1950), p. 17-26.

[e] 1948-49 income.

[f] Information not available.

Three of the economic index figures are shown in the same table: (1) per capita income expressed in U.S. dollars, (2) per capita calorie supply, and (3) density of population.[7]

Ranking the countries in the order of their "satisfaction," "security," "flexibility" of class structure (i.e., giving those with the highest scores in column 3 the lowest ranks), "income," "food supply," and "living space" (i.e., giving those with the highest populations in column 7 the lowest ranks) shows all these variables to be positively, though often moderately, correlated. "Income" and "food supply" indices are high for the same countries because they measure substantially the same things. "Satisfaction" seems to be a product of both the *actual* standard of living as registered by these two and the national level of "security," which involves not only economic conditions but also their *impact* on the individual. "Living space" is more closely related to the three dependent variables than to the two independent ones.[8]

In Table 4, Australia, Norway, and the United States are among the top four countries on all the variables—attitudinal and economic. At the bottom there is more shifting of position: Germany is one of the bottom three in every column, Italy one of the bottom four in six of the seven.

Possibilities for Further Research

The "security index" experiment holds out some promise. Individual scores are found to be related to class variations within a country.[9] For a geographical area—West Berlin—the index is shown to be sensitive to

[7] Since not all of these statistics were available for 1948, the nearest year for which the data appear is used. Real per capita income for 1947 is also given for the six countries for which available.

[8] Rank-difference coefficients for these variables were used as a rough measure of relationship in this analysis. Dependent variables include a percentage, an index, and a coefficient; independent ones are based on economic and demographic data from several sources; hence the accuracy implied by a more precise measure would not be warranted. (See Margaret J. Hagood, *Statistics for Sociologists* (New York: Henry Holt & Co., 1947), pp. 677-78.) The *rhos* are as follows:

	Security	Flexibility	Income	Food Supply	Living Space
Satisfaction (Col. 1)	.77	.67	.74	.74	.58
Security (Col. 2)		.37	.45	.55	.68
Flexibility (Col. 3)			.48	.48	.63
Income (Col. 4)				.95	.08
Food Supply (Col. 6)					.25
Living Space (Col. 7)					

[9] In certain countries individual security is also found to be related to ideas about peace and world government, although it is entirely possible that this is not an immediate connection but a common relation to some other factor, such as education (see p. 64).

changes over a period of time and to move in the direction that alterations in the economic and political environment would have led one to expect.

As a national index, it scales the majority of the nine countries in the order that other, independent statistics—such as wealth and diet—would rank them. To this ranking, however, there are certain notable exceptions: high security in Mexico with other factors comparatively low;[10] low security in France with other factors higher than would be expected. In this connection, one might define those elusive concepts variously known as "national character" or "national morale" as "the factors which cause security in a nation to be higher or lower than the point where objectively measurable effects, such as population or income, would place it."

This index, with further refinements, offers an opportunity for testing the "threshold of stress" theory by comparing conditions both from nation to nation and over a period of time. Since the occasions when aggressive tendencies lead to outright war are, fortunately, rare enough that generalizations may not be readily derived, it would be necessary to compare "security indices" with other measurable manifestations of tension—strikes, statistics on crimes of violence, changes of government, irascible editorials, flag-waving speeches, etc.—in order to determine whether these phenomena increase as personal security decreases for the nation as a whole.

In this way it may be possible to test the "threshold of stress" theory and determine the limits and variability of such a threshold.

A long-term experiment of this nature is being undertaken by Service de Sondages et Statistiques in France, although its public opinion questions are designed to cover a wider area than that of economic security. Three factors will be compared in this study: (1) daily observations of current events; (2) "statistics of certain social facts," such as crime, suicide, birth and marriage rates, emigration, and economic indices; and (3) national and international "averages of opinions" obtained by polling.[11]

One of the major prerequisites for the development of an index that will measure tensions is further research in individual psychology to determine the constituents of actual "security" and develop simple questions that enable this quality to be reliably assessed. Even if a totally new set of questions is developed, repetition of the Unesco questions along with them will permit this survey to be used as a base line—within a country as a point in time from which trends may be charted and between countries as a yardstick that has been applied at the same time to nine nations.

[10] There was a slight difference in the wording of Q.6a in Mexico, which could account for part of this effect. See pp. 184-85.

[11] Max Barioux, "A Study of Psycho-Sociology by Public Opinion Polls," *International Social Science Bulletin*, Vol. III, No. 3 (autumn, 1951).

It may be assumed that the national indices of morale achieved here are in a sense "corrected" economic indices—adjusted, that is, to take into consideration the *human, social* reaction to economic environment. It is possible, then, to supplement the "maps" that show relative resources, diet levels, and population density of various geographical areas with "maps" that point to the national groups, and the social groups within them, where inequality between food supply and mouths to feed has exacerbated insecurity.

If the fluctuations of these morale indices are accompanied by demonstrations of aggressive behavior, and if these "maps" point out the potential trouble spots in the world, we may advance in our understanding of the basis of international tensions. The virtue of this method is that it need not necessarily be confined to national studies. Security levels of smaller groups and narrower geographical areas may be used in developing the technique.

─────── **Chapter** 4

Explanations of the source of hostilities that lead to war are innumerable: threats to national security, ideology, ethnocentrism, envy due to economic differences and population pressure, propaganda, "incidents" of various sorts, imperialism, nationalism—these ideas and many others have served to "explain" tensions at various levels of abstraction.

Respondents to the Unesco survey were asked to name the "peoples" to which they were "most" and "least friendly." In each survey one or two nationalities drew the great bulk of mentions, and six or eight others were picked by more than one per cent of respondents. Certain patterns stand out clearly on examination of the results for the nine surveys as a whole. The following analysis is an attempt to arrange in some sort of order the types of relationships suggested by these patterns—relationships which presumably underlie the respondents' choices.

Problems of Category

Studying international affairs statistically, as has frequently been pointed out, is complicated by the fact that the nation, if it serves as the unit, exists in a great variety of forms. Relations between nations are so complex that it is virtually impossible to find enough pure cases to come to a generalization. For these reasons, the historical method has been more popular.

An attempt is made here to subject the material to numerical evaluation using the respondent as the unit, his feelings toward another "people" as the case, and the actual relationship between that people (or nation) and his own as the category or context. The substantive results of such an attempt may be meager in the present instance, but the technique deserves attention if "wars begin in the minds of men." As wider surveys, and more intensive ones, become possible, it may become a valuable supplementary tool.

The questions used for the direct measurement of tensions were:

Q.11: *Which foreign people do you feel most friendly toward?*

Q.12: *Which foreign people do you feel least friendly toward?*

The relationships between nations, determining the context or frame of reference within which it is considered most likely that respondents answered the questions, are classified as follows:

Context I: "The Bi-Polar World"

II: "World War II"

III: "Common Boundaries"

IV: "Common Language/Culture"

V: "Neutrality"

This categorization scheme is subject to several limitations. One is the difficulty of setting up indisputable criteria. What constitutes, for example, a "common language"? Do Denmark and Norway have one? Germany and the Netherlands? The Netherlands and Belgium? Switzerland and Italy? Somewhere along the continuum a line must be drawn, and it was therefore necessary to make some quite arbitrary decisions. Another difficulty is the wide variety of relationships that exist simultaneously between two nations or peoples. This made it impossible to establish mutually exclusive categories.

While it is ordinarily a questionable practice to add or average percentages obtained in several countries, that liberty is taken here in the attempt to examine the *kinds* of relationships between peoples and to bring out the common characteristics of those people who occur to respondents when they are asked the above questions. The set of relationships and the relative strengths of the various contexts are, of course, affected by the particular nine countries selected for study. These might be altered considerably by studying nine other nations or these same nine at a different time.

Further, a really rigorous investigation would demand setting up the categories in advance of the survey, rather than *a posteriori*, as is done here.

The purpose of these sundry qualifications is to mitigate the impression of preciseness which quantitative treatment might otherwise give the study. They should not, however, weaken the important disclosures: that *certain nations are regarded with more friendliness than others*, and *that these nations have certain common cultural or historical characteristics*.

"People" or "Government"

In general, the results suggest that the word "people" should not be interpreted literally by the reader. It clearly was not so interpreted by the respondents, which is, in itself, a rather significant fact. In other surveys the word "government" and the word "people" as used in this context have been found to be *almost* synonymous. Some of the material which bears on this point is given in Appendix B (p. 116).

Milton D. Graham, in a study of British attitudes toward Americans, has examined the carry-over effect of impressions of a people to estimates of their governmental actions. He finds that when unfavorable characteristics are attributed to Americans as a people, these opinions

affect the observers' appraisal of America as a nation and as a dominant world power as certainly as the unfavorable aspects of American international and national policies affect the observers' appraisal of the Americans as a people.

The Americans are generous, mechanically adept and not domineering; the Americans provide generous economic assistance and good technological advice without interfering in domestic political affairs. Similarly, the Americans are cocksure, over-confident and rather simple and over-patriotic; the Americans are naive about international trade difficulties and the intricacies of international diplomacy.

This mixture of people and policies continues in the all-important ambivalent category of responses. The American people are materialistic and not well-educated; the value of the American cultural effort is questionable, their leadership more questionable from the cultural point of view, and the American conduct of domestic affairs is not reassuring to those who believe that domestic leadership and international leadership are very closely related, if not identical; there are fitful bursts of often misdirected energy, lack of consideration for the individual, and a general uneven temper in the conduct of public affairs.[1]

One of the criteria which Svalastoga sets up for "a condition of high hostility for one nation (A) toward another (B)" is a situation in which the members of A "make no discrimination favorable to the non-governing members of B between the attitude of the government of B toward A and the attitude of the non-governing members of B toward A." [2]

While the Unesco survey does not bear directly on the relation in the public mind of the concepts "people" and "government" applied to any foreign nation, it is a topic that deserves further study since it underlies the whole paradox of war.

What Governs "Friendliness"?

This is how the five contexts into which responses were classified compare with each other:

[1] "British Attitudes Toward America," Ph.D. Dissertation at the University of London (1951), Ch. 1, p. 13.
[2] Kaare Svalastoga, "A Progress Report on International Tensions in the State of Washington" (Washington Public Opinion Laboratory, University of Washington, Seattle, 1949). (Mimeographed.)

Context I: "The Bi-Polar World"

The immediacy of the East-West conflict makes this the most obvious factor in the selection of "peoples" as liked or disliked. The percentage-mentions [3] of the Americans and Russians as either most or least liked comprise 38% of the responses in the other eight countries. "Likes" and "dislikes" in this category are about evenly balanced; i.e., *the "Bi-Polar World" appears to influence about as many respondents to like one people as to dislike another.*

Context II: "World War II"

In the seven Allied nations in which the survey was made, 28% of percentage-mentions are Germans, Japanese, and Italians on the "least friendly" question, but only 2% on the "most friendly." In Allied countries, 20% of "most friendly" percentage-mentions are of Dutch, French, Belgians, British, or Canadians—all Allied or Occupied countries—while only 2% of "least friendly" percentage-mentions are of these peoples.[4]

In Germany and Italy, 23% of percentage-mentions for "least friendly" are Poles, French, Dutch, Czechs, British, and Yugoslavs while these peoples get 13% of percentage-mentions for "most friendly." There are no mentions of Japanese, and between Germany and Italy there is only 2% of percentage-mentions "most friendly," compared to 8% "least friendly."

While these percentages are quite obviously products of factors other than the war,[5] it is nevertheless clear that *the last war serves as a frame of reference for many respondents in making their selections.* The combined percentage-mentions in both Allied and Axis countries for allies liked and enemies disliked is 18%.

Thus, combining Contexts I and II, it becomes evident that somewhat over half the respondents took sides either in an immediately past war or a threatening war in determining which peoples they felt "most friendly" and "least friendly" toward. *The tendency to select an impending rather than a concluded conflict was more apparent among the losers—Germany and Italy—than among the winners.*

Context III: "Common Boundaries"

While the shrinking world has made adjoining neighbors relatively less a threat for each other (as indicated by the large number of respondents selecting Amer-

---

[3] Percentage-mentions = the sum of the percentages in each survey mentioning a particular people or category of peoples divided by the sum of the percentages in each survey mentioning all peoples. The latter total is sometimes larger than 100% times the number of surveys being considered, because some survey agencies permitted respondents to name more than one country.

[4] Americans and Russians were excluded because they had already been listed in Context I; Norwegians· because in some surveys they are included under the category "Scandinavians." Since both the French and Mexican surveys lumped peoples mentioned by less than 5% under "All others," the percentages totaled here are conservative.

[5] Proximity of countries, "Bi-Polar" alliances, elimination of Russians and Americans as belonging exclusively to the previous category, the disproportionate number of nations on the two sides in World War II, Italy's position on both sides, and inconsistencies among survey agencies in their methods of comprising the "all other" category.

icans and Russians—peoples tangent to none of the countries surveyed except Mexico and Norway), respondents might be expected to name those peoples closest to them with whom they have presumably the most frequent opportunities for contact, friendly or unfriendly. Furthermore, possession of a common boundary is a definite standard for setting up a category although it excludes the islands of Australia and Britain.

The other seven countries surveyed have a total of 29 immediate neighbors, of whom 20 were mentioned by 1% or more of respondents in these countries. Of these, *nine countries were in the "most friendly" class—all of them smaller nations than the ones in which the choices were made;* five were in the "least friendly," and six in both. The nine peoples not mentioned were Austrians by Germans and Italians, Belgians by Germans, Luxemburgers by Germans and French, British Hondurans and Guatemalans by Mexicans, Mexicans by Americans, and Spaniards by the French. Of the 20 nations mentioned, 13% of percentage-mentions were "most friendly" and 16% "least friendly." [6]

Context IV: "Common Language/Culture"

English-speaking peoples mentioned in the United States, Australia, and Britain; Spanish-speaking peoples mentioned in Mexico; other Scandinavians mentioned in Norway; Belgians in France and the Netherlands; Swiss in Italy, France, and Germany; and common mention between the Germans and the Dutch account for 26% of the "most friendly" percentage-mentions, but only 5% of the "least friendly." (This latter figure would be 1% except that 36% of the Dutch cited the Germans.)

Context V: "Neutrality"

Peoples of the nations which for various reasons remained neutral in World War II received 10% of percentage-mentions for "most friendly," but less than 1% for "least friendly." These included the Irish, Swiss, Swedes, Spaniards, and Argentines. "Scandinavians" were also included when mentioned or tabulated as a group.[7]

It will be noted that in Contexts I, II, and III, which deal with tension, war, and territorial security, "likes" are about evenly balanced with "dislikes" while in Contexts IV and V, dealing with common culture and neutrality, "dislikes" amount to only a fraction of the percentage-mentions that "likes" do. The similarity between these Contexts and the categories set up for Q.8 (see p. 32) is striking, due to the incidence with which respondents selected the same countries. It is not surprising that one is friendly to the people of a country that offers him "the kind of life he wants to lead."

---

[6] Whereas Contexts I and II were made mutually exclusive by eliminating Americans and Russians from Context II, the remaining categories overlap each other, as well as I and II. Contexts II and V are mutually exclusive.

[7] Since Scandinavians were both participants and neutrals in World War II, they could be counted either way. The 10% figure becomes 8% if they are excluded.

"Bi-Polar World" Tensions: Context I Examined

Only Americans and Russians were picked by enough respondents in the eight remaining countries to make a breakdown by groups in the population feasible. The averages for the eight countries are as follows:

	"Most friendly" to Americans on Q.11	"Least friendly" to Russians on Q.12
National Total	33%	36%
Socio-economic Status		
A—wealthy	38	50
B—average	33	41
C—below average	34	34
D—very poor	30	28
Class Identification		
Upper	34	52
Middle	34	42
Lower	30	30
Politics		
"Leftists"	28	26
"Rightists"	34	49

Dislike of Russians is far more directly related to income and class identification than is a liking for Americans. One might hazard a guess that two factors are working against each other in the American figure: (1) the choosing of sides in the "Bi-Polar" conflict, which would make for friendliness to America in the upper brackets, and (2) a need and desire to migrate, which is more forceful in the lower brackets.[8] There appears no appreciable difference in the effect of "objective" and "subjective" class affiliation.

These averages obscure national patterns, particularly on the "most friendly" question where differences are smaller, and some countries clearly contradict the pattern suggested here. The groups selecting the United States are the same ones that picked it as offering them the best opportunity (p. 31).

Narrow Area of Choice

The great majority of peoples, numerically, who occupy the largest part of the globe, appear infrequently on either the "most" or "least friendly" lists. There is one mention of China, one of Argentina, one of "Asiatics," and several hostile mentions of Japan; otherwise the *natives of South and Central America, Africa, the Near East, the Far East, and Southeast Asia are entirely ignored.* Technology, economics, and threat of war may have

---

[8] It is impossible to determine how much of the drop in the lower income and class group percentages is due to "Don't know's" since these were not separately tabulated.

linked the real world, but the mental world of the individual in these Western countries remains small and ethno-centered. His "map of the world," if he lives in Europe, remains the Greenwich-centered Mercator. The peoples whom he sees as important to him would occupy only the small central area on this map. The "maps" in the heads of extra-Continentals (Mexicans, Australians, and Americans) differ in orientation, but are no less self-centered.

Summary

This exercise in categorization suffers because only a few nations were surveyed, because the categories were set up after examining the data, and because some rather arbitrary assignments were necessary. However, these shortcomings need not apply to further studies along this line. Among some of the possibilities are:

1. A repetition of the same questions in the same nine countries employing the same categories. (A great many of the errors of classification will thus cancel out for trend purposes.) This would make it possible to estimate the degree to which popular pre-occupation with the East-West conflict has, since 1948, pushed into the backbround attitudes held over from World War II. It might be valuable to project a "forgetting curve" in which the residual hatred from a past war is plotted against intervening time and events. This general technique may be useful in gauging the ebb and flow of international tensions. What effects do diplomatic breaches and *rapprochements* have? *Coups d'états?* Are friendships based on common language or traditional neutrality more stable than those produced by the pressure of a momentary power situation?

2. Further probing as to what reasoning underlies an individual's choice of the "people" toward whom he is "most" or "least friendly." The categories used here involve the assumption that respondents pick certain peoples for one reason or another, but there is no evidence that this is their real reason, nor is there any allowance for difference between respondents in the reason for their selections. Additional "why" questions could lead to clearer and more realistic categories. A list of nations handed to the respondent might diminish the factor of "attention" (see Appendix B).

3. Inclusion of a larger group of nations in the "sample" might lead to some generalizations about an individual's reactions to other nations or peoples which would have broader significance than those given here.

National Stereotypes[1]

— Chapter 5

A central question in the matter of national attitude and belief is the way the members of any given nation perceive the members of another. Generally, the people of one nation—and the United States is no exception—harbor stereotyped images of other nations, starkly simple and exceedingly inaccurate. . . .

The nature of the various types of images . . . their comparison with reality, and the identification of causal factors are attackable problems. Until some headway is made, international relations must always be in danger of decisions based on fantasy.[2]

The Unesco questionnaire utilized a technique to attack this problem that had been used by social psychologists since early in the 1930's to investigate stereotypes of both races and nationalities, so there exists a body of previous research using comparable methods. However, aside from some surveys by the Office of Public Opinion Research during the war, it had not been frequently combined with the polling technique of gathering cases.

The Unesco question read:

Q.13: *From the list of words on this card, which seems to you to describe the American people best? Select as many as you wish and call off the letters and the words that go with them. If you have no particular feelings one way or the other, just say so.* The words listed were: HARD-WORKING, INTELLIGENT, PRACTICAL, CONCEITED, GENEROUS, CRUEL, BACKWARD, BRAVE, SELF-CONTROLLED, DOMINEERING, PROGRESSIVE, PEACE-LOVING, IMPOSSIBLE TO CHARACTERIZE.

---

[1] This chapter is an edited version of "Stereotypes and Tensions as Revealed by the Unesco International Poll" in the *International Social Science Bulletin*, III, No. 3 (autumn, 1951), 515-28.

[2] Leighton, *op. cit.*, pp. 102-03.

TABLE 5 SUMMARY OF Q.13 RESULTS (Percentage of respondents in each country selecting each adjective)

Country in which survey was made	AUSTRALIA			BRITAIN					GERMANY					
People Described	U.S.	Russ.	Self	U.S.	Russ.	Self	Fr.	Chin.	U.S.	Russ.	Self	Brit.	Fr.	Chin.
Adjective														
Hardworking	33%	52%	43%	32%	53%	57%	24%	40%	19%	12%	90%	13%	4%	18%
Intelligent	46	16	53	38	12	52	32	17	34	4	64	34	22	6
Practical	49	19	49	38	21	47	20	11	45	8	53	20	5	3
Conceited	42	14	17	52	13	11	29	2	15	3	15	23	20	—
Generous	40	4	63	52	3	48	14	7	46	2	11	14	5	1
Cruel	2	37	—	3	39	1	5	18	2	48	1	3	10	6
Backward	3	28	9	4	36	6	9	37	1	41	2	3	10	12
Brave	21	26	57	19	31	59	14	21	6	11	63	8	7	6
Self-controlled	18	15	26	10	9	44	3	15	11	3	12	24	5	5
Domineering	23	57	4	37	42	6	11	2	10	12	10	21	12	1
Progressive	77	25	39	58	21	31	14	8	58	2	39	17	7	1
Peace-loving	42	7	71	39	6	77	21	22	23	5	37	15	12	5
Impossible to characterize	ᵃ	ᵃ	ᵃ	8	18	5	30	32	17	34	5	34	49	71
Average no.: Positive adj.	3.3	1.6	4.0	3.0	1.6	4.1	1.4	1.4	2.4	.5	3.7	1.4	.6	.4
Neg. adj.	.7	1.3	.3	1.0	1.3	.2	.5	.6	.3	1.0	.3	.5	.5	.2

ᵃ Not tabulated.

This procedure was repeated for "the Russian people," then with reference to the people of the country in which the survey was being made. In certain surveys respondents were also asked to describe in the same manner the British, French, and Chinese peoples. Results of the Mexican survey were not cross-tabulated, so they are omitted from the following analysis.

Difficulties in the Word-List Method

Several qualifications should be made concerning generalizations from results of a survey using this technique:

1. The wording on the question to some degree implies that a "people" may be described in one or a few words, and so may evoke from the compliant respondent an answer that can be classified as a stereotype, although the respondent is well aware that he has been forced into fallacious thinking. Eysenck and Crown found that 136 of 204 English middle-class subjects in a similar experiment gave some indication that they were aware of this. A majority indicated that "they did not know any representatives of the races concerned, and had quite unanimously to fall back in most cases on what they had heard or read about the unknown nationalities, or seen

FRANCE			ITALY			NETHERLANDS						NORWAY			UNITED STATES		
U.S.	Russ.	Self	U.S.	Russ.	Self	U.S.	Russ.	Self	Brit.	Fr.	Chin.	U.S.	Russ.	Self	Russ.	Brit.	Self
37%	51%	46%	39%	22%	67%	49%	36%	62%	23%	6%	12%	56%	36%	43%	49%	43%	68%
37	15	79	34	13	80	33	8	49	22	8	7	31	6	32	12	49	72
81	11	17	59	5	24	61	6	36	24	5	3	54	9	22	13	32	53
24	14	30	22	12	24	15	10	14	24	10	2	11	7	19	28	38	22
34	7	62	60	5	41	40	3	23	7	16	2	39	5	31	3	13	76
4	41	—	3	55	3	2	53	—	3	2	12	1	19	1	50	3	2
2	56	4	2	58	7	1	43	1	2	8	20	1	25	7	40	11	2
26	42	56	18	22	45	25	21	37	20	20	9	16	20	42	28	43	66
34	9	12	16	4	5	16	3	36	34	3	9	15	5	21	14	35	37
46	49	4	11	45	8	16	50	5	21	5	2	10	51	3	49	33	9
75	19	34	32	13	17	57	15	43	17	10	4	42	7	27	15	25	70
26	10	69	29	6	27	40	6	68	26	15	9	35	7	69	7	42	82
4	12	3	9	20	7	10	13	8	22	46	54	13	31	8	17	15	3
3.5	1.6	3.7	2.9	.9	3.1	3.2	1.0	3.6	1.7	.8	.5	2.9	.9	2.9	1.4	2.8	5.2
.8	1.6	.4	.4	1.7	.4	.3	1.6	.2	.5	.3	.4	.2	.8	.3	1.7	.9	.4

at the cinema, or picked up in casual conversation. They were recording stereotyped opinions, certainly, but in a high proportion of cases were fully conscious that their ideas were based on meager evidence." [3]

By including the "impossible to characterize" category, and in the last sentence of the question, the Unesco survey drafters provided two possible escape routes for those sophisticated respondents who felt strongly that the test was unfair.

2. The limited choice of twelve words may not give the respondent enough material to reproduce with any accuracy his mental image of one or several of the peoples to be described. Therefore, this survey is more useful in comparing stereotypes held among different groups of describers than in exploring the content of stereotypes. Free answer techniques are better adapted for the latter purpose.

3. The variations in familarity between one word and another—some being in everyday, colloquial use, others met with more rarely—make it dangerous to assume that departures from chance expectations are due

[3] H. J. Eysenck and S. Crown, "National Stereotypes: An Experimental and Methodological Study," *International Journal of Opinion and Attitude Research* (spring, 1948), pp. 26-39.

solely to stereotyping. In earlier studies using somewhat the same method, Schoenfeld [4] found that a control group picked from the Katz-Braly [5] word list certain adjectives which they would use more frequently to describe *any* race or nationality.

This difficulty is aggravated in an international survey because it may be impossible to find a familiar word with even the approximate connotation of the term in the English-French text. Hence one should be slow to attribute a deviation from the international norm to a propensity on the part of a particular "describer nation" to stereotype a certain people in terms of one adjective; on the other hand, the existence of such a norm (i.e., the tendency of a large proportion of respondents in eight countries, speaking six languages, to apply the same term to one people and not to another) is indicative either of a stereotype or the sextuple coincidence of a canceling-out effect in the translating process.

4. There is no proof that certain of these words cannot be objectively shown to be more applicable to certain peoples than to others. A comparison, for example, of the average work week and rate of production might show one people as more "hardworking." This "kernel of truth" hypothesis is discussed by Schoenfeld and Klineberg.[6] Mace [7] sees a stereotype as the possible result of both "cognitive" and "emotional" factors.

In view of the public unavailability of such information, if it ever has been compiled, the word "stereotype" is used consistently herein because it conforms to the definition of stereotype as a view that is "not well thought out" even though it may not be provably "deceptive."

5. All the figures in Table 5 are no more than percentages of a sample which selected certain words. This fact, as well as the use of the term "describer nation," imputes a collective character to what is actually the sum of a common aspect of a number of individual stereotypes. It is necessary occasionally to remind oneself that, for example, the use of the values 25% in Australia and 13% in Italy in conjunction with the word "progressive" as applied to the Russians does not mean that Australians think of Russians as twice as progressive as Italians do, or that the penchant for thinking of Russians as progressive is twice as strong in a given Australian, or an

---

[4] N. Schoenfeld, "An Experimental Study of Some Problems Relating to Stereotypes," *Archives of Psychology*, No. 270 (1942).

[5] D. Katz and K. W. Braly, "Verbal Stereotypes and Racial Prejudice," in T. M. Newcomb and E. L. Hartley, *Readings in Social Psychology* (New York: Henry Holt & Co., 1947), pp. 204-10. This summarizes two experiments conducted in 1932, which led to wide use of the word-list technique in American studies of stereotypes.

[6] Klineberg, *op. cit.*, pp. 118-23.

[7] C. A. Mace, "National Stereotypes—Their Nature and Function," *Sociological Review*, January–April, 1943.

average Australian, as in an Italian. The use of the term "describer nation" is an example of that compulsion to economy in thought and word which Lippmann originally advanced as the motive which underlies the stereotyping process!

The Existence of Stereotypes

Table 5 brings together the percentages choosing each adjective for every country except Mexico, where this information was not tabulated. Many of the differences are "significant." However, vertical differences (i.e., between two adjectives applied to the same people) may be due to a variation in the familiarity of the words or to their place on the list; and horizontal differences (i.e., between the same adjective as applied to different peoples) may be due to the relative familiarity of the population with the peoples described, as evidenced by variations in the "impossible to characterize" category. If these factors could be held constant, the residue might fairly be labeled a pure "stereotype." Since they cannot, it must be cautioned that the characteristics which are to be analyzed contain an unspecified amount of impurities and that the indices computed are to be considered as qualitative rather than rigorously accurate.

It has been noted that respondents were given adequate opportunity to avoid responding with a stereotype. Were all those who fell in the "impossible to characterize" cell (ranging from 71% of Germans asked to describe the Chinese down to 3% of French and Americans asked to describe themselves) respondents who avoided the choice of adjectives on rational grounds? There is evidence that they were not. Four surveys (Germany, Netherlands, Norway, and the United States) were cross-tabulated by educational groups, and in all of them this category, "Impossible to characterize," attracted a higher percentage of uneducated than educated respondents. This is in line with an almost universal tendency in opinion polling for the less advantaged group to prefer the "no opinion" and "no answer" boxes.

So it must be supposed that this category contains a mixture of sophisticated respondents, respondents who may have had stereotypes not describable in the adjectives on the list, respondents unfamiliar with the peoples asked about, and along with them a sprinkling of the taciturn, illiterate, and totally uncomprehending.

Standardization of Stereotypes

Each respondent was given a choice of twelve adjectives. In all, five peoples were described: the Russians by eight other nations, the Americans by themselves and seven others, the British and French by themselves and three others, and the Chinese by three others. All eight described their own countrymen. Table 6 gives the adjectives selected by the three highest percentages in each country, and the total in each cell represents the number of countries in which that adjective was among the three most popular. Table 7 gives the rank order of the six adjectives most frequently used.

The picture of the Russians is quite consistent from country to country, that of the Americans somewhat less so. There is an indication that the British, French, and Chinese are even less consistently pictured, but the lower percentages of respondents who found any adjectives applicable and the fact that these peoples were described in only three surveys make comparisons difficult.

TABLE 6   Number of Countries in Which an Adjective Was One of the Three Most Frequently Chosen to Describe Their Own Countrymen or Another Country; (e.g., "Hardworking" was among the three adjectives most often used to describe Americans in 3 out of the 7 countries describing them) [a]

People Described and Number of Countries Describing Them	Russians (8)	Americans (U. S.) (7)	British (3)	French (3)	Chinese (3)	Own Countrymen (8)
Adjective						
Hardworking	5½	3	1	1	3	5
Intelligent		1	2	2	⅓	5
Practical		6	½			
Conceited		1	1½	2		
Generous		3		1		3
Cruel	6				1⅓	
Backward	5				3	
Brave			1	1	⅓	5
Self-controlled			2			
Domineering	7½	1		½		
Progressive		6				
Peace-loving			1	1½	1	6
Total	24	21	9	9	9	24

ᵃ Fractions represent ties for third place.

These consistencies, which surmount the translation barrier, suggest that *stereotyped views of certain peoples are common property of the Western culture rather than the effect of bilateral national outlooks that differ from one country to another.* The consistency of the Russian and American stereotypes might also be counted an effect of the so-called "Bi-Polar World."

TABLE 7 THE SIX ADJECTIVES MOST FREQUENTLY USED TO DESCRIBE FIVE NATIONS (Brackets Indicate Tie in Percentages.)

Description of Russians by

Australians	*British*	*French*	*Germans*
Domineering	Hardworking	Backward	Cruel
Hardworking	Domineering	Hardworking	Backward
Cruel	Cruel	Domineering	⎰Hardworking
Backward	Backward	Brave	⎱Domineering
Brave	Brave	Cruel	Brave
Progressive	⎰Practical	Progressive	Practical
	⎱Progressive		

Italians	*Dutch*	*Norwegians*	*Americans (U. S.)*
Backward	Cruel	Hardworking	Cruel
Cruel	Domineering	Domineering	⎰Hardworking
Domineering	Backward	Backward	⎱Domineering
⎰Hardworking	Hardworking	Brave	Backward
⎱Brave	Brave	Cruel	⎰Conceited
⎰Intelligent	Progressive	Practical	⎱Brave
⎱Progressive			

Description of Americans (U. S.) by

Australians	*British*	*French*	*Germans*
Progressive	Progressive	Practical	Progressive
Practical	⎰Conceited	Progressive	Generous
Intelligent	⎱Generous	Domineering	Practical
Conceited	Peace-loving	⎰Hardworking	Intelligent
Peace-loving	⎰Intelligent	⎱Intelligent	Peace-loving
Generous	⎱Practical	⎰Generous	Hardworking
		⎱Self-controlled	

Italians	*Dutch*	*Norwegians*	
Generous	Practical	Hardworking	
Practical	Progressive	Practical	
Hardworking	Hardworking	Progressive	
Intelligent	⎰Generous	Generous	
Progressive	⎱Peace-loving	Peace-loving	
Peace-loving	Intelligent	Intelligent	

Description of British by

Germans	*Dutch*	*Americans (U. S.)*
Intelligent	Self-controlled	Intelligent
Self-controlled	Peace-loving	⎰Hardworking
Conceited	⎰Practical	⎱Brave
Domineering	⎱Conceited	Peace-loving

Description of British by—continued

Germans	Dutch	Americans (U. S.)
Practical	Hardworking	Conceited
Progressive	Intelligent	Self-controlled

Description of French by

British	Germans	Dutch
Intelligent	Intelligent	Brave
Conceited	Conceited	Generous
Hardworking	⎰ Domineering	Peace-loving
Peace-loving	⎱ Peace-loving	⎰ Conceited
Practical	⎰ Cruel	⎱ Progressive
⎰ Generous	⎱ Backward	⎰ Intelligent
⎨ Brave		⎱ Backward
⎩ Progressive		

Description of Chinese by

British	Germans	Dutch
Hardworking	Hardworking	Backward
Backward	Backward	⎰ Hardworking
Peace-loving	⎰ Intelligent	⎱ Cruel
Brave	⎨ Cruel	⎰ Brave
Cruel	⎩ Brave	⎨ Self-controlled
Intelligent	⎰ Self-controlled	⎩ Peace-loving
	⎱ Peace-loving	

Description of Own Countrymen by

Australians	British	French	Germans
Peace-loving	Peace-loving	Intelligent	Hardworking
Generous	Brave	Peace-loving	Intelligent
Brave	Hardworking	Generous	Brave
Intelligent	Intelligent	Brave	Practical
Practical	Generous	Hardworking	Progressive
Hardworking	Practical	Progressive	Peace-loving

Italians	Dutch	Norwegians	Americans (U. S.)
Intelligent	Peace-loving	Peace-loving	Peace-loving
Hardworking	Hardworking	Hardworking	Generous
Brave	Intelligent	Brave	Intelligent
Generous	Progressive	Intelligent	Progressive
Peace-loving	Brave	Generous	Hardworking
⎰ Practical	⎰ Practical	Progressive	Brave
⎱ Conceited	⎱ Self-controlled		

The Stereotype as Extension of Ego

The last column in Table 6 gives the adjectives picked by the three highest percentages in each nation to describe their fellow countrymen. There is evident a universal tendency to appropriate the complimentary adjectives for one's own countrymen and, by reflection of virtue, for oneself. Lippmann said: "A pattern of stereotypes is not neutral. . . . It is not merely a short cut. . . . It is a guarantee of our self respect; it is a projection upon the world of our own value, our own position, and our own rights. . . . They are the fortress of our own tradition and behind its defenses we can continue to feel ourselves safe in the position we occupy." [8]

Stereotype Direction and Tensions

The drafters of the questionnaire designated four of the adjectives—conceited, cruel, backward, and domineering—as negative in connotation, and eight—hardworking, intelligent, practical, generous, brave, self-controlled, progressive, and peace-loving—as positive. This is a rough measure, since it makes no allowance for varying degrees of attractiveness or repugnance of the qualities concerned; but in view of the variations in connotation, familiarity, and forcefulness of the adjectives when translated into six different languages, no more precise index was practicable. The correctness of this division was demonstrated when the least popular positive adjective was found to have been chosen by a greater proportion of respondents than the most popular negative adjective in describing their countrymen, with the single exception of "conceited" in three of the nine countries.

The average number of mentions of the positive terms and of the negative terms (i.e., the total of the times each such term was applied to a particular people divided by the number of respondents in the sample) is given at the bottom of Table 5.

To get a "stereotype score" which evaluates the "direction" or tone of the stereotype, the average number of negative words used to describe a people was doubled (to adjust for the two-to-one ratio of positive to negative terms) and subtracted from the positive average. This provides an index which could vary from $+ 8.0$ (if every respondent had selected all positive but no negative adjectives) to $- 8.0$ (if everyone had selected all negative but no positive adjectives). This "stereotype score" was computed for the 29 instances in which one nation described the people of another and is given in Column 1 of Table 8.

[8] Walter Lippmann, *Public Opinion* (New York: Harcourt, Brace & Co., 1922), p. 96.

TABLE 8   "STEREOTYPE" AND "FRIENDLINESS SCORES"

			"Stereotype Score"[a]	"Friendliness Score"[b]
Dutch	toward	Americans	2.6	26%
Norwegians	"	Americans	2.5	21
Italians	"	Americans	2.1	50
Australians	"	Americans	1.9	60
French	"	Americans	1.9	11
Germans	"	Americans	1.8	24
Americans	"	British	1.0	31
British	"	Americans	1.0	26
Dutch	"	British	0.7	8
British	"	French	0.4	9
Germans	"	British	0.4	9
Mexicans	"	Americans	0.3	18
Dutch	"	French	0.2	4
British	"	Chinese	0.2	0
Mexicans	"	French	0.1	0
Germans	"	Chinese	0	0
Mexicans	"	British	0	0
Dutch	"	Chinese	−0.3	0
Germans	"	French	−0.4	−2
Mexicans	"	Chinese	−0.6	−10
Norwegians	"	Russians	−0.7	−26
Mexicans	"	Russians	−0.8	−24
Australians	"	Russians	−1.0	−34
British	"	Russians	−1.0	−37
Germans	"	Russians	−1.5	−56
French	"	Russians	−1.6	−22
Americans	"	Russians	−2.0	−51
Dutch	"	Russians	−2.2	−36
Italians	"	Russians	−2.5	−39

[a] "Stereotype Score"—average number of positive adjectives applied to a people, minus twice the number of negative adjectives.

[b] "Friendliness Score"—percentage designating themselves "most friendly" toward a people, minus percentage designating themselves "least friendly."

For each of the "stereotype scores," the percentage of respondents designating that country as the one which they felt "least friendly" toward on Q.12 was subtracted from the percentage designating it as the one they were "most friendly" toward on Q.11 in order to get a "friendliness score." (Less than 1% was counted as zero.) This could range between + 100 (if 100% of respondents had been friendly toward the same country and none unfriendly) and − 100 (if 100% had been unfriendly and none friendly). It may be worth reiterating that this represents friendly respondents minus unfriendly ones, rather than the degree of friendliness shown by any or all the people; whereas the "stereotype score" summarizes over a group of people positive and negative tendencies which may be exhibited by the same individuals. The "friendliness score" is given in the last column of Table 8. Table 9 shows the relationship of the two scores. This bears out on an international level the conclusion, which Katz and Braly drew from a survey of 100 Princeton students, that "there is a marked similarity between the relative ranking on the basis of preference for group names and the average scores representing an evaluation of typical traits."

TABLE 9 RELATIONSHIP OF "STEREOTYPE" AND "FRIENDLINESS SCORES" IN TABLE 8

"Friendliness Score"	"Stereotype Score"										
	−2.1 and over	−1.6 to −2.0	−1.1 to −1.5	−.6 to −1.0	−.1 to −.5	0	.1 to .5	.6 to 1.0	1.1 to 1.5	1.6 to 2.0	2.1 and over
40% and over										1	1
31 to 49%								1			
21 to 30%								1		1	2
11 to 20%							1			1	
1 to 10%							3	1			
0					1	2	2				
−1 to −10%				1	1						
−11 to −20%											
−21 to −30%		1		2							
−31 to −40%	2			2							
−40 and over		1	1								

Changes in Stereotypes

In 1942 the Office of Public Opinion Research asked a sample of 1,200 Americans to select those adjectives from a list of 25 which best described the Russians.[9] Seven of these adjectives were also used on the Unesco survey. The results are as follows:

	1942	*1948*
HARDWORKING	61%	49%
INTELLIGENT	16	12
PRACTICAL	18	13
CONCEITED	3	28
CRUEL	9	50
BRAVE	48	28
PROGRESSIVE	24	15

A "stereotype score" was computed for these percentages in the manner outlined above, except that the negative average was multiplied by 2.5 rather than 2 to adjust for the different ratio of positive to negative adjec-

[9] Hadley Cantril and Mildred Strunk, *Public Opinion 1935-1946* (Princeton, N. J.: Princeton University Press, 1951), p. 502.

tives. For 1942 the score is $+ 1.4$; for 1948 it is $- 0.8$. (For all twelve adjectives it is $- 2.0$ in 1948. This is indicative of the effect that the alteration of only a few words can have.)

Allowing for the difference between the length and content of the two word lists, it still seems obvious that some other factor is at work, and it is most reasonable to believe that this is the deterioration in Russian-American relations. In this case, stereotypes may be more flexible than is often assumed.[10] In 1950 G. M. Gilbert repeated the Katz-Braly experiment on the same small segment of Americans—Princeton University undergraduates—a generation after the original study. He found those students more aware of the fallacy of describing a people in a few words, and much less addicted to the old popular stereotypes. He also found that World War II had radically altered the picture of the Germans and Japanese.[11]

This alteration over a period of time suggests that *stereotypes are less likely to govern the likes and dislikes between nations than to adapt themselves to the positive or negative relationship based on matters unrelated to images of the people concerned.* Rather than summing up the characteristics of a people as "pictured in his head" and deciding whether this is a portrait of a "nice" or a "bad" person (a subjective method which would be somewhat analagous to the compilation of the "stereotype score" above), it seems that the individual is first brought to a feeling of like or dislike, after which he refocuses his mental image to correspond.

Schoenfeld, in comparing the content of the stereotypes he found just after Pearl Harbor with those found by Katz and Braly in the early 1930's, concludes that "the influence of historical events has changed somewhat the quality of the German, Italian, and especially the Japanese stereotypes. Many of the old qualities have been retained, but to them have been added new ones, such as 'arrogant,' 'conceited,' 'cowardly,' 'deceitful.' In addition, some former qualities of a pejorative nature have increased in frequency of assignment. To the traditional stereotypes of those nations with which we are allies, there have also been added new qualities, but these are generally of a likeable kind, while former complimentary qualities have in some instances increased in frequency of assignment—apparently it is possible for a nationality stereotype to undergo marked changes of direction or intensity without correspondingly great changes in quality."[12]

Further light on this process is obtained if the 1942 and 1948 stereotypes

---

[10] Mace, *op. cit.*, "current usage tends to restrict the term to ideas that are fixed when fixity is inappropriate, or appropriate on other than intellectual grounds. It implies most frequently fixity of ideas or invariability of responses in circumstances which call for plasticity or adaptability."

[11] G. M. Gilbert, "Stereotype Persistence and Change Among College Students," *Journal of Abnormal and Social Psychology*, 46, No. 2 (April, 1951), 245-54.

[12] Schoenfeld, *op. cit.*

above are divided into two patterns—a positive and a negative. The rank order and the rough proportions of the percentages are the same for both periods within each pattern. In both, more respondents think the Russians cruel than think them conceited; in both, more think them hardworking than brave, brave than progressive, progressive than practical, practical than intelligent. But in the interim all the bad qualities have come to the fore and the good ones receded.

These isolated findings are, of course, indicative rather than conclusive; but repetition of word-list studies over a period of time long enough to relate national stereotypes to events of international significance may shed further light on their swiftness of change and susceptibility to events. (Additional material on the choice of adjectives from the word list by different educational and socio-economic groups in the Dutch population is given on p. 80.)

Summary

The results on the stereotype question indicate: *(1) that there exists in all eight countries surveyed a tendency to ascribe certain characteristics to certain people; (2) that there is a uniform tendency of respondents of all countries, taken as a whole, to describe the Russians in the same terms, and somewhat less agreement on the Americans; (3) that stereotypes of one's own countrymen are invariably in flattering terms; and (4) that the prevalence of complimentary over derogatory terms in a national stereotype is a good index of friendliness between nations.*

There is limited evidence that national stereotypes are flexible over a period of years; and thus that they may follow and rationalize, rather than precede and determine, reaction to a certain nation.

The tenor of the findings as a whole is in the direction of minimizing the causative effect of either favorable or unfavorable stereotypes in relations between nations, and suggests that stereotypes may not exist until objective events demand their creation. Perhaps their important function is the wartime one of providing a rationale within which men are able to kill, deceive, and perform other acts not sanctioned by the usual moral code.

Evidence in Chapter 4 strongly suggests that friendliness or unfriendliness to another people may be attributed to relationships between their governments: whether they were in the allied or enemy camp in the past war or in the present "cold" war, whether one can understand the language they speak, and whether they are traditionally neutral. Yet here friendliness and unfriendliness are found to be related to the predominant stereotypes held in the various countries. This is, once again, evidence that *stereotypes should not be thought of as causative, but as symptomatic.* "These people threaten us, they have fought against us, they are just across our border, we cannot understand what they say, hence they *must be* cruel, conceited, domineering, etc."

Possibilities for Further Research

This material was analyzed almost entirely for evidence of stereotypes as related to international tensions. It is obvious that there remains to be done a great deal of research toward describing and accounting for stereotypes. Unsummarized results of this type, in the form of punch cards, might reveal more about the extent to which stereotypes are phenomena of individual personality or class outlook; certainly these findings suggest that differences within a nation might be more extreme than those between nations.

Stereotypes of only five foreign peoples were delineated—too few to be fitted into the categorization scheme in Chapter 4. An investigation designed to show what characteristics are assigned to near-by peoples, to peoples speaking one's language, and to allies or former allies might produce useful information.

Graham recently found that a sample of British respondents reacted to individual Americans on the basis of immediate personal contacts but formed their impression of the American "type" on the basis of

. . . superficial contact or observation or on consistent portrayal over a long period of time in books, the press, or the films. . . . The trend from the individual to the "type" is from the specific to the more general, and from the strongly favourable to the moderately favourable. These trends continue as the still more general concept of the "American people" comes into consideration. Here, much greater reliance is placed on second-hand information such as press and literary accounts; personal attributes become more blurred, generalizations become more sweeping, considerations of American national and international policy begin to affect some respondents' replies, and the circle from the individual American friend to the U.S.A. as a dominant world power is closed.[13]

It is unquestionably one of the less personal, more generalized contexts which the word-list technique used in the Unesco survey taps. This is the context in which "peoples" and governments merge; it is the least favorable one in the British-American study, but this should not necessarily be true in every case.

There is a great need for more study of the processes of perception by individuals of acts of foreign governments and the intent behind these acts. Media of communication obviously must bear some responsibility for the

---

[13] Milton D. Graham, "An Experiment in International Attitudes Research," *International Social Science Bulletin,* III, No. 3 (autumn, 1951), 538-39.

stereotypes held by members of their audience. So must the leaders of the people who are the subject of the stereotype, since their acts, perceived at second hand through these media, are the events which form and change the stereotypes. The popular assumption that personal contacts between people will improve relationships between them is not necessarily true. The absurdity of a stereotype of a people as a whole does not apparently discourage individuals from holding it, even though they may recognize it as a stereotype [14] and even though they may have a first-hand acquaintance with individual representatives of the people.[15] The stereotype seems to serve to explain acts of a distant entity (seen either as a government or as a "people") which would otherwise be inexplicable to the perceiver.

Leighton says of stereotypes that "these images are the basis upon which people feel for or against other nations, interpret their behavior as villainous or good, judge their actions, and judge what *they themselves as a nation should do in relation to others*. It follows, of course, that if the images are false, the resulting action can hardly ever be adequate." [16]

The Unesco survey indicates that stereotypes are less effective in producing a positive or negative reaction than Leighton's appraisal implies. The danger lies, instead, in the inadequate action we may take on the basis of false notions of the intentions of other governments, notions which result from attributing a particular set of characteristics to the peoples which these governments represent.

We must know accurately at least two things to get on amicably with another nation: (1) what the purposes of these people are, and (2) how they see our purposes. Otherwise, both parties, traveling by different "maps," are likely to collide inadvertently.

---

[14] See p. 46.

[15] "Some of my best friends are Jews."

[16] Leighton, *op. cit.* Italics are supplied by the authors of this study.

"Human Nature,"
"National Character,"
World Peace, and
International Government

Chapter 6

The individual's assumptions concerning the nature of the world, of which ideas concerning men and nations and war and peace are fragments, form the intellectual framework within which he considers proposals for change. The four questions which deal with these more or less abstract ideas differ from the other questions in that the "you" element is subordinated. They demand that the respondent exercise logic, pass on matters of fact or probability, and judge proposals rather than merely describe his position in life or his subjective relations to others.

Since they demand more of an "intellectual" than an "emotional" reaction, these questions were not intended to get at the "real" reasons for the individual's view of international affairs but rather to get at his rationalizations and assumptions. This should not imply that these opinions are any less firmly held, or necessarily less important to the individual.

These questions test the prevalence of the sort of thinking embodied in the phrase "War is inevitable because you can't change human nature." While this sort of reasoning may not itself motivate people to resist proposals for change, it does supply them with a satisfying rationale, and if it goes unchallenged, presents a stumbling block to any efforts of those who seek to re-order the world along more amicable lines.

One set of data may be anticipated from this block of results to illustrate the importance of these ideas and how they are believed to function. In Germany 59%, and in Italy 51%, of respondents said their national characteristics were "born in us." In the United States, 15% gave this response, in Norway 23%. Nazi–Fascist teachings unquestionably account for the large difference, but they cannot be considered the sole cause, for the figures in the Netherlands (44%) and Britain (39%) are almost as high. The difference is that in Germany these beliefs supported a program of policy, and for the individual rationalized actions on the part of his government against "non-Aryans" which he could not otherwise have justified. What were the "real" motives behind these national acts is far more important, but there are no data on them here. The important point is that this belief sanctioned actions, just as the belief in the inevitability of war may support those who for other reasons oppose international government and hinder those who want to work toward it.

The Questions

The authors of the questionnaire recognized the danger of probing a basic attitude with a single question. Nevertheless, they were interested in having an off-the-cuff reaction to a series of issues which are often discussed, hence are well-verbalized attitudes and, therefore, fit subjects for opinion polling.

The questions were:

Q.1a: *Do you believe that human nature can be changed?*

Q.1b:[1] (If Can): *Do you think this is likely to happen?*

Q.2: *Do you think that our* (British, French, Italian, etc.) *characteristics are mainly born in us, or are they due to the way we are brought up?*

Q.3a: *Do you believe that it will be possible for all countries to live together at peace with each other?*

Q.3b:[1] *Do you think that this is likely to happen?*

Q.4: *Some people say that there should be a world government able to control the laws made by each country. Do you agree or disagree?*

The totals for each of the nine countries on Q.1-4 are given in Table 10. Except in Mexico the answers tend to group around the middle of the scale on Q.1, 3, and 4. Those believing human nature can be changed run from 34% to 59% in the eight other countries; those believing world peace possible, between 30% and 58%; those agreeing there should be a world government, between 35% and 56%. These are apparently matters on which there is little consensus and no distinct international pattern.

These national percentages fall around the 50-50 point, where random replies by respondents would have put them. There is a large percentage of "Don't know's" in many countries. The percentage saying "Likely" does

---

[1] Q.1b and 3b ("Do you think that this is likely to happen?") sharply reduced the previous "Yes" percentages. However, they were percentaged on different bases by different survey agencies, in several cases in such a manner that it was impossible to reconvert them, so they are disregarded here although they are given in Appendix D. The French and Norwegians recalculated the figures for Q.2 to combine the "Both" with the "Don't know" responses; it is not clear how such qualified answers were handled in the other countries.

TABLE 10   TOTALS FOR EACH OF NINE COUNTRIES ON Q.1-4

Type of Answer	Austral.	Brit.	Fr.	West Ger.	Ital.	Mex.	Neth.	Nor.	U.S.
Human nature *can* be changed	43	40	59	54	34	32	44	56	50
Human nature *cannot* be changed	51	48	22	30	43	55	43	31	40
Don't know	6	12	19	16	23	13	13	13	10
Nat'l characteristics *born in us*	23	39	35	59	51	28	44	23	15
Due to *way brought up*	74	55	45	29	39	64	43	57	79
Both or *Don't know*	3	6	20	12	10	8	13	20	6
Believe world peace *possible*	42	47	47	58	30	18	46	43	49
Believe world peace *not possible*	54	44	41	35	59	74	49	52	45
Don't know	4	9	12	7	11	8	5	5	6
Agree there should be world government	35	44	45	46	56	19	46	48	42
Disagree	58	40	36	33	28	72	32	35	46
Don't know	7	16	19	21	16	9	22	17	12

not always show a consistent relation to the percentage saying "Possible."
In several countries, 6% to 8% of those saying "Likely" on Q.3b had already
said "Impossible" on Q.3a. These questions deal with matters of the intellectual rather than experiential knowledge of the respondents; their
pertinence to his life is not immediately obvious. For all these reasons,
one should expect less validity from these questions than from more personal ones.[2]

There is somewhat clearer division on the question of national characteristics. *In Australia and the United States, more than 70% say these are
due to upbringing; in Germany only 29% say this; the others fall in between.*

Mexicans do not differ strongly from the others on the questions relating

[2] This is further borne out by the following replies obtained by Gallup affiliates in five
of the nine countries in September, 1948. Although the subject matter is connected, the
national totals show little consistency with those obtained in the same countries on Q.3a
and 3b as comparison with Table 1 will indicate.
"Do you think there will be another big war within the next ten years?"

	Will	*Will not*	*No opinion*
Italy	58	26	16
United States	57	26	17
Norway	53	27	20
Netherlands	52	34	14
England	35	36	29

From *World Opinion,* October, 1948, p. 5.

to human nature and national characteristics, but they are very pessimistic on matters of world peace and world government.

Italians exhibit still a different pattern: they tend to be undecided about human nature, to follow the Germans in their view of national characteristics, and to follow the Mexicans in the pessimism about the possibility of peace. However, they reverse themselves and outdo all the others in their espousal of world government.

The French are particularly optimistic about changing human nature, otherwise their answers are not atypical.

These gyrations suggest either that these are matters where the teachings of national school systems or national cultural norms differ sharply between countries or else that there is a large degree of incompatibility in the translations of the questions (Q.1-4). (These translations are given in Appendix D.)

Neither the sex nor the age of respondents seemed to have a "consistent" or "significant" effect on the answers to any of the questions (Q.1-4). Socioeconomic status was not related in any way that could not be accounted for by its connection with education.

In Britain and Mexico, the proportion believing that human nature could be changed was higher among those with secondary and university education [3] than among those with primary or no education. In Germany it was just the opposite: there, those with less formal education were more likely to say human nature could be changed than those who had reached a higher level.

The proportion believing their respective national characteristics were due to the way they were brought up was higher among respondents with secondary or university education in France and the United States and with secondary education in Germany.[4] Italy reversed the trend: those with little or no education were most likely to say their national characteristics were due to the way they were brought up.

All these differences were "significant," and all of them remained when the respondents who replied "Don't know" (or "Both" on Q.2) were eliminated and the percentages recalculated with 100% equal to the number of respondents who gave a definite, unequivocal reply.[5]

In other countries, differences were either not "significant" or did not

[3] These groups were combined in the analysis because in many countries there were not enough university-educated respondents to calculate significances.

[4] Figures on the university educated in Germany were such that it was impossible to draw any conclusions.

[5] This adjusts for the tendency of the uneducated to answer "Don't know" to any question, which in this instance would reduce the percentages giving either of the other two answers and which would make a direct comparison with educated respondents misleading.

remain when the "Don't know's" were eliminated; and they were not consistently in the same direction. Opinions on peace and world government showed no relation to education.

This suggests that the content of the educational system, particularly the teaching of biology, sociology, and philosophy, may in the past have varied considerably between nations. This is known to have been the case in Germany, and the amount of shift attributable to revised teaching under the occupational authorities is suggested below (p. 86).

The Political Factor in Opinions

When divided by political views, the results are less equivocal. *"Rightists" tend to believe human nature cannot be changed and that national characteristics are inborn.* This is evident in most countries, but the percentages are only occasionally "significant." "Leftists" do not consistently take the opposite view, a fairly high proportion of them falling in the "Don't know" category.

On the possibility of peace, "Leftists" in every country tend to be optimistic; "Rightists," pessimistic. The differences are "significant" in six of the nine countries. The "Leftists" favor a world government, and the "Rightists" oppose it in eight of the nine countries, and by significant margins in four of the nine.

To summarize: of the four clearly independent variables, three (sex, age, and socio-economic status) show no relationship, while the fourth (education) seems to have some effect, but not always in the same direction.[6] The fifth background variable (political predisposition) is in itself a matter of opinion and cannot be considered independent. It is clearly related to views on international affairs and somewhat less clearly to views of human nature and national characteristics.

In gauging the effect of security on answers to questions about peace and world government, it is necessary to use the "Security Scores," which eliminates France and Australia (for which the scores are not available). These two were the nations with the lowest, and highest, security indices, respectively. In the seven remaining countries, there was a "consistent" tendency for the more secure respondents to believe that peace was possible. The difference between the "least secure" and the "medium secure" groups was not "significant," however, and between the "least secure" and "most secure" groups it was "significant" only for Germany and Mexico. There was some tendency for the most secure respondents to feel world

---

[6] This finding for Q.3a checks with those of Kaare Svalastoga, "Factors Associated with Belief in Permanent Peace," *International Journal of Opinion and Attitude Research*, V, No. 3 (fall, 1951), 391-96.

government necessary, but the converse was not true; that is, the least secure did not "disagree," they merely dropped into the "Don't know" group. For this reason, the tendency did not reach the point of "significance." And even this slight trend was not visible in Norway.

Cross-Relation of Questions

In every country those who believe human nature can be changed are more likely to believe their national characteristics result from upbringing, and those who believe human nature inflexible are more likely to attribute national characteristics to heredity. These differences are "significant" in seven of the nine countries.[7]

The two questions on international relations were also closely related. *In every country those who thought peace possible were more likely to want world government than those who thought it impossible.* The differences were "significant" in all nine countries, ranging from 9% to 41%.

In every country those who thought human nature could be changed were more likely to be hopeful of peace than those who said it could not be. The differences ran from 10% to 34%, all "significant." More in the former group also thought peace likely, though by considerably smaller and only occasionally "significant" margins. *Those who thought human nature could change tended to accept world government in eight of the nine countries,* by "significant" margins in six of them.

Whether respondents thought national characteristics were inherited or acquired had no strong relation to their views on peace or world government. There was a slight tendency in seven countries for those who thought their national characteristics due to upbringing to say peace was possible, but this was "significant" in only two.

All these relationships are presented in tabular form in Table 11.

Conclusions and Suggestions

Throughout the areas surveyed, opinions on the possibility of peace and world government are closely related to each other, and to views of human nature and politics as well. It is not apparent that these constellations of opinion conform to the age, sex, or status reference groups of their holders.

Opinion divides into two patterns somewhat as follows: on one hand there are the *"optimists"—those who believe human nature perfectible, national*

---

[7] To be sure, those views may be logically connected; however, just over a third of the 12,000 interviewees did not find them so—saying either that human nature can be changed but that national characteristics are inborn, or that while human nature is inflexible their national traits result from upbringing.

TABLE 11 RELATION OF CERTAIN OPINIONS TO EACH OTHER AND TO BACKGROUND FIGURES

	Human Nature	National Character	Peace	World Gov't
National character..	"Consistent" and "Significant"			
Peace............	Strong	"Consistent"		
World government..	"Consistent" and "Significant"	None	Strong	
Political views......	"Consistent" for "Rightists" only	"Consistent" for "Rightists" only	"Consistent" and "Significant"	"Consistent" and "Significant"
Education.........	Inconsistent	Inconsistent	None	None
Socio-economic.....	None	None	"	"
Sex..............	"	"	"	"
Age..............	"	"	"	"

Key:

None: Differences between groups not "significant" in more than one country, not in the same direction in more than six countries, or did not remain when adjusted for "Don't know's" (see p. 63).

Inconsistent: "Significant" differences were found in certain countries, but were not in the same direction in every country where found.

"Consistent": Differences were in the same direction in seven or more countries, but were not "significant" in more than one; differences for the variant countries were not "significant."

"Consistent" and "Significant": Differences were in the same direction in seven or more countries, and "significant" in half or more of these; differences for the variant countries were not "significant."

Strong: Differences were in the same direction in all countries and were "significant" in all.

For meanings of "consistent" and "significant" as used here, see p. 112.

character pliable, world peace attainable, and world organization advisable; on the other hand are the *"fatalists"—those who believe that "you'll always have wars because you can't change human nature," and that change is hardly worth trying.* Along the continuum between them stand the bulk of the population, choosing among these various beliefs with magnificent disregard for consistency.

Do these findings offer any hope for Unesco's educational program? They leave unanswered an important question: What purpose does the "fatalistic" view of the world serve for those who hold it? Age, sex, and status give no clue. Politics suggest that this may be part of a philosophy of ultraconservatism in which those who see their own government, regardless of its actual complexion, as "too much to the left" also derive some grim satisfaction from believing that all these efforts toward change will come to nothing, while only human obstinacy and national bloodlines remain constant. If this is actually the case, the prospect for shaking these beliefs is hardly bright. However, the presence of a considerable body of Communists among the group finding these same governments "Too right" puts an entirely different connotation on the questions. Then the issue becomes: Are these changes to be achieved gradually or by revolution?

A third possibility is that the key phrase may be "human nature"—a phrase which translates with ease from language to language (la nature humaine, das Wesen des Menschen, la natura umana, naturaleza humana, manselijke natuur, menneskenaturen), which provokes about the same patterns of response in every country and which perhaps has no really specific meaning anywhere.

If the "fatalist's" glib generality about human nature were no more than a useful cracker-barrel debater's point, one would not expect to find it so well integrated in his outlook on politics, heredity, peace, and internationalism. It would be naive to expect a campaign designed to deny the aphorism that "wars are inevitable because of human nature" would by itself improve international understanding.

The contemporary studies of anthropologists, biologists, psychologists, and sociologists demonstrate the infinite variety of cultures and the flexibility of human behavior. Wider dissemination of these findings through schools and universities should (aside from its intrinsic worth as enlightenment) have a beneficial effect on ideas about peace and international cooperation. "To the best of our knowledge, there is no evidence to indicate that wars are necessary and inevitable consequences of 'human nature' as such" was the first point in a statement issued by eight social scientists at a Unesco conference.[8]

The comparative strength of the relationships suggests that perhaps hope for peace is the central attitude and that the others are part of a supporting rationale—the whole constellation being provoked by shock at the possibility of another war.

Whether or not any one, all, or none of these lines of speculation proves fruitful, there is enough evidence to conclude that *attitudes toward peace and world government are part of a more or less coherent philosophy of life that in its broad lines extends to all Western nations and all classes within them and that remedial programs should attack at more than a single point.*

[8] Hadley Cantril, editor, *Tensions That Cause Wars* (Urbana: University of Illinois Press, 1950), p. 17.

The Nine
National Surveys

Chapter 7

In addition to the patterns that are revealed by examining the results, in all of the surveys, of a particular question or a group of related questions, one may consider each national survey as a unit, highlighting the especial combination of attitudes characteristic of that nation, and the cross-relationships of these attitudes. This is tantamount to treating the survey as though it had been made as a unique investigation. In the attempt, however, it becomes inevitable that the other surveys must be taken into consideration. Their existence as a standard of comparison increases tremendously the power of the research technique. Ignoring them is possible as an intellectual *tour de force,* but it leaves standing only the shell of the investigation.

Australia

Australians were found to be the most "secure" of the nationalities studied.[1] The Australian government was the one considered farthest "Left" by the people under it (see p. 25). Australia also rated high on the index of "national satisfaction" (see p. 30) and was one of the countries characterized by a "loose" class system (see p. 17).

The high security index resulted largely from a greater feeling of security in their jobs (Q.6a) than was exhibited in other nations. Australians were also more likely to feel that they were able to "plan ahead" (Q.6b). They were somewhat disappointed at the way their postwar expectations had failed to materialize (Q.7), and their expression of "general satisfaction" was lower than in Norway or the United States.

---

[1] For the distinction between "security score" and "security index," both of which will be used in these discussions, see p. 26.

On the subject of human nature, Australians presented a fairly typical picture: 51% believed it could not be changed. The most influential background factor here was education: of the primary group, only 39% said human nature could be changed, while among the small group with a university education, this figure was 61%.

Along with other non-European peoples, most Australians were likely to attribute their national characteristics to upbringing (74%) rather than to heredity (Q.2), and only Americans (79%) believed more widely in the influence of environment. Since both countries are well populated with immigrants, this is not surprising.

A small majority of Australians (54%) did not believe world peace was possible (Q.3). It is interesting to note, however, that Australians had more reservations about world government than any other country except Mexico (Q.4). Some explanation of this may be found, possibly, in Australia's peculiar geographic and ethnographic position: her nearness to Asia, the "white Australia" sentiment, and the realization that a world government would necessarily have a majority of non-white representatives.

Social self-rating by the Australian respondents (Q.9) resulted in a fairly even split between "middle"- and "working"-class replies. Australians, despite their suspicions of world government, revealed strong feelings of kinship with members of their own class abroad (67% felt they had "something in common"). They also were higher than others in the proportion (78%) feeling "something in common" with Australians of other classes.

Satisfaction with life in Australia was high, 83% picking it as the country offering them the life they would like to lead (Q.8). This was exceeded only by the United States (96%).

Asked what foreign people they were most friendly toward, 61% of Australians named the Americans. (The British were not considered "foreign.") This is the highest proportion of respondents in any country naming any one people. Russians and Japanese were each cited by about a third of the respondents as the people toward whom they felt least friendly (Q.12). Nowhere else were the Japanese mentioned by nearly so large a proportion.

Britain

The answers of Britons to the Unesco questions showed the influence of geography and history, reflecting in some particulars their proximity to the Continental nations, in others their affiliation with other English-speaking peoples, as represented in the survey by the United States and Australia.

A small margin of British respondents believed human nature could not be changed (40% said "Can"; 48%, "Cannot"). Only 24% thought this change likely: groups in which there were more "Can's" than "Cannot's." And of all those believing change was possible, only 57% thought it likely.

Belief that British national characteristics were due to upbringing rather than heredity was expressed by 55% of the respondents. However, the "Born in us" point of view increased with age, as was the case in most Continental countries. Although the samples are too small to be reliable, there is an indication of conflicting views among the more privileged respondents. On most other questions the self-styled "upper" class, the "A" socio-economic group, and the university educated, being overlapping groups, deviate in the same direction from the bulk of respondents. On this question the "upper" class is the only group where a majority (53%) picks heredity, and the "A" group also picks heredity in greater numbers than the "B" and "C" groups. However, the university educated [2] were the strongest believers in environment (65%), along with those who believe the government "Too right" (67%).

The British were fairly evenly divided on the possibility of world peace; 44% said "Not possible"; 47%, "Possible"; and there was little variation from these totals among the various background groups. But only 21% thought such a peace was "Likely."

Opinions on world government (Q.4) corresponded rather closely to results on Q.3. In general those who believed peace was possible also agreed with the idea of world government, although there was a larger "Don't know" response on Q.4 than on Q.3. The small groups believing in environment (see above), that is, the university educated and the "Leftists," were outstandingly in favor of such international control.

Britain's security index ranked it midway among the nine countries. Postwar expectations had been more widely disappointed in Britain than anywhere else except in France: 58% of all respondents (and 64% of the youngest age group) were not doing so well as they had expected at the end of the war. The history of the immediate postwar years can easily account for this result. Taking into consideration this fact, and also the fact that England had a Socialist government at the time of the survey, it is interesting to compare security scores of the top and bottom British socio-economic classes with similar groups in the United States:

Security Scores

		High (12-10)	Medium (9-5)	Low (4-0)	Total
"A" group:	U. S.	42%	49%	9%	100%
	Britain	24	49	27	100
"D" group:	U. S.	4	39	57	100
	Britain	6	47	47	100

[2] See p. 135.

This indicates that the well-to-do are more secure in the United States, but that the lowest economic group is more secure in England than in the United States, despite the higher *total* American security. The British show a smaller range between the security level of the "well-to-do" group and the security level of the "very poor" than any country, except Norway, of the seven for which Security Scores are available.

When security breakdowns are further examined, it appears that women were less secure than men, and that the youngest and oldest respondents had lower scores than the two middle age-groups.

Britain was chosen by 51% of the respondents as the country offering them the life they wanted. Although this is far below the Australian and American figures, it is the highest of the other nations, and somewhat higher than either the total security index or its general satisfaction component would lead one to expect. The youngest respondents were least disposed to choose Britain, only 38% did so. They were correspondingly more likely to choose the United States and Australia, which were the next most popular choices among all Britons.

When choosing a name for their social class, 60% of the respondents placed themselves in the "working" class. Only in the Netherlands was the proportion this high.

On Q.10 the British revealed a high degree of both international and national commonality. Only Australia and the Netherlands had a higher percentage than the British (58%), saying they felt something in common with their class abroad. Women were more inclined than men to say "No" or "Don't know," and there is the usual tendency toward internationalism as well as more feeling of commonality toward Britons of other classes, as status, education, and occupation rise.

The United States was named by the largest proportion as the country toward which Britons were most friendly. The "middle" class was the group in which the United States was most popular, the "Leftists" the group in which it was least popular. The Russians were named by 37% of the British as the group they felt least friendly toward, and hostility rose with both "subjective" and "objective" status. The Germans were named by 16%, but the background influence is reversed: the "D" group and the "working" class were most hostile.

France

France had much the lowest security level of any country surveyed. The national security index was 20, which is far below the next country on the scale (Germany, 26), and in all but one of the components of the index France ranked as the least secure, by a large margin. This low level of security,[3] and the Frenchman's ideological position, caught between the massive pressures of the "Bi-Polar World," are exhibited throughout the replies (see p. 20).

In spite of the pervading atmosphere of despair (or perhaps because of it), respondents in France were more hopeful that human nature could be changed (59%) than in any other nation. When *all* respondents [4] were asked whether this change was likely, 38% thought it was.

National characteristics were attributed to environment rather than heredity (Q.2) by almost half the respondents. This was about the same proportion as in the Netherlands, but contrasts sharply to France's other neighbors, Germany and Italy, where the apparent effects of "super race" doctrines were still in evidence.

French opinion was rather evenly divided on the question of world peace: 47% thought it possible, 41% thought not. Only 24% of the respondents thought such a peace likely. These figures do not differ appreciably from those in Britain, Germany, and the United States.

The balance of French respondents favored the idea of world government; the pattern of replies of those who agreed with the idea generally following the optimistic answers about the possibility of world peace, although, as in other countries, "Don't know" replies to Q.4 were more frequent than to Q.3a.

Asked to choose the country which offered the best kind of life, 43% of the respondents named France; not as low a percentage as the security level would have indicated (see discussion, p. 28). Next in popularity was America, picked by 12%—a much lower figure than in other continental countries. Russia was chosen by 4%, the highest proportion of the nine nations surveyed, with most of the pro-Russian replies coming from the "D" group, the "working" class and the "Leftists."

Of all respondents, 46% said they were "working" class, 44% "middle" class. Respondents tended to place themselves higher on the social scale as their age increased. This is in striking contrast to their security level, which became lower with increasing age. Perhaps it indicates a more intense desire to "keep up with the Joneses," or "save face" as respondents grow older and less secure.

Nearly half the respondents (48%) felt they had something in common

---

[3] A release by AIPO November 26, 1949, giving results from seven countries on questions as to how "happy" respondents considered themselves, showed France again as the most pessimistic country surveyed. "Not happy" responses in Australia, Britain, the Netherlands, Canada, Norway, and the United States ranged from 3% to 12% of the sample; in France, 33%. "Very happy" proportions in the other countries ranged from 26% to 43%; in France they comprised 11%. Perhaps there is some cultural norm in France which provokes respondents to give the most pessimistic answer possible to this sort of question. If so, the validity of security measurements by the survey process is open to serious question.

[4] See p. 144.

with others of their own class abroad—higher than any other Continental people except the Dutch. French "working" class respondents were *more* likely than those of the "middle" class to express this aspect of internationalism (see p. 20). France is thus a unique exception to the general pattern of an increase in international class consciousness as status rises.

French respondents gave almost equal mention to Swiss, Americans, Belgians, and British, as the people to whom they felt most friendly, with replies ranging from 18% to 14%. In no other country were the choices so evenly distributed. Russians were named by 10%, more than in any other country, which substantiates the comparatively high proportion on Q.8 picking Russia as offering them the kind of life they would like to live.

Germans and Russians were named by 34% and 32% of French respondents as the people toward whom they were least friendly. The Americans were named by 6%, the Italians by 7%. No other nation named these two latter peoples as frequently.

Germany

The German survey was conducted in the British Zone of Germany with the cooperation of the British Occupation authorities. Although the sample (3,371) was three times as large as the other surveys, it cannot be considered geographically representative of even the West German people, since it omits the Southern Catholics. Another factor which may affect the comparability of results is the high "Don't know" responses on a number of questions, particularly the more abstract ones. While this in itself is a revealing finding (and one, incidentally borne out by other surveys in postwar Germany), it interferes to some extent in comparing to other surveys the proportions of those who *did* have opinions.

Germans were, compared with other nations, fairly optimistic about changing human nature—54% replied "Can." No significant background differences were evident in the breakdowns when the "Don't know's" were eliminated.

Germany had the highest proportion of any country saying their national characteristics were inborn (59%), which seems indicative of the remaining effects of Nazi ideology. Again, background factors seemed to have little influence on this belief, since the opinion was widespread; in no group of the population did less than 47% say German characteristics were "born in us." However, there is some evidence in the Berlin survey that this belief is decreasing (see p. 85).

Replies to Q.3 reveal Germany to have been the most optimistic of all countries about the prospects of world peace: 58% thought it "Possible." However, only 15% believed it "Likely." The age breakdown was the only one revealing any great difference of opinion. The youngest respondents (46% "Possible") were the most pessimistic of all Germans, while the 50-65 age group and the "most secure" group were most optimistic. As in several other countries, there is evident some measure of confusion regarding the two parts of the question—8% of those who said world peace was "Likely" had just said it was "Impossible."

The Germans were generally in favor of world government, reflecting again their optimism about world peace and human nature. Women were less sure of their opinion than men: 37% and 57% "agreed," respectively, the 20-point spread being largely accounted for by "Don't know" replies. Optimistic replies increased with socio-economic status and security scores, suggesting that this general optimism was *not* the hope inspired by desperation at Germany's postwar plight. Germans in the 30-49 age group were notably more opposed to world government than were the others.

The German security index figure was 26, halfway between France and Italy; 54% of respondents scored as "insecure" and only 5% as "secure," the remainder falling in the middle group. The comparatively high German score on the postwar expectation component probably indicates a low level of expectation rather than a high level of fulfillment. The women were more disappointed than the men. On the other components of the index, German answers were at about the level of the French. The most striking figure is the 81% who said they were unable to "plan ahead," a far higher proportion than in any other country, but not surprising in view of economic conditions in Germany in 1948.

Germany was chosen by only 30% as the best place to live, again the lowest proportion, although the Netherlands had only 31% choosing their homeland. The United States was chosen by 25%, the second highest proportion to do this in the nine countries.

Germans were somewhat more likely than others to claim "middle"-class status (52%), while 41% claimed to be members of the "working" class. But as has been noted above (p. 17), there was greater agreement between interviewer's and respondent's judgment of the latter's status than in other countries. On the question regarding affiliation with class members abroad and others at home, only 30% picked the internationalist response, while 38% said "Don't know"; but 64% picked the nationalist answer, while only 20% in this instance said "Don't know." Women again accounted for a disproportionate number of "Don't know's."

On the "most friendly" question, 23% named Americans, 11% British and 7% Swedish, but again there was a large number of respondents (37%) who refused to choose. Germans were "least friendly" toward the Russians (50%) and the Poles (14%). Only Americans chose the Russians this frequently, and no more than half of 1% in any other country chose the Poles. Differences of opinion between men and women are evident throughout the German survey. A large part, although not all of this, appears to stem from the women's refusal to commit themselves on the questions. Their "Don't know" percentage is always higher than the men's.

Italy

The national security level in Italy was not so low as others, but there are evidences that what "security" is present in Italy is not very well distributed, which seems to heighten the difference between responses of different socio-economic and occupational groups to a number of the Unesco questions.

The "security index" for Italy was 32, compared to France's 20, Germany's 26, and the Netherlands' 33. Postwar expectations had not been so severely crushed as in other countries, perhaps because Italy's ambiguous status at the war's end had not encouraged optimism. One of the most striking tendencies was the relation of socio-economic status to the general satisfaction component (Q.7): 79% of the "D" group were dissatisfied, but only 22% of the "A" group were "dissatisfied," the "Very satisfied" among the "D" and the "A" groups were 3% and 18%, respectively. The 57-point spread on "Dissatisfied" answers was almost twice that of any other country (France's spread was 30 points) and was larger than the spread between educational and occupational groups. There was a 31-point socio-economic spread on Q.5, also large compared with other countries, and the other security questions also showed fairly large differences.

On Q.1, 34% of Italians thought human nature could be changed, fewer than in other countries; but 73% of them said that the change was likely.[5] Those with secondary education were more likely to say human nature was changeable than either the respondents with more education or those with less. Optimism, however, decreased with socio-economic status, even when the "Don't know's" are included.

While Italy showed almost as high a belief in hereditary national characteristics as Germany (51% compared to 59%), the sex difference in Germany is not apparent in Italy and the age effect is precisely reversed. With "Don't know's" excluded, those over 49 years of age were equally divided between heredity and environment, while younger Italians split 60-40 in the direction of heredity. Belief in heredity *increased* with education, with "objective" status, and with "subjective" status as well, indicating that the whole social system, formal and informal, has apparently been coordinated to promote nationalist values.

Only 30% of Italians thought world peace possible, a degree of pessimism surpassed only in Mexico (18%). There was a high degree of consistency

[5] The survey agency reported some confusion on the question (see p. 173).

in the proportions of the various groups in the population making this response.

Despite this figure, Italy had the highest percentage of all agreeing with the idea of world government, surprising in view of the fact that *individuals* in *all nine* countries who believed in the possibility of peace were more likely to support world government. In all nine countries the total percentage believing in peace was within a few points of the percentage believing in world government, but in Italy these percentages were 26 points apart.

A larger proportion of Italians (54%) considered themselves members of the "middle" class than was the case in other countries. Women were particularly likely to inflate their status, and less than half of 1% of the respondents were unable to place themselves in a class.

There was a rather high "No" response (26%) to the question as to whether respondents felt something in common with Italians of other classes (Q.10a), and both "No" and "Don't know" responses increased as education, "objective" and "subjective" status decreased.

The occupational breakdown shows up more accurately the focal point of dissatisfaction on the security questions and the source of class differences on the class identification questions. The "farm worker" and "manual worker" groups were extreme in proportion of those who had been disappointed after the war, who felt least secure in their jobs, and who were most dissatisfied with things in general. These are, of course, the groups who overwhelmingly considered themselves members of the "working" class (91% and 88%, respectively). About half the "workers" in the sample fell into one of these two occupational groups.

Both groups felt isolated from their countrymen (37% of farm workers and 34% of manual workers answered "No" to Q.10b, compared to a national average of 26%). Of the farm workers 40% said they had nothing in common with members of their class abroad (compared with a national average of 27%, and a figure of 29% for manual workers), a finding which fairly pinpoints the center of Communist appeals.

In striking contrast to farm workers were the farm owners: [6]

	Farm Workers (70)[a]	Farm Owners (193)[a]
Expected to be getting along better at war's end	54%	37%
Feel less secure than average Italian	46	12
Feel unable to plan ahead	67	33
Dissatisfied with way they are getting along	63	32
Belong to "working" class	91	34
Feel nothing in common with class abroad	40	22
Feel nothing in common with other Italians	37	26

[a] Number of persons in sample.

[6] See p. 175 for a note on the constitution of these groups.

The Italian farm workers' "security index" was 21, compared to 32 for the nation as a whole.

It is not unexpected that Italy was one of the countries in which comparatively few respondents (36%) picked their native land as giving them a chance to live the kind of life they would like. Of the rest of the respondents, the bulk selected America,[7] as would be expected where the motive factor is economic insecurity. However, a large "Don't know" response—up to 20% in the "D" group—suggests that, even when asked to do some wishful thinking, many of the respondents who were worst off hardly knew where to turn.

Friendliness to Americans (Q.11) extended through all groups, but diminished among men, young people, and particularly the "D" group ("working" class and "Leftists"). The percentage most friendly to Russians increased almost exactly in proportion to the loss in American popularity. There was an even more pronounced socio-economic effect on unfriendliness to Russia (Q.12).

Mexico

Mexico's 'security index" of 39 places it near the top of the scale, together with Norway and the United States, and it is surpassed only by Australia. Among all nine nations, Mexicans were least disappointed in the realization of their postwar expectations (Q.5). This seems reasonable in view of the fact that they were probably less affected by the war than the others: expectations had not been deferred during the war years, hopes did not bound upward so strongly in 1945, and hence the letdown in 1948 when the postwar Utopia failed to materialize was not as disappointing as in the other nations. Mexicans felt relatively secure in their jobs (Q.6a),[8] and they topped the scale again in their ability to plan ahead (Q.6b). Despite all this, 61% on Q.7 were dissatisfied with conditions in general—a degree of insecurity equivalent to France, Germany, and Italy. Thus the security index shows less internal consistency in Mexico than in any of the other eight nations.

Furthermore, the pessimistic answers to questions about human nature, world peace, and world government do not support the supposition of a high degree of security. Only 32% of Mexicans said it was possible to change human nature, but four-fifths of these respondents said it was likely—making Mexico at once the most pessimistic country but the one

[7] See p. 176.
[8] But note that one alternative, "About the same," was omitted from the questionnaire.

in which the few optimists were most consistent. The effect of both education and socio-economic status was to increase optimism.

Mexicans, along with Australians, Norwegians, and Americans, were inclined toward the environmental rather than the hereditary view of national character (Q.2). Belief in heredity was highest at the middle levels, that is, the secondary educated, the 30-49 age group, and the "C" socio-economic group. Class identification seems to have had little effect.

Of all nine nations, Mexico reached the greatest depths of pessimism concerning world peace; only 18% believed it possible, and half of these thought it unlikely. Optimism was appreciably greater among the "A" socio-economic group, the university educated, and those with high Security Scores.

Again on Q.4 a very large proportion (72%) disagreed with the idea of world government, while only 19% agreed. Opinions did not vary widely from group to group in the population.

Mexico was chosen as offering the best life by 45% of the respondents, and the United States by 31%. The influence of their prosperous neighbor was strongest among the youthful respondents, those of the "B" and "C" socio-economic status, members of the "middle" class, and, surprisingly in view of responses in other countries, the "Leftists."

In rating their own social class, 51% replied "working" class, 45% "middle" class. The men rated themselves socially somewhat lower than the women, and age brought a steady lowering of respondents' self-rating, a situation found in no other country.

A comparatively high degree of personal isolateness was evident from the replies to Q.10; fewer respondents than in most other countries felt they had something in common either with their class members or fellow countrymen.

Americans were the foreign people toward whom the Mexicans felt most friendly, 28% gave this reply. Another 10% named the Spaniards. A misunderstanding (see p. 185) resulted in 28% choosing Mexicans, which reduced these other percentages proportionately.

Two points worthy of mention show up on the "least friendly" question. The Russians were mentioned by the largest proportion (24%), but the next two in order of frequency were the Americans and the Chinese, each named by 10% of the respondents. This is the highest unfriendly mention of Americans and the only mention of the Chinese among all nine nations.

Thus, on all three questions calling for reactions to other people, proximity to the United States resulted in a Mexican view of Americans which differed from that prevalent in the other seven countries.

The Netherlands

If it were necessary to designate one of the nine nations as "typical," that one would be the Netherlands.

Its "security index" was low—about on a level with Italy but not so low as Germany or France. Like other Allied peoples who had borne the brunt of war's devastation, the Dutch were disappointed with the fruits of victory (Q.5). Events in Indonesia also may have played a role in this. A low proportion (31%) picked the Netherlands as offering them the opportunity they wanted (Q.8), but there was a smaller proportion than in other Continental countries picking the United States, and a larger proportion picking the British Dominions. Although the percentages are too small to be "significant," it appears that Canada and South Africa were particularly favored among the less well-off respondents and the "workers."

In the Netherlands fewer respondents than in any other country identified themselves as members of the "middle" class (33% on Q.9) and more with the "working" class (60%, the same as Britain).

There was relatively high identification with class members abroad (61% on Q. 10a) and low identification with Dutchmen of other classes (56% on Q.10b). Holland is the only country where more people identified with the former than the latter.

As in Italy, manual and farm workers were the least secure. The "security index" of Italy is 24, compared to 33 for the Netherlands as a whole. However, in Italy there was a violent contrast between farm owners and farm workers which was not evident in the Netherlands, nor did farm workers differ as radically from the national average on replies to the class- and national-identification questions. On the other hand, there was a great difference in Holland between the net security scores of the "A" and "D" socio-economic groups.

On the more abstract questions (Q.1-4) the Dutch were so evenly divided that the results might have been obtained by flipping a coin. Only on the question about world government (Q.4) was there a "significant" difference between the major response categories: only 32% "Disagree," while 22% "Don't know."

As in other countries, the eldest group was most pessimistic about changing human nature, but so were the wealthiest, and, surprisingly, the best educated. Samples in all three groups are too small to be conclusive. Men were more likely than women to believe in heredity as the source of national characteristics (a contrast to Germany, the only other country in which a sex difference is noticeable). Belief in heredity increased with age, but neither the educational nor the socio-economic breakdown is very revealing.

To the questions about the possibility of peace and the desirability of world government (Q.3 and 4), the eldest group contained more optimists than the younger group. This is true in no other country, and is more remarkable because the oldsters were not sanguine about changing human nature, a view generally connected with belief in the possibility of peace and espousal of a world government. The long history of Dutch internationalism, the Hague conferences, and the establishment of the World Court, all events which took place close to these respondents while they were younger, may have given them personal and continuous interest and hence a personal stake in these concepts. The group is small, so the figures are not "significant," but this explanation, if valid, is important in its implications to those who would strengthen international loyalties.

Friendship toward the Americans was expressed by 28% of the respondents. Among those sixty-five and over, this proportion dropped to 13%; and "Leftists" were considerably less likely than "Rightists" to make this choice (19% compared to 37%). The British, Belgians, and Canadians were mentioned next, and the inclusion of the last by such a high proportion is unique.

Russians and Germans shared almost equally in the total proportion of respondents choosing them as "least friendly"; (39% and 36%). However, background factors influenced replies to this question. As age-level decreased and "objective" and "subjective" status rose, there was an increase in the incidence of mentions of the Russians, with a corresponding decrease in frequency of naming the Germans. The "Leftists" showed notably less animosity toward the Russians, as in other countries.

The Dutch survey agency was one of those which tabulated each adjective on Q.13 according to the sex, age, socio-economic status, and education of the respondent. Although these results may not be generalized to other nations, they are worth examining in several aspects. (The data on which this discussion is based do not appear in the Appendices.)

The better-educated respondents and those higher on the socio-economic scale selected *more* adjectives to describe every people than did the less fortunate ones. This is undoubtedly due to their better ability to verbalize, which has been noted universally in public opinion surveys.

The higher socio-economic groups selected more positively valued words than the lower group to describe the Americans, British, French, and the Dutch themselves, and more negatively valued words to describe the Russians. Of the positively valued adjectives chosen—"Practical," "Progressive," "Peace-loving," "Hardworking," and "Self-controlled" as descriptive of Americans—and of the negatively valued ones—"Cruel," "Backward," and "Domineering" as descriptive of Russians—are chosen in constantly increasing proportions as the income-level rises. This straight-line relation does not apply, however, to the words "Conceited" and "Domineering" as applied to Americans, and "Hardworking," "Intelligent," and "Progressive" as applied to Russians. These words show a curved relationship to status. More people employ them in the "A" and "D" brackets, fewer in the "B" and "C" brackets.

This curved effect is apparent in the educational breakdown. Respondents with secondary education were considerably more likely to apply "nice" words to Americans and "bad" words to Russians than were the primary educated, but they were also slightly more likely to use them than were the university educated.

These results suggest that a rather complex set of factors is at work. One of these factors, a result of the word-list method, is the wider familiarity with the adjectives which education (formal or informal) gives the respondent. Another is the reaction to Communism, which influences the direction of the stereotypes in different economic groups. Another might be the variations in the quality of descriptions of Americans and Russians to which the people at different educational levels have been exposed. Perhaps the better educated are also more reluctant to describe a "people" in black-or-white terms.

Of the four negative adjectives, "Cruel" and "Backward" were virtually ignored by all respondents in describing the Dutch themselves, but "Conceited" and "Domineering" were somewhat more frequently used among the "D" group and the primary educated than among more fortunate respondents. These were the *only two* among the twelve adjectives used more frequently among lower than among higher-status groups to describe their own nationality. This is not a common effect, or at any rate, it did not appear in Germany and Norway, the other two countries in which the adjectives were separately tabulated. The fact that these two adjectives are the ones that might be most accurately used by an "inferior" group to describe those above them throws light on the finding (mentioned above), that only 39% of the "D" group feel they have something in common with Dutch people of other classes (national average, 56%) while 31% say they have nothing in common (national average, 23%).

Norway

The Norwegian lack of class consciousness was perhaps the most outstanding national phenomenon revealed by the Unesco survey. In reply to Q.9, about the same number claimed "middle"—and "working"—class status (43% and 45%). A far larger proportion than in any other country (11%) could not make up their minds. Only 1% considered themselves members of the "upper" class (see p. 15 for further discussion of this point).

The breakdown reveals that while a third of the "D" socio-economic group called themselves "middle" class, 12% of the "A" group said they were members of the "working" class, indicating that these terms have a very nebulous significance for many Norwegians. This resulted in the lowest national score on the index of class discreteness (see p. 17). Another indication of national homogeneity is the fact that breakdowns by social self-rating for the fourteen questions revealed less range than in other countries between the opinions in each class group.

In spite of their unawareness of class distinction, however, only an average proportion of respondents felt they had something in common with other Norwegians not of their class; 64% gave this reply, which is as high as Germany, Britain, and France, but far lower than the United States and Australia, where respondents were less class conscious. Nor did Norwegians differ notably from others in the percentage feeling something in common with members of their class abroad.

Of all respondents, 43% thought world peace was possible, and 48% favored world government, both fairly typical responses. The Norwegian "security index" was 39, which ranks it as the most secure of the Continental nations. Three-fourths of respondents were rated on the Security Score as "very" or "moderately secure," and only Australia had fewer people than Norway in the "least secure" group. Compared to other nations, there was a very small difference between the Security Scores of the well-to-do ("A") respondents and the very poor ("D") group. Norwegians ranked comparatively low in the postwar expectation component of security, and here there is a marked sex difference. At the end of the war 45% of the men had hoped to be getting along better than they actually were, whereas 60% of the women gave this answer. The Norwegian Gallup Institute attributed this to continued shortages of certain kinds of food and clothing. On security in their jobs and ability to plan ahead, however, Norwegians felt better off than other Continental peoples, and apparently these factors counted heavily in their general satisfaction (Q.7), for here Norwegians ranked highest of all, 88% of respondents feeling "Very satisfied" or "All right" about the way they were getting along.

In view of these indications of contentment, it is not surprising to find that 50% of Norwegians chose their own country as the one offering the best opportunity (Q.8), again the highest proportion of any continental country. The United States was chosen by 21%, and a similar number replied "Don't know."

Americans were named by 22% of respondents as the people toward whom they felt the most friendly, and the Danish were chosen by 20% (Q.11). Russians and Germans were the "least friendly" choice of 28% and 22%, respectively. Only the Netherlands and France showed a higher hostility toward the Germans, while Mexico was the only country which revealed less animosity for the Russians.

Norwegian respondents may be summarized as being democratic with regard to class, believers in the adaptability of human character, secure personally, and satisfied with life in Norway. They did not reveal the optimism about peace and world government or the international-mindedness in regard to class and national friendships which one might expect of a representative of Scandinavia.

United States

The United States, together with Norway and Mexico, had a "security index" of 39, which was topped only by Australia's high of 42. However, there was a wide range in security between the "A" and "D" groups—a phenomenon also found in the Netherlands. At the other extreme of the scale in this respect—i.e., the countries where "security" is evenly distributed—are Britain and Norway.

A fairly high proportion of Americans (50%) thought human nature could be changed, but only half of them said it was likely. Opinions were fairly homogeneous throughout the groups in the population.

Americans were the firmest believers among all the nine nations in the influence of environment on national characteristics; only 15% said "Born in us" to Q.2, a phenomenon easily explainable where a fifth of the population are immigrants or children of immigrants. Older respondents were somewhat more likely to believe in heredity than younger ones. Otherwise the most privileged respondents were adherents of the "environmentalist" school, a tendency which contrasts with some European countries.

As in Britain and France, the balance of sentiment in the United States regarding world peace swung toward the optimistic side; 49% said it was "Possible"; 45%, "Not possible."

American opinion on world government was again quite evenly divided; 46% disagreed with the idea, 42% agreed. Only in the two other non-European countries, Australia and Mexico, did the balance of sentiment go against the idea, and by even greater margins, especially in Mexico. The only groups in the American population favoring world government were the youngest respondents, the university educated, the "Leftists," and those who believed world peace possible.

The highest proportion by far selecting their own country as offering the best life (Q.8) occurred among Americans, 96% of whom chose the United States. The nearest was Australia, and other countries varied from 30% to 51%. All groups within the population seemed to believe they were living in the "land of opportunity," for there was no significant variation in their replies. Even among the "D" group, 57% of whom were scored as "insecure," 92% picked the United States.

On Q.9, 51% claimed membership in the "working" class, while 42%

said "middle" class, and 4% "upper" class. However, there is a noticeable sex difference in the replies to this question: women were inclined to place themselves lower socially than were the men, a phenomenon which was not found elsewhere. There is a sudden rise in "subjective" status among those 65 years of age and older: 51% put themselves in the "middle" class, only 35% in the "working" class.

Affinity with their own class abroad was acknowledged and denied by about an equal number of respondents (42% and 40%). Americans' feeling for their countrymen of other classes was much stronger: 77% replied they had something in common. The difference between the percentages identifying with nation and with class—35 points—was equaled only in Germany. The trend in the United States for both these questions followed the usual pattern of a high positive answer among the wealthy, those with a college education, and the younger respondents.

It is evident from replies to the questions concerning attitudes toward other countries and nationalities that the United States was in 1948 still (1) somewhat isolationist and (2) definitely Europe-oriented in its outlook on the world. Mention of Japanese by 11% on the "least friendly" question, easily accountable to the war, was the only exception. The answers to these two questions also point up a tendency toward extremism: a third of Americans felt most friendly toward the British, but no other nation got more than 8% of mentions; similarly Russians (51%) monopolized the "least friendly" mentions, and no other people, not even the enemies of the past war, received more than 11% of the mentions. This suggests that the American picture of the outside world is somewhat oversimplified.

— **Chapter** 8

In the Western sector of Berlin, the Unesco questionnaire was asked of two samples of respondents (sample sizes: 644 and 430) at different times. One was the original survey in August, 1948; the other a follow-up by the British government's Public Opinion Research Office in October, 1949.

When the first survey was made, the blockade of Berlin was in progress, and the atmosphere was one of tension, with the cold war in imminent danger of becoming a shooting war. In October, 1949, five months after the blockade was raised, the impending danger had passed, although Berlin remained a place of tension even when compared to the unquiet situation all over the world.

The pertinent figures for both surveys are given on pages 160 to 169.

Opinions on Human Nature, World Peace, etc.

In both Berlin surveys, the younger respondents were more confident that human nature could *not* be changed. Of those who believed that change was possible, approximately four-fifths in both surveys believed this was "likely to happen." There was no more than 6% difference between the two surveys in any answer category.

There was more change in the answers to the question about national characteristics. Those attributing German traits to environment rather than heredity had grown from 28% to 37%, principally at the expense of the "Don't know's," who had dropped from 15% to 9%. This increase in the be-

[1] Much of the analysis of these questions is based on a report by Dr. James R. White, who directed the two surveys. Dr. White's report has been revised and edited to eliminate duplication with other sections of this study.

lief in environment had come from the younger age groups, and in the second survey the belief obviously decreased as respondents' age increased. The self-styled "working" class, which in 1948 had been the stronghold of beliefs in heredity, was in 1949 somewhat less likely than the higher classes to believe in it.

On both these questions the influence of educational level on the answers, which had been clear in 1948, was becoming blurred by 1949. This could not be attributed to the change in teachings in the formal school system since all but a few respondents had graduated before either survey was taken. The reduction in "Don't know" replies among the less educated was the major difference between the two surveys, but on the whole there is somewhat less adherence to the static, hereditary viewpoint. This effect may have been achieved by the efforts of occupying nations to correct Nazi race doctrines. It may be an actual change of viewpoint, or may merely reflect a wider knowledge of the sort of answers that the occupation authorities—whose sponsorship of the survey must have been recognizable—would approve.

Agreement that there should be a world government increased from 58% to 66%; disagreement decreased commensurately. In both surveys "Don't know's" were twice as frequent among older respondents.

Belief in the possibility of peace increased in about the same measure, while "Don't know's" remained constant at 4%, a rather low figure for a German survey. The youngest group was most pessimistic in both surveys; other breakdowns were unrevealing. While the percentage of all respondents saying "Possible" increased, the percentage saying "Likely" decreased by the same amount (8%) at the expense of both "Unlikely" and "Don't know" responses. This imparts an equivocal flavor to the findings, which discourages interpretation.

Questions Regarding Personal Security

There was an appreciable change in the answers to all the questions dealing with personal conditions and security. This may be attributed to the raising of the blockade, and perhaps in some measure to currency reforms.

Of the August, 1948, respondents, 78% said on Q.5 that they had expected better conditions than they were in fact experiencing. By October, 1949, this percentage had fallen to 52%. Those who had anticipated worse conditions than they were actually undergoing rose from 5% to 22%. The younger people were responsible for most of this change; respondents 66 years of age and up remained almost as despondent as they had been.

Q.6a asked for a comparison of job security with *all* Germans, not Berliners. Unemployment had increased much more rapidly in Berlin than in the Western Zone, and answers may reflect this situation. Various respondents might have considered the "average German" to be an inhabitant of either the Eastern or Western zones, hence, without a definite point of reference, results of this question should be interpreted with care. At any rate, the trend was pessimistic: those feeling less secure than their countrymen had increased from 30% to 42%, those saying "about the same" dropped from 43% to 27%.

The number who said they were sufficiently secure to plan ahead increased from 6% to 13% despite the drop in actual job security. However, those who felt life too insecure for planning still remained high, at 86%. In the age group 21-29, those unable to plan dropped from 90% to 72%, but among all respondents over 50 it remained above 90%.

In 1948 less than 1% of respondents were "Very well satisfied" with conditions, and only 31% said "All right." In 1949 these percentages had increased to 4 and 48, respectively.

As a result of these changes—three for the better and one for the worse—the "security index" for West Berlin as a whole rose from 16 to 23. Comparison with the national indices (see p. 27) shows that the 1948 Berlin level was below that of any country, including West Germany, but that in the following fourteen months Berlin moved up past the point occupied by France in 1948.

Where in 1948 less than 1% of respondents had personal Security Scores of 10 to 12, in 1949 this had increased to 4% and the least secure—those with personal scores of 4 or less—had dropped from 79% to 62%.

In both surveys men had higher Security Scores than women, and younger respondents were more secure than older ones. Those over 65 years of age were striking in their pessimism in the second survey. There is not enough difference between the two middle socio-economic groups, and not enough cases in the two extreme groups, to come to any conclusions about the extent to which security conforms to status as judged by the interviewers, in either survey.

However, the change in a fourteen-month period in the total scores suggests that this group of questions is an effective index for measuring over-all security since it is most reasonable to assume that removal of the blockade and currency reform would achieve a real increase in sentiments of confidence among West Berlin residents.

Questions Regarding Relations to Other Groups

There was an increase in the total who said "Don't know" to the question (Q.10a) as to whether they felt anything in common with their own class abroad; a fact which is more interesting because in 1948 the "Don't know" responses to this question (34%) had been the highest of any of the fourteen questions. The increase in "Don't know's" was entirely on the part of women. Only 25% of men gave this reply in 1948, and this percentage remained constant. "Don't know" responses also increased appreciably among the "working" class.

There was no "significant" change in the number of "Yes" and "No" responses to either this question or the following one on identification with Germans of other classes. On the latter question, however, women were again responsible for whatever change occurred. The follow-up question (Q.10c) did not show any consistent change of opinion.

On the question regarding friendliness to other peoples, there is a slight shift from Britain to the United States. Britain led in 1948 with the United States two percentage points behind; in 1949 the United States led by four points. The change could be accounted for by the dismantling program for which Britain had been the target of German propaganda, American espousal of *laissez faire* while Britain supported economic controls, and the German belief that the United States was "tougher" toward the Russians.

Britain had lost most support among men, younger respondents, and the "working" class. In both surveys the United States and Britain combined obtained about two-thirds of all mentions.

There was no change in the percentage picking Russia as the nation they were least friendly toward. In both surveys women were somewhat more aggressive than men. Nor was there any change of stereotypes, as measured by the word lists. The summarized results, in the form of percentages of total mentions (rather than percentage of respondents, as in other surveys), indicated that not a single one of the twelve adjectives has altered its place on the lists selected to describe the Americans, the Russians, and the Germans themselves. The percentages themselves change as much as 4% on only two adjectives: "Cruel" and "Backward" are more frequently used to describe the Russians.

Other Questions

Between the two surveys there was a 7% increase in the number of respondents saying they were members of the "working" class. Although this sector of Berlin is not normally a workers' residential area, evacuation due to bombing had confused prewar boundaries, and a certain migration of population may have taken place between the two surveys. Interviewers placed more persons in the "below average" socio-economic group in 1949. The increase in the "working"-class response and the corresponding decrease in the "middle"-class response was more obvious among men than among women.

As the country which Berliners felt offered them the "kind of life they would like to lead," there was a slight shift from the United States to Germany. Women accounted for most of the shift. This might therefore be attributed to the increase in younger males in the German population, as prisoners-of-war returned to their homes. Respondents under thirty still tended to prefer the United States, but there was no clear tendency among older respondents.

The final questions, as to whether the government was too far "Right" or "Left" showed an increasing belief that it was "Too right." However, this is not particularly important, since the question was virtually meaningless in 1948, when there was no German government aside from the economic union of the West zones.

Categories of Opinion and Opinion Change

Table 12 indicates the changes over the fourteen-month period between the two surveys. A "significant" difference is about 6½%. Of the 16 dif-

TABLE 12 PERCENTAGE DIFFERENCES BETWEEN REPLIES TO UNESCO QUESTIONNAIRE IN BERLIN BETWEEN AUGUST, 1948, AND OCTOBER, 1949

Question	Direction of Change (response category)	Amount of Change	Don't Know in 1948	
1a	Human nature *can* be changed	+4	8%	Questions dealing with abstract ideas
1b	*Likely* to happen	+6	6	
2a	National character due to *upbringing*	+9	15	
3a	World peace *possible*	+8	4	Average change = 7%
3b	*Likely* to happen	−8	20	Average Don't Know = 12%
4	*Favor* world government	+8	18	
	Security Scores of 5 or above	+17	—	
5	Conditions *better* than expected[a]	+17	2	Questions dealing with personal living conditions
6a	Feel *less* secure than average	+12	6	
6b	*Able* to plan ahead	+7	2	Average change = 14%
7	*Satisfied* with conditions[b]	+21	1	Average Don't Know = 3%
8	*Germany* offers best opportunity	+4	—	
9	Belong to *"working"* class	+7	3	
10a	Identify with *own* class *abroad*	−5	34	Questions dealing with relations to other groups
10b	Identify with *other* classes in Germany	−4	17	
11	*Most* friendly to British	−4	21	Average change = 3%
12	*Least* friendly to Russians	0	15	Average Don't Know = 22%

ᵃ Table C, Col. B, p. 164.

ᵇ Table D, Cols. A and B, p. 165.

ferences recorded here (Security Scores are excluded, being a recalculation of other percentages), seven were of 6% or less, nine of 7% or more. It is, of course, possible that alterations in the population components of West Berlin account for some of these.

Nevertheless, it is apparent that the greatest change occurred in the answers to questions dealing with personal security. These are also the questions on which there were the fewest "Don't know" responses originally. Three of the four changes were in the direction of greater optimism.

On questions dealing with abstract ideas, there was considerably less change, but still enough to rise above the level of "significance." Five of the six were in an optimistic direction, and in the direction which the military government education program would presumably have approved.

However, in the third category, which deals with relations to other peoples and other classes, there was a high "Don't know" percentage to begin with, and the change was not "significant."

The relations of these three groups of questions may be tabulated as follows:

	Personal (Q.5-7)	Abstract (Q.1-4)	Relation to Group (Q.10-12)
Average change:	14%	7%	3%
Average "Don't know":	3%	12%	22%

Berlin was selected for the follow-up study because it was an atypical area, one in which a startling change in conditions had taken place. Hence one must be slow to surmise that this sort of connection between personal conditions, abstract opinions, and group relationships has any wider validity. This is another topic for further research.

— **Chapter** 9

As a Pilot Study

The Unesco survey developed and expanded a technique which had often been used nationally in social science research but had not been attempted over a wide enough area to make cross-national comparisons possible. A number of obstacles appeared: some were overcome in the process of making the survey; others led to suggestions that might be used in future surveys of this type, others (mostly semantic) still remain. These difficulties are discussed, for the most part in Appendix A.

Most important, the survey demonstrated that the existing facilities for surveying public opinion may be utilized in studying the phenomena of international relations as products of individual, personal thoughts and behavior. These facilities are already in existence; as of 1952 there are research organizations of this kind in 20 to 25 countries, including Japan and Israel in addition to Western-oriented nations such as the nine covered here. Opinion surveying has also been done by Stuart C. Dodd, Paul Lazarsfeld, and others in the Near East. Thus the possibility is now open for expanding the technique to cover even more widely differing cultures.

Substantive Results

Earlier research (notably on stereotypes and class identification) that had been done only in one or two countries was substantiated in the wider area of Western culture. Within a limited sphere of subject matter, the survey disclosed that certain ideas and certain relationships between ideas were general while others were restricted to only a few nations. As an index of latent tension, it plumbed the national level of individual security in a number of countries in comparable terms.

More specifically, the major substantive findings may be summarized as follows:

1. The survey accentuated a phenomenon that has frequently been remarked—the narrow limits of the individual's horizon. The individual respondent is quick and definite in answers about conditions that affect him personally—his job, his security, his location in the class structure.[1] He is quicker to see his relationship to his countrymen than to members of his class in other nations—although these do not appear to be mutually exclusive or contradictory affiliations.[2] While his view of the world beyond his borders is out of the perspective in which the geographer or the demographer might draw it, still it may be quite accurately pictured *for the individual* since those people who seem most likely to have an impact *on him* loom larger than life-size, while others are lost in the background.[3]

A novelist once said of middle-class Parisians that "they thought of the world as a sort of a dish, the bottom being France and all foreign lands the peoples being grouped together around the narrow, slanting rim, so that stray objects and personalities slid down into their ken now and then."[4] The Unesco survey indicates that this phenomenon is confined to no single city or country.

2. There is an evident connection between the individual's position in his national life and his view of the world. Involved in this position are his income and "status," his occupation, his education, and his feeling of personal security.[5] These factors are, of course, interrelated; persons who rate high on one generally rate high on the others.[6]

An improvement in one or several of these background characteristics produces in the individual an increased identification with his countrymen and with members of his class (that is, the "middle" or "upper" class) abroad as well.[7] This is probably because wealth increases his commitments, and hence his susceptibility to international political events, while education produces an awareness of relationships between peoples that might otherwise not be realized. An improvement in one's position in life also

---

[1] See pp. 28 and 15-16.

[2] See p. 18.

[3] See pp. 43-44.

[4] Elliot Paul, *The Last Time I Saw Paris* (New York: Random House, 1942); Bantam edition, 1945, p. 150.

[5] See pp. 30 ff. and Chap. 7.

[6] The technique of tabulating each of these variables singly, and percentaging results for the country as a whole, prohibits in this survey the higher order breakdowns that would make it possible to single out the *most* important variable in every case.

[7] See p. 20.

results in friendliness to the United States and dislike of Russia; and in certain countries it is also accompanied by increased satisfaction with life in that country.[8]

3. A person's occupation, income, and education determine what class he feels he belongs to in all these countries. Although virtually every occupational group in every country has some members who claim affiliation with each of the three classes, the norms within different groups vary considerably.[9] Manual and farm workers always occupy the bottom rung of the class ladder, but there is considerable shifting of occupations from country to country on the higher rungs. Moreover, in certain countries the class boundaries are much more distinct than in others.[10]

4. Respondents generally indicated that the "kind of life they would like to lead" involved economic advantages. Nations with higher standards of living were recognized as offering this life, by their own natives and by outsiders as well.[11]

An individual "security index," which was based on questions about employment and expectations, and summarized for the nation as a whole, proved able to differentiate between nations and to reflect changing conditions.[12]

Taking each nation as a whole, three measures—security as gauged by this index, satisfaction with opportunities offered in a nation, and the tightness of class boundaries—were found to be roughly related to each other, to per capita income, to food supply, and to population pressure. However, several countries proved exceptions in certain of these respects.[13]

5. Whether respondents in one nation express themselves as "friendly" or "unfriendly" to another "people" seems to be influenced by the proximity of the latter, their language, and the policies of their government which are discernible in the history of their neutrality or military and ideological alliances. These aspects determine how much attention a nation attracts abroad and whether it stimulates confidence or apprehension.[14] It appears that the individual, after deciding whether a nation threatens or reassures him, then fills in with a description of the people of that nation, coloring them in predominantly attractive or predominantly unattractive characteristics to suit his purposes.[15]

6. Stereotypes of certain peoples were found to be fairly consistent among

[8] See pp. 30, 43.
[9] See p. 14.
[10] See p. 17.
[11] See p. 32.
[12] See p. 28.
[13] See Chap. 4.
[14] See pp. 34-36.
[15] See p. 56.

all the nations studied, and peoples everywhere were prone to stereotype their own nationality in favorable terms.[16] The raw material from which stereotypes are formed may be transmitted from generation to generation [17] and may be absorbed by a child before he realizes what a "nation" or a "people" is.[18] But the manner in which these materials are combined at any moment to produce a pleasant or an unpleasant image apparently will vary with the current state of relations between the governments of the two peoples.[19]

7. Certain ideas about human nature, national characteristics, peace, and world government, with national politics also involved, combine to form a rationale within which the individual views international affairs.[20] Ideas on these topics run in certain patterns so that, knowing an individual's views on one or two of them, one might predict the others with better than chance results, regardless of the individual's nationality. However, these ideas are not consistently related to sex, age, status, and education. They apparently have been influenced by the subject matter of the formal educational system in certain countries.[21]

Two very obvious patterns of response appear in every one of the nine countries, and in each of the nine they are "significant." These are:

1. The respondents who "believe human nature can be changed" are more likely than others to believe that "it will be possible for all countries to live together in peace with each other." [22]

2. Those respondents who believe that such a peace is possible are more likely than others to agree that "there should be a world government able to control the laws made by each country." [23]

(The belief that human nature can be changed is also related to belief in world government, but not with equal force.)

Our Picture of Other Peoples

From the evidence internal to this study alone, it is impossible to describe or explain the phenomenon of our reaction to affairs beyond our borders or to draw in full detail our "map of the world." These fourteen

[16] See p. 50.

[17] Graham (*op. cit.*, p. 535) found that words and phrases written about Americans prior to 1860 were more popular than those of more recent origin.

[18] J. Piaget and A. M. Weil, "The Development in Children of the Idea of the Homeland and of Relations with Other Countries," *International Social Science Bulletin*, III, No. 3 (autumn, 1951), 561.

[19] See p. 56.

[20] See p. 66.

[21] See p. 63.

[22] See p. 65.

[23] See p. 65.

questions are analagous to fourteen frames from a long cinema reel. In reconstructing the plot, one must rely on a few brief, static flashes and fill in the remainder by speculation. One possible interpretation of these results would go about as follows:

Everywhere we work toward our personal ends surrounded by conditions —some of them close by, some distant, in both space and effect. Of these, the conditions with the greatest impact are those that affect us personally: our jobs, our prospects for security, and our place in the class structure which govern our relations with others. Our countrymen, who affect us only indirectly, and our fellow men across the border, who generally appear to affect us not at all, are only vaguely perceived.

Even at this great distance, however, there is a hierarchy of importance of various nations. Those whose borders touch ours, those we have acted against or cooperated with in the course of a recent war, those whose contest with each other threatens to involve us, those that offer us—through hope of immigration—a better opportunity than we now have, those whose dogma offers us an improvement of our station, those who speak our language or a language we can understand, those whose history of neutrality incites our admiration or confidence—all those nations attract our attention with varying force to the exclusion of more populous, far-off countries or of closer ones not large enough to affect us vitally. Our "map" is drawn in proportion to our purposes, not to the area covered by a people or their members.

But beyond our borders we do not spontaneously differentiate between "peoples" and "governments." We recognize the distinction—when it is called to our attention—but it is not ordinarily an important distinction because whatever effect these people have on us is customarily transmitted through the entity called their government. Thus "people" and "government," as they affect us, are more or less of a piece. The connection we see between the two, of course, varies widely from nation to nation.

Certain acts of these governments come to our attention. Because we are unable to "see" these acts personally, we are dependent on interpreters —usually the mass media of communication—to describe them to us. Since even the best informed are too far removed and too ill informed on the context in which these acts occur to understand the motives that underlie them, we must either ignore them or find some simplified explanation. The sort of explanation that is most intelligible is one in terms of individuals, since it is with individuals that our daily transactions occur. We have found it useful in the past to type persons by the characteristics which they have exhibited toward us ("Jones shortchanged me; he is dishonest; I shall not trade with him again."); it is, therefore, not unreasonable to employ the same device in assigning characteristics to foreign peoples as reflected by the acts of their representatives, official or unofficial.

However, this cannot be the whole story, since it does not account for the richness and verisimilitude of the stereotypes, and only partially accounts for their similarity from country to country. Apparently there are latent in fiction, in folklore, and in the educational system certain images of various peoples, images of centuries' standing, perhaps. Within these images may be a "kernel of truth"; or there may be a dried hulk of what might have been truth decades ago. Once a people or government has come to our attention, and we have reacted positively or negatively toward that people or government, we then select the images that support and fill out the stereotype until a credible picture of that unreal concept—a "people"— is before us.

Thus we can account to ourselves in familiar, everyday terms for otherwise inexplicable events and actions. We are also able to act ourselves (or, more frequently, approve or object to the actions of our leaders), since we are now confronted by a "real" and reasonable phenomenon. We know what to do with "Backward" people—educate them; we know what to do with "Generous" people—thank them and return the courtesy; we know what to do with "Cruel" and "Arrogant" people—obliterate them. Thus these stereotypes permit us, especially in a war situation, to act, where we might hesitate if we continued to hold the thought that across the border were individuals as varied and as human as we.

The danger of stereotypes is not so much that nations are hostile to other "peoples" because they have unfavorable stereotypes; it begins to appear that they have unfavorable stereotypes *because they are hostile.* The greater danger is that we will act irrationally on the basis of these simple, satisfying, realistic, but entirely fanciful images. Since in international relations we do not act personally, as we do with our baker, but through a complicated chain of representatives and agents, we never have a chance to test and revise our image, as we would our image of the baker if we discovered that transactions with him based on that image were frequently unsuccessful. We never know precisely what effect our action had, or whether our picture is incorrect, or whether our agents have been inefficient, or whether uncontrollable events have altered the situation in the meantime.

A series of events that occurred in World War II illustrates this point: [24] the Foreign Morale Analysis Division of the U.S. Office of War Information concluded in May, 1945, on the basis of a statistical analysis of Japanese prisoner-of-war interviews, confiscated diaries, and similar intelligence data:

---

[24] Leighton, *op. cit.,* Ch. VII.

(1) that loyalty to the Emperor could not be shaken; but

(2) that home front morale was badly weakened and that surrender by the Japanese was a possibility.

At that time neither conclusion coincided with the opinions prevailing in American policy circles and among the public as well. The current view, based on a particular stereotype of the Japanese "people" as fanatics who would never surrender, was that the war would last until 1946. These preconceptions were not revised until after Hiroshima. Had they been revised before, that holocaust might have been avoided; had they not been revised when they were, the war might have continued until invasion and attrition, costly to both sides, had completely shattered the Japanese nation and forced a deposition of the Emperor. The important observation is that, in this latter case, *the stereotype would have been "proved" to be correct.* Morale could be said to have continued firm to the end and the final remnant of Japan to have been disloyal to the Emperor.[25]

Such speculation runs the usual danger of "rewriting history." But the very caution against "rewriting history" is evidence that, because historical —i.e., social—situations are so seldom similar, nations find it virtually impossible to learn by experience as the individual does in his daily affairs. Moreover, national policy-directing organizations do not have the well-integrated physiological and nervous mechanism which register for the individual organism the consequences of his actions.

Suggestions for Action

The Unesco survey was descriptive and experimental, designed to explore the way for further accumulation of facts about tensions and stereotypes and how men in one country perceive those in another. The process of improving relations between peoples is a long-term one, and there is time for more research to be done, and for its results to be fed back into policy decisions. But because certain choices and actions are demanded in the here-and-now of those who work toward this goal, it may be worth while to relate the survey findings to a somewhat broader body of research in an attempt to make them more useful as a guide to action. It should be emphasized, though, that the following suggestions are interpretations of the data and not demonstrated conclusions.

To make each individual citizen of any country a citizen of the world, capable of acting for the best interests of all citizens of the world, we must:

[25] For a similar example in Germany, see O. Klineberg, "The Scientific Study of National Stereotypes," *International Social Science Bulletin*, III, No. 3 (autumn, 1951), 505-06.

1. *Enlarge his own perceived world.* This involves making him aware of others outside his own immediate environs and their effect on him. This is particularly necessary among the less fortunate groups in every nation, who exhibit a greater isolateness than their countrymen. Since this isolateness is related to economic and status variables, a prerequisite for breaking through it would seem to be a certain minimum of personal security—food, clothes, job, and future—and a certain minimum feeling of self-respect and status.

2. *Bring this world into perspective.* More is demanded here than an increased dose of academic geography and economics. The individual must be made conscious of the relationships which he has with other peoples, perhaps far distant from him, and the *importance* of these relationships to him.[26] He may at present realize only that a wave of feeling in one or another particular country could involve him in a war. This is the negative aspect. He is less likely to realize the impact of peoples abroad on the value of the coin in his pocket, the quantity of food on his table, and his chances for remaining employed.

However, awareness of the importance of others will make him lean more rather than less heavily on his stereotypes. The man who is ignorant of others really has no use for a mental picture of them. Inadequate and inaccurate ideas about other peoples cannot simply be eradicated, leaving the canvas blank. Another picture must be substituted, one equally plausible and equally satisfactory to the individual in interpreting the events that have, or seem to have, personal importance to him.

3. *Improve his facilities for communication and perception.* Communication here does not necessarily imply more and louder international broadcasts. It is rather an increased effort to find out what peoples in other lands want and need, how these wants and needs affect our individual, how he can cooperate in supplying them, and how he can make his own wants and needs known to people abroad. This also involves making clear the motives and purposes behind these wants and needs, and his intentions toward other peoples, and theirs toward him.

The role of government communication abroad (i.e., "propaganda") is to translate national policies into terms that are understandable to the peoples abroad whom they affect. It demands a greater knowledge of what these peoples want than is currently utilized by most governments.

The role of the media of communications is to report events adequately, and also to interpret the purposes of the people who have brought these events about. A French cabinet change or a blow-off by an American iso-

---

[26] See Hadley Cantril, *The Why of Man's Experience* (New York: The Macmillan Co., 1950), Chs. 7, 8.

lationist congressman, to take trite examples, are meaningless to the foreign newspaper reader unless he is supplied with two facts: What do the people in France or America want that is manifested by these events? and How do these wants affect the purposes of the reader of the newspaper? This explanation must, ideally, be couched in terms of personal reference, that is, the tangibles of income, opportunity, and security.

4. *Give him an opportunity to act.* Perhaps the key to the whole psychological problem of international tensions is the fact that the individual can think of no way in which he can act personally to cope with international situations which threaten him. Asked: "Can you think of anything that you personally can do that would help prevent another war?" 64% of Americans answered "No." To a similar question in Canada, 48% answered "No." Even those who answered "Yes" were able to suggest only actions that personally could bring little satisfaction or relief—"study and teaching," "voting," "stop talking and thinking of war," "pray," "mind our own business," "develop character." [27] Some of these are negative actions; the imperative to "stop thinking" is especially likely to develop rather than reduce tensions.

International organizations as a channel for this sort of action encounter some unfortunate obstacles. One of these is the prevalence of certain widespread beliefs, such as those about human nature and the inevitability of war, which inhibit any action, personal or national. Some of these beliefs, however, may be weakened by a wider dissemination of the present body of knowledge in the social sciences. Another obstacle is the inability of the individual to see the *personal* implications of these efforts. The futility of even a full-scale promotional campaign if the individual cannot see the immediate, personal effects was demonstrated several years ago in Cincinnati. After a steady bombardment by all the advertising media— radio, posters, newspapers, club meetings, sermons, etc.—no measurable change in attitude toward the United Nations was achieved. The net result was typified by the remark of one woman when asked about the principal slogan of the campaign, "Peace begins with the United Nations—the United Nations begins with you," which had been broadcast on the local radio

---

[27] See National Opinion Research Center, *Where Unesco Begins,* Rept. No. 34 (Denver, Colo., 1947), and *Unesco and Public Opinion Today,* Rept. No. 35 (Chicago, Ill., 1947). The editors of the former report comment (p. 32), "The apparent paradox of defeatism . . . is highlighted by the fact that, during the war, 83% felt that they as individuals were doing something specific (war job, volunteer defense work, buying bonds) to further the United States' total war effort . . . more than 80% of the public said that national leaders and the press had given them 'a good idea' of how they as individuals might *help the war effort,* but only a third as many felt that leaders and the press had given practical suggestions of what they as individuals could do to *help prevent another war.*"

150 times per week. Her response was: "Why yes. I heard it over and over again—but I never did find out what it means." [28]

5. *Create opportunities for common action.* Stereotypes which lead to irrational, self-destructive action do so because they are based on incorrect apprehensions of what others will do when confronted by a certain situation. They may be corrected only by experience—by noting the unfortunate effects of these misapprehensions. Since the chain of action and perception, via governments and communication media, is so complex and attenuated in the international sphere, it has become difficult for the individual to draw the proper conclusions about the effectiveness of his actions.

However, opportunities are more frequent for action in common with other peoples, in the individual's private capacity. Attempts to improve health conditions, participation in mutual trade, cooperation in scientific or historical research, exchange of literature and art, international religious conferences and foreign missionary work, Olympic games, youth organizations such as the Boy Scouts, international trades unions—all these efforts to reach the goals of security, knowledge, health, faith, beauty, and self-respect are common endeavors of men everywhere simply because they are human beings. Attempts to work together to reach these goals will, in addition to their own immediate ends, build up a body of experience and common assumptions in working together which will enable the individual to check with reality his pictures of other people. To achieve this fully, contacts must be predominantly first hand, and they must involve cooperation toward a common objective. Tourist travel for "broadening" effect, assignment of drafted troops to foreign stations, the study of exotic cultures for the sake of study will not serve the purpose as effectively as the exchange of students who want to learn specific techniques, the incorporation of volunteers into an international army, or the exchange of workers or teachers who must earn their way in their temporary jobs.

In terms of the map analogy, these suggestions might be summarized:

(1) Enlarge the territory which the individual's "map" covers.
(2) Make it more "accurate" for his purposes.
(3) Enable him to revise it from time to time.
(4) Let him use it.
(5) Arrange for him to compare it with others' "maps."

Although these suggestions have been confined to the realm of international relations, it would contradict virtually everything the survey has shown to imply that international affairs fall into a separate context so far

---

[28] S. A. Star and H. M. Hughes, "Report on an Educational Campaign—The Cincinnati Plan for the United Nations," *American Journal of Sociology*, Vol. LV, No. 4 (January, 1950), p. 397.

as the individual is concerned. There is hardly an answer in the survey that does not in some way emphasize the effect of the respondent's position in the life of his own community and country on his views of other peoples. National and class loyalties are not conflicting claims but wider circles of relationships to other men. Few of the opinions registered show wider divergences between nations than between groups within nations.

In the final analysis, this enlargement of contact and cooperation must begin at home, on local levels, and perhaps in routine or trivial affairs. The nation-state that has supplanted the tribe, city-state, and barony is in essence held together by a multiplicity of contacts between its citizens for a common purpose. The state enters into a period of schism when irreconcilable, conflicting purposes transcend in importance the body of common purposes. The individual who feels he is isolated from people abroad has been shown to be the one who also feels his isolation from his countrymen. Lack of education, lack of income, and lack of status narrow the number of groups of people with which our individual is able to come into fruitful contact.

Only as he is able to learn in his daily give-and-take with neighbors and co-workers, and then to enlarge his experience to include participation with those at greater geographical and social distance, will the individual be able to expand his experience in the area of international relations and thus become a citizen of the world.

Appendices

Problems of Meaning,
Methodology,
and Evaluation

—— Appendix A

In the present state of development of opinion surveying, even on a national scale, there remain many baffling and controversial problems.

One of the least soluble of these problems revolves around the wording of questions. Until recently it had been recognized widely, and almost as widely ignored. The appearance of Stanley Payne's *The Art of Asking Questions* [1] has initiated a more fruitful study of the semantics of polling.

An example, pertinent to the Unesco survey, is the drastic difference in the percentage of replies caused by changing one word—"working"—to its dictionary synonym—"laboring"—in a question quite similar to the class question (Q.9) used here (see p. 13).

Translation

The semantic problem that exists in a single survey is vastly complicated in an international survey where translations must be made into seven languages. Radvanyi [2] shows that definitions of "democracy" vary from country to country; for example, one definition given by 51% of respondents in the United States was given by only 4% in Denmark. Stern tells how "washing machine" in some European countries means a fairly expensive electrically operated mechanism, while in others it is a simple, hand-cranked gadget. [3]

While the word "war" was not used in the Unesco survey, the idea of it

---

[1] Princeton, N. J.: Princeton University Press, 1951.
[2] L. Radvanyi, "Problems of International Opinion Surveys," *International Journal of Opinion and Attitude Research*, I, No. 2, 1947, 32-51.
[3] D. Wallace *et al.*, "Experience in the *Time* International Survey," *Public Opinion Quarterly*, XII, No. 4, 708-21.

was implicit in several questions, hence Radvanyi's discussion of it is pertinent:

It would seem that the meaning of the word "war" should be identical in all countries, quite particularly after the recent experiences. In reality, the experiences many peoples had in relation with the war were quite different. In many parts of the world the last war signified tremendous destruction of human life and property, foreign occupation, appalling misery and starvation. However, elsewhere (for instance in Latin America), the same war signified, for broad strata of the population, chiefly greater employment because of the considerable increase in exportation, and higher wages. Although the price increases largely eliminated the increase in wages, today, when the boom produced by the war has already vanished and unemployment is rapidly increasing, the term "war" may continue to have for many of these peoples a meaning not only very different from that of the destroyed countries of Europe, but even of something desirable: a period when employment could be obtained easily, when salaries increased, etc. The example cited demonstrates how different experiences in relation with the same phenomenon can produce different meanings of the same term and thus create serious problems for international opinion surveys.[4]

The Mexican percentage in the Unesco surveys believing world peace possible is lower than that of any other country. Is this due to a different meaning of the word "peace" to a Mexican? Assuming that it is, a corollary question immediately arises: Is this purely a semantic difficulty—like the washing machine problem—which could be resolved by explaining the term? If not, then the difference in the meaning of the term reflects a true difference in opinion, resulting from the nature of the national experience with the phenomena of "war" and of "peace."

Barioux[5] sees the problem as "reducing to a minimum" the "difference resulting from varying emotional reactions to the words used." This is an apt statement of the problem of choice between "working" and "laboring" in the United States, but it is questionable whether it applies to "war" in the circumstances discussed.

In the present study, the list of adjectives (Q.13) gave the most trouble to translators, as the comments of the various agencies indicate (see pp. 127, 153, 171-72). Yet it was perhaps the most useful single question in the inquiry, since it showed that, despite translation differences, respondents everywhere picked the same adjectives to describe the same peoples.

Another concept which caused some difficulty was "too far to the right (left)" (Q.14). Apparently a large group of Americans, and perhaps some Australians (see pp. 127, 210) found that neither these words nor available synonyms had the clear meaning they did on the Continent. The absence of meaning is in itself a significant finding.

In Australia and Italy, the concept of "the average Australian (Italian)"

---

[4] Radvanyi, *op. cit.*, p. 35.
[5] D. Wallace *et al.*, *op. cit.*, pp. 715-18.

(Q.6a) seemed to give trouble (see pp. 127, 171). There was also some variation in translating the ideas of contrasted heredity and environment (Q.2), especially in the French and Italian texts.

It will be noted that all these are rather abstract ideas, suggesting that it is in this realm that national cultures differ to the extent that communication becomes difficult. This is a handicap to the drafter of an international questionnaire, who sees it merely as a limitation on the subject matter he can deal with. To those who are interested in cultural differences and "national character," it may appear in a different light. Comparative philology has often been a useful tool for them; and the survey technique, which deals with words in a considerably more pragmatic manner than dictionaries and grammar texts, may open up new possibilities.

One development of recent date, the invention of Jan Stapel of the Netherlands Institute of Public Opinion, is the so-called "scalometer" device, in which respondents indicate the degree of approval or disapproval of persons, parties, proposals, and other controversial concerns by "putting" them in positively or negatively marked "boxes." This reduces to a minimum the verbal element and may be useful in international surveys on those questions which seek only the net reaction to certain clearly identifiable entities. It has been tested in Dutch and British election polls, with particularly satisfactory results among those with limited education. Of the Unesco questions, those dealing with friendliness toward particular nations might be verified by "scalometer" questions.

Language problems are the most serious ones confronted by international polling. However, in the broadest sense of the word "semantic," the whole problem of international tensions is a "semantic" one. If the fourteen questions in the Unesco survey could be phrased so that they meant precisely the same thing to every respondent in all nine countries, then there might be no need of asking them, perhaps no need of Unesco. Social research encounters the same translation difficulties in this survey that beset any attempt to communicate between peoples. Polling technique, however, focuses attention on differences of meaning that in a less rigidly controlled communication might never be realized, or might be attributed to unshakable differences of opinion. Here at least, language can be *considered*, even if its effects cannot invariably be separated out.

Language, after all, is one of the bases of attitudes, of decisions, and of action. Thus words, however illusory they may be to begin with, acquire a reality when they are acted on—a reality that affects both the actor and the object of his attention. The victims of religious wars are as dead as the victims of economic wars.

The "Universe" and Sub-Groups

Of the other sources of difficulty inherent in international polling, two of the most important may be mentioned:

1. Definition of the "universe": The nine samples here are either political cross-sections used in election studies or consumer samples for commercial surveys. All available information about the sampling process is given in Appendices A, C, and D. Summarizing the results of all nine countries into one sample would presumably make it representative of the populations of all nine countries, to the extent that each individual sample is representative. Since these particular countries comprise no political, geographical, or cultural unit, any expression of the sum of their opinions as a whole would have no significance. Therefore the data should be added or averaged principally as a technical device for reducing an already visible tendency to a single figure for comparison with another such tendency.

2. Comparability of groups: A great deal of what we know about public opinion has been derived by classifying respondents according to their external appearance and what they tell the interviewers about themselves —their education, wealth and status, age, sex, occupation. Within the range of interviewer and response errors, these groups within a country are relatively homogeneous. One could describe with some accuracy a member of a particular socio-economic group in such absolute terms as the type of house he is likely to live in, the diet he is accustomed to, and the facilities for recreation at his disposal. If an individual has reached a certain level of education, one could specify within limits what or how many foreign languages he can read or speak, and what facts about the world are at his disposal.

In an international survey these groups of the population may not be homogeneous from country to country. The standard of living or educational system may vary more between countries than between groups within a country. The rich in one place may have the same standard of living as the poor in another. Only sex and age groups are equivalent; although even here there may be differences of custom and usage governing their treatment and status.

However, in a relative sense these groups do have something in common from nation to nation. Members of the topmost socio-economic group in any country, regardless of their absolute standard, have more to lose by radical change than other groups. Those with only primary education, regardless of what they have been taught (and this may vary considerably between systems of education) are always alike in that they think of the rest of their countrymen as being better informed than they are. These viewpoints may also influence their opinions.

While studies have demonstrated unequivocally that opinion varies between groups, no technique has been refined to the point that it indicates when the individual's point of view is governed by his *absolute* condition in the world, and when it is governed by his *relative* position in the society.

Cross-national groups then are equated in this study, in the absence of knowledge of why these opinions vary, but caution is necessary in interpreting the results.

Coding and Tabulation

A procedure different from that employed in the Unesco survey might justify in sharpened analysis its cost in time and expense during the survey period. This would be to code and tabulate centrally the results of all surveys, using the original ballots. In this case, the interviewers would be instructed to indicate as accurately as possible the respondent's position in respect to each background variable: exact age, number of years of schooling, income if obtainable or some other criteria of economic status (such as the French radio, auto, real property, servant classification scheme, see p. 144). This would make it possible for tabulators to divide each national group into descending halves, thirds, or quarters on each variable, giving larger sub-samples. Or, for other purposes, absolute rather than relative categories might be set up (say, radio owners or those with less than six years of schooling) which would apply to all nations regardless of whether these groups were large or small. With these two processes available, differences in national standards of living, education levels, and life expectancy could be taken into account.

Central tabulation would also permit consolidating groups and making higher-order breakdowns.

The choice of "check-box" or "open-end" questions is even more vital to an international than to a national survey. The former choice runs the risk of obscuring variations of meaning that occur in the translation process, thus *forcing* the results to be comparable. The latter runs the risk of producing results so divergent in context that they cannot be compared at all. The Unesco surveyors chose the first risk, leaving only three open-end questions (Q.8, 11, and 12), all of which demanded simply the names of nations or nationalities. Even here, however, problems arose which could hardly have been foreseen without recourse to a trial run of several hundred interviews in each country. For example: Does "America" on Q.8 mean North and South America, North America, or the United States of America, or does it mean different things to different respondents, or are many respondents ignorant of the distinction between them? (See p. 171 for one answer.) Does "South Africa" mean Southern Africa or the Union of South

Africa? Does "foreign people" in Australia and Britain include British and Commonwealth natives?

In addition to these questions, which could be fully answered only by elaborate pre-tests and instructions to interviewers, there were similar coding problems that arose when results were being tabulated. Since the Unesco tabulation was decentralized, these were answered differently from country to country. Among these were the categorization of responses like "Scandinavians," "Asiatics," and "Jews" on Q.11 and 12; "Dominions and Colonies," and "South America" on Q.8; and "None," "All," "Any," "None in particular," "Don't know," "No answer," two or more choices by the same respondent, and the "All other" category on Q.8, 11, and 12.

It is virtually impossible to foresee all these difficulties, even in a national survey, but in a national survey it is easier to overcome them in the coding stage.

Assorted Biases

Among the biases known to entrap social surveyors, local, national, and international, are:

Those biases originating with the respondent: failure to answer truthfully for prestige reasons, distrust of auspices of the survey, dislike for the interviewer, suspicion of his motives, or mere politeness; failure to understand the question or the alternatives, complete refusal to cooperate.

Those biases that originate with the interviewer: failure to record correctly, failure to ask one or all of the questions, prompting the respondent or antagonizing him, conscious or unconscious prejudice reflected in his tone and emphasis, deviating from instructions in selecting respondents, consciously or unconsciously misreporting age, occupation, or economic status for any number of reasons.

Those biases that originate with the survey agency: sampling design that does not reach a representative group of respondents, choice of a poor time for seeking them out, errors in coding and tabulating the issue, misinterpretation of results, failure to caution the reader about limitations of the data.

Some statisticians even list among the biases in surveys the misinterpretation or misuse that readers make of otherwise impeccable data.[6]

Some of these biases exist in the Unesco survey, to large or little extent, but there is no way of calculating them.

While this survey was being made, employing the "quota sampling"

---

[6] Of the many discussions of such matters may be cited Mildred Parten, *Surveys, Polls and Samples* (New York: Harper & Bros., 1950); and W. E. Deming, "On Errors in Surveys," *American Sociological Review*, 1944, 9:359-60.

methods then in almost universal use, the American pollsters were in the process of demonstrating that they could not pick the winner in the 1948 presidential election. The fact that they used this method may have been one of several reasons for their failure. But even if this were accepted as the sole reason, the error is not great enough to invalidate the results of the Unesco survey.[7]

A more recent judgment of the merits of "quota" versus "probability" sampling, based on field tests, is that "while probability sampling is sound in theory its practicability for public opinion measurement is open to question"; and that, when "quota" sampling was rigidly controlled, "the answers obtained by the two methods differed very little." [8]

The process of "quota" sampling is adequately and critically described in *The Pre-Election Polls of 1948*.[9] Subject to the modifications noted in Appendix D, these are the methods used by all the agencies cooperating in the Unesco surveys.

Calculation of "Significance"

In addition to all these biases, there are random errors; these at least are measurable on a probability basis. Given the number of cases in a sample, or sub-sample, one may determine the amount of confidence to be placed in that sample as representing the universe from which it was drawn. For a national sample this may be expressed in the following form: "the chances are 19 out of 20 that the percentage of 'Yes' answers actually recorded in a random sample of (   ) cases will not vary by more than (   )% from the percentage that would have been recorded if everyone in the nation had been asked the question." Combining two of these calculations shows the difference between two percentages that is "statistically significant" at the "19 in 20" level; that is, would not have been caused by chance more than once in twenty surveys. These calculations for samples of various sizes at various levels have been combined in graphic form by S. S. Wilks.[10]

Such a table has been applied to the differences found in the Unesco survey, especially in the treatment of Chapter 6. It may be reiterated that calculation of significance is based on the assumption that respondents

---

[7] The *maximum* errors of the three American polls were 5.3%, 4.8%, and 12.4%. F. Mosteller *et al.*, *The Pre-Election Polls of 1948*, Social Science Research Council Bulletin 60 (New York, 1949), p. 17.

[8] Charles F. Haner and Norman C. Meier, "The Adaptability of Area-Probability Sampling to Public Opinion Measurement," *Public Opinion Quarterly*, Vol. 15, No. 2 (summer, 1951).

[9] Mosteller, *op. cit.*, Ch. VI.

[10] S. S. Wilks, "Confidence Limits and Critical Differences Between Percentages," *Public Opinion Quarterly*, IV, No. 2, pp. 332-38.

were picked entirely at random, which is not the case in "quota" sampling. Since no method of surveying practicable for social studies completely achieves randomness, this calculation is used as the best achievable estimate of the error than can be caused by chance.

Throughout the text certain differences are labeled "significant," but the term is always used in quotation marks to indicate that it does not have the force that it would in a random sample. The process is a convenient one because it eliminates from consideration a host of minor differences which could well have been caused by chance even if sampling had been perfectly random and the answers free of all bias.

Even in this restricted sense, the "19 in 20" probability should be qualified because of the method of working over the material. The data were eyed for differences, those that appeared substantial were tested for "significance" and commented on in the text if they appeared in a number of countries. This method, hardly defensible in a study attempting to test a hypothesis, is justifiable in a pioneer study, especially an expensive one, where maximum use must be made of the data.

If we first inspect the data for relationships and analyze only those results which appear to be statistically significant, we may come up with statistically significant differences. However, these differences may be attributable to *non-chance* inspection of the data rather than to variables operating within the data.

One cannot, of course, give any interpretative import to these "chance-occurring" relationships unless they are borne out in further investigations designed to test them. However, these relationships, especially if they can be given sensible interpretation, are a likely source of hypotheses for further research.[11]

The risk of highlighting purely random resemblances is reduced to some extent by introducing another standard—"consistency"—that is, *the degree to which groups in several countries showed differences in the same direction.* Purely random figures would give "significant" differences one time in twenty, and half of the differences, "significant" or not, would be in one direction (for example, in half the countries wealthy respondents would be more likely to say "Yes," in the other half poor respondents would be more likely to give this answer). Therefore finding "significant" differences in the same direction in five or more countries is far less likely to be accounted for by chance.

These various qualifications are too numerous to mention repeatedly throughout the text, especially since they apply with equal force to almost all the figures. Consequently, a sort of shorthand is adopted, which consists of treating the data *as though* there were no biases, no translation difficulties, and as though the questions meant precisely what they said to every respondent. This is, after all, substantially what the economist does

[11] M. Jahoda, M. Deutsch, and S. W. Cook, *Research Methods in Social Relations,* Part I (New York: The Dryden Press, 1951), p. 285.

when he bases his rules on the assumption that "all other things are equal," when he is quite well aware that they are not.

Summary

The international opinion survey, as a tool of social science, is heir to all the ills of a national survey, plus a few of its own.[12] Some of these latter might be avoided by two procedures, which would, of course, increase materially the expense of gathering the data:

1. Pre-testing the ballot with several hundred interviews in each country to get a leverage on the translation problems, and to standardize the coding.

2. Central coding and tabulation of results from ballots which show as precisely as possible the background information on each respondent.

More open-end questions are preferable, but they might involve prohibitive translation costs, if coding were done centrally.

The international survey is a powerful tool because each national result serves as a standard for considering results in other nations. It cannot, without further development, give as precise and valid quantitative information as a national survey, but it shows up qualitative differences between nations more forcefully than other techniques for examining international relations, because its demands for precision discourage sweeping generalizations.

---

[12] For a recent discussion of these, see the *Public Opinion Quarterly's* special issue on "International Communications Research" (Vol. 16, No. 4, winter, 1952-53), especially Susan Ervin and Robert T. Bower, "Translation Problems in International Surveys," pp. 595-604.

——————— **Appendix B**

Class Identification

Q.9: *If you were asked to use a name for your social class, would you say you belonged in the middle class, working class, or upper class?*

The Unesco percentages for the United States conform rather closely to the patterns discovered in previous surveys, as indicated in Table 13.

TABLE 13 POLL QUESTIONS ON CLASS IDENTIFICATION IN THE UNITED STATES

	Survey Organization	Upper	Upper Middle[a]	Middle	Lower Middle[a]	Lower	Working	Laboring	DK[b]
To what social class in this country do you feel you belong: middle class, upper class, or lower class?	1. AIPO, 3/3/39 1,711 cases[c]	6	14	63	11	6			
	2. AIPO, 6/24/41 3,027 cases[c]	4.9	10.5	65.8	11.1	7.7			
What income group in our country do you feel you are a member of: the middle income group, upper income group, or lower income group?[e]	3. AIPO, 3/3/39 1,610 cases[d]	1	6	41	21	31			
	4. AIPO, 6/24/41 3,072 cases[d]	1.4	6.8	40.9	23.6	27.3			

TABLE 13 continued

	Survey Organization	Upper	Upper Middle[a]	Middle	Lower Middle[a]	Lower	Working	Laboring	DK[b]
If you were asked to use one of these four names for your social class, which would you say you belong in: the middle class, lower class, working class, or upper class?	5. AIPO, 2/13/46 2,298 cases[c]	4		36		5	51		4
	6. OPOR, 7/17/45 1,097 cases[f]	3		43		1	51		2
	7. AIPO, 3/26/47 1,518 cases[d]	3		38		3	52		4
Same question except "laboring" substituted for "working" class (split ballot).	8. AIPO, 3/26/47 1,501 cases[d]	4		53		4		35	4
If you were asked to use a name for your social class, would you say you belong to the middle class, working class, or upper class?	9. UNESCO, 1948 (U.S. results)	4		42			51		3

[a] Check boxes were provided for interviewers in case respondents volunteered these answers.

[b] "Don't know," "Don't believe in classes," and "No answer."

[c] Cantril and Strunk, *op. cit.*, p. 116.

[d] This information taken from the files of the American Institute of Public Opinion results, maintained by OPOR.

[e] The 1939 question was a split-ballot question. On the 1941 ballot, the social class question followed the income question, and was asked of the same respondents.

[f] From the survey which provided the data for Centers' *The Psychology of Social Classes, op. cit.* (White males only.)

Surveys 5, 6, 7, and 9 show almost no change in a three-year period. There is less than four percentage points difference in any of the replies to the two pairs of AIPO questions (Surveys 1 and 2; 3 and 4). The OPOR survey was confined to males, but still remained close to the others.

In contrast to these similarities, the changing of one word—"working"—to its dictionary synonym—"laboring"—cuts by 16% or 17% the number of respondents who assert they belong to that class (Survey 8). Most of them choose the "middle" class. Had the Unesco ballot been originally drafted in some other language and translated into English, the translator might well have chosen either of the words!

An indication of the difference in the connotations of the two words is given by the answers to an open-end question which followed them on the Gallup ballot: "What would you say puts a person in the working (laboring) class?"

	"Working"	"Laboring"
Working for a living	26%	17%
Manual labor, common labor, mill workers, factory workers, etc.	23	32
Amount of income, lack of income	14	14
Lack of education or training	8	14
Other responses	24	21
No opinion, don't know	11	10
Total (More than 100% because more than one answer was possible)	106	108

Questions asked in three European countries, though not strictly comparable to the Unesco wording, are:

Swedish Gallup Institute June, 1943	French Institute of Public Opinion January, 1947	British Institute of Public Opinion October, 1951
Dividing the nation into four classes of society, the upper class, the upper middle class, middle class, workers and those of similar standing, to which class do you consider that you belong? [a]	Do you regard yourself as belonging to the prosperous class, the poor class, the upper middle class or the lower middle class? [b]	If you *had* to say what social class you belong to, which would you say? [c]

Upper	1%	Prosperous	1%	Upper	1%
Upper middle	3	Upper middle	20	Upper middle	5
Middle	24	Lower middle	56	Middle	28
Workers, etc.	57	Poor	19	Lower middle	16
Don't know	15	No answer	4	Don't know	2

[a] Cantril and Strunk, *op. cit.*, p. 116.
[b] OPOR files. The French text ran: "riche," "pauvre," "moyenne plutôt riche," "moyenne plutôt pauvre."
[c] OPOR files, BIPO Survey 269.

It will be noted that in these varied questions the total of "middle"-class responses runs to 27%, 76%, and 49%, respectively. Comparison of these figures with the United States average for the eight independent surveys in Table 13 (61% total for "middle"-class responses) does not substantiate the claim that the United States society is obviously more "middle-class oriented" than others.

"People" vs. "Government"

Q.11: *Which foreign people do you feel most friendly toward?*
Q.12: *Which foreign people do you feel least friendly toward?*

The results of the Unesco survey in all nine countries suggest that the word "people" in this question had very little force so far as most respondents were concerned—that they reacted toward the government involved. Other poll findings have shown that under certain circumstances there can be a very real distinction in the minds of respondents between the two.

Fortune magazine in the United States asked in 1939: "Toward which of these foreign peoples do you feel most friendly and least friendly?" On a second question, the word "governments" was substituted for "peoples," and the word "British" for "Great Britain," "Swedes" for " Sweden," etc., on the card handed the respondents.[1] The results were as follows: [2]

	Most Friendly	
	Government	People
Great Britain/British	45.3%	40.3%
Sweden/Swedes	10.0	8.5
Finland/Finns	9.7	3.4
France/French	8.6	8.2
Germany/Germans	1.9	6.9
U.S.S.R./Russians	1.3	.9
Italy/Italians	1.0	2.3
Japan/Japanese	.2	.3
All	4.8	13.9
None	5.1	4.0
Don't know	12.1	11.3

	Least Friendly	
	Government	People
Germany/Germans	56.2%	28.8%
Japan/Japanese	11.9	19.3
Italy/Italians	5.7	7.0
U.S.S.R./Russians	4.3	3.4
Great Britain/British	1.1	1.0
France/French	.9	1.1
Sweden/Swedes	.2	.2
Finland/Finns	.1	.3
All	.9	.9
None	8.6	24.2
Don't know	10.1	13.8

It appears that considerably more people claimed to be friendly to "all people" and unfriendly to none than asserted friendship for "all governments" and dislike for none. This is hardly surprising. Dislike for Germany was focused primarily on the government, while dislike for Japan was

---

[1] It is not clear whether this was a split ballot, two questions on the same ballot, or two separate surveys.
[2] Cantril and Strunk, *op. cit.*, p. 948.

focused on the people. The Japanese, it will be noted, are the only Orientals on the list. Friendliness to the Finnish government rather than the Finnish people may be due to public recognition of the war debt settlement when the word "government" is brought in, although the percentages are too small for safe generalization.

During World War II there was a slight tendency for American opinion to shift its dislike from the German government to the German people, as indicated by these selections from a series of questions by the American Institute. The wordings varied slightly: "Do you feel that our enemy is the German people [as a whole] or simply the Hitler [Nazi, German] government?" [3]

	People	Government	Don't Know	Both
February, 1942	6	75	6	13
September, 1943	10	66	4	20
February, 1945	12	64	3	21

When an even more forceful distinction is made, as by the National Opinion Research Center in March, 1951, the number of respondents who will condemn a people can be reduced considerably.

> "Now I'd like to ask you how you feel about the *people* who live in certain countries, as distinct from the *governments*. In general, do you have a favorable or unfavorable impression of . . . the Russian people?"
> Favorable 46%   Unfavorable 41%   Don't know 13%

List vs. Open-End Questions

A second consideration regarding question wording, as applied to Q.11 and 12, is the effect of the open-end question, adopted in the Unesco survey, as opposed to a list of peoples from which the respondent would choose.

In general, it has been found that nations selected appear in roughly the same order, and with roughly the same proportion of respondents selecting each nation, when the two methods are compared. The *Fortune* results above compared with the 1939 figures in Table 14 and the questions asked in France in 1939, 1948, and 1950 (see Table 15) will bear this out. A list of nations reduces the variety of responses; but at the same time it may suggest nations that would not occur otherwise to the respondents. The advantage of the open-end question is that it does not in any way prompt the respondent. At the same time it weights his answer heavily in favor of the nations which are the object of immediate attention in the press and radio—those that would leap to his mind in almost any context in which

[3] *Ibid.*, p. 1075.

TABLE 14   UNITED STATES POLLS: "FRIENDLINESS" TO SPECIFIC EUROPEAN NATIONS[a]

	FORTUNE "What foreign country do you feel most friendly toward?" Oct. '35		AIPO "Which foreign country do you like best?" Jan. '37		AIPO "Which of the European countries (which European country) do you like best?" June '37		Jan. '39		July '39		UNESCO "Which foreign people do you feel most friendly toward?" Oct. '48	
	% of all countries	% of these five	% of all countries	% of these five	% of all countries	% of these five	% of all countries	% of these five	% of all countries	% of these five	% of all countries	% of these five
Britain	28.6	72	54	74	55	71	48	70	43	72	31	69
France	4.7	12	10	14	11	14	12	17	11	18	5	11
Germany	4.4	11	5	7	8	10	4	6	3	5	5	11
Italy	1.2	3	3	4	3	4	3	4	2	3	4	9
Russia (U.S.S.R.)	.8	2	1	1	1	1	2	3	1	2	—	—

[a] Data, except for Unesco survey, from Cantril and Strunk, *op. cit.*, pp. 948-49.

he is asked to name a nation. There may be peoples liked or disliked more heartily than any of these (some head-hunting tribes, for an extreme example) who would never have occurred to the respondent.[4]

It is difficult to separate out the changes in Table 15 which are due to time, from those due to question wording. However, it seems obvious that omission of Belgians and Swiss on the 1950 question forced respondents who might otherwise have selected them to choose Americans and British. The difference in the wording of the question can hardly account for the shift from dislike of Germans to dislike of Russians. Otherwise, these results indicate considerable stability of attitude toward certain peoples.

TABLE 15   OPEN-END VS. LIST QUESTIONS (Comparison of Unesco Result with Those of Two Questions Asked by the Institut Français d'Opinion Publique)

	Best liked, 1939, IFOP[a]	Most friendly, 1948, Unesco	Most (Rank 1), 1950, IFOP[b]	Least liked, 1939, IFOP[a]	Least friendly, 1948, Unesco	Least (Rank 8), 1950, IFOP[b]
Swiss	15%	18%	not inc.		*[c]	not inc.
Americans	26	17	29%		6%	6%
Belgians	9	16	not inc.		*	not inc.
British	23	14	23		*	1
Swedes	2	*[c]	19		*	0
Russians	7	10	10	5%	32	39
Spaniards	1	*	2		*	2
Italians		*	2	10	7	5
Yugoslavs		*	2		*	3
Roumanians		*	1		*	2
Germans		*	1	70	34	27

[a] What foreign country do you like best (least)? Cantril and Strunk, *op. cit.*, p. 375.

[b] Parmi les peoples suivants, quel est celui pour lequel vous avez le plus de sympathie? Quel est celui pour lequel vous avez le moins de sympathie? Essayer de classer les autres. *Sondages*, Paris, Vol. 1951, No. 1, p. 53.

[c] Asterisk (*) = less than 0.5%.

With these considerations in mind, the Unesco results might equally well be interpreted as answers to the question: "Which foreign people, or government, comes to your attention most forcibly at the moment in a favorable (unfavorable) context?"

---

[4] If one has any doubt that America and Russia loom large in the ideas of the bulk of respondents, he may refer to the poll questions asked in 1945 and 1946 in eight countries regarding the nation expected to be most influential in postwar affairs. These two were mentioned first in all eight countries. See Cantril and Strunk, *op. cit.*, pp. 1058-61.

Excerpts from
Instructions to
Survey Agencies[1]

—— **Appendix C**

No. of interviews: 1,000

Cross section composition: Usual political cross section, adult men and women.

Age groups: 21–29
30–49
50–65
66 and over

Socio-economic: Four are required:
Well-to-do, AV +
Middle class, AV
Working class, AV —
Very poor, Group D

Education: Two are required:
a) Number of years of formal schooling, including university.
This should be secured in order to check the replies to
b) What stage of education was reached, i.e., primary, secondary, college, and so forth. Since types of schools vary among countries, each survey administrator should make up these educational groups in the way best suited to his own country. But the basis of the classification must be the broad threefold division given here.

Occupation: Please use the following code:
a) Professional { i. Higher professions [2]
workers { ii. Lower professions [2]

---

[1] These are the pertinent paragraphs taken verbatim from the mimeographed instruction sheet that was sent, along with copies of the English and French texts, to each of the participating survey agencies.

[2] Because of the small sample, these are combined in the final tabulations.

b) Owners of businesses, and large, medium shops

c) Workers on own account, owners of small shops

d) Salaried—managerial and top-grade clerical workers

e) Other clerical workers, shop assistants, personal services including catering

f) Manual workers

g) Farm workers, fishermen, gardeners

h) Farm owners

i) Housewives (who will go into their husbands' socio-economic grouping)

j) Retired: independent

This code will go into one column on the Hollerith card.

Questionnaire: Please keep to the order of questions as given in the draft. If you think that there is a better lead off than Q.1, then tell your interviewers that if they wish they can start with that question, but even if you do this, please *print the questionnaire as set out in the draft,* keeping to the same order of question numbering.

Q.8, 11, 12 can be given, say, six countries, or peoples, as precoded answers with "Other _____" for cases where the choice happens to be some other than the precoded names.

In tabulating replies to these three questions, group together as "Miscellaneous" all countries (peoples) mentioned by 4% or less of the sample.

N.B. All sub-questions, e.g., Q.1b *should be percentaged on the basis of the total sample*: do not use the number of answers as the base.

Report: Would you please set it out as follows:

1. Specimen questionnaire.

2. Details of cross section: No. of interviewers engaged: No. of areas covered: any groups or areas of country excluded, if this happens to be the case and the reasons for the exclusions.

3. Numbers in each of the standard categories, including occupational grouping.

There is no need to write up the report but it would be very helpful to have any general or particular conclusions which the surveyor regards as warranted.

It would be most useful to be told any background which seems relevant to the understanding of a result which may at first sight seem a trifle odd. This should be given as a comment at the end of the Tables.

Tabulations Required for Unesco Survey

Q.1a: Sex; age; socio-economic; education. (These four are referred to below as "Standard 4.") X Q.14.

Q.1b: Standard 4.

Q.2: Standard 4; X Q.9; X Q.1a; X Q.3a; X Q.4; X Q.14.

Q.3a: Standard 4; X Q.3b; X Q.4; X Q.14; X Q.1a. This means for Q.1a, and similarly in all other such instances:

	Q.3a	Possible	Not possible	Don't know	
Q.1a	Can				= 100%
	Cannot				= 100%
	Don't know				= 100%

Q.3b: Standard 4; X Q.1a.

Q.4: Standard 4; X Q.3a; X Q.1a; X Q.14.

Q.5: Standard 4; occupational.

Q.6: Standard 4; occupational.

Q.7: Standard 4; occupational.

Q.8: Totals: analyze leading four countries by sex; age; socio-economic; X Q.14; X Q.9.

Q.9: Standard 4; occupational.

Q.10a: Standard 4; occupational; X Q.9.

Q.10b: Standard 4; occupational; X Q.9.

Q.10c: Sample here may be very small. If so, give only absolute figures.

Q.11: Totals: analyze leading four countries by sex; age; socio-economic; X Q.14; X Q.9.

Q.12: As for Q.11.

Q.13: TOTALS: Analyze as follows:

Hardworking	+ (plus)	
Conceited		− (minus)
Intelligent	+	
Total:	8	4 The "Like/Dislike" score

Accordingly, if a person chose all the terms as being characteristic of one people (an impossibility of course) their score would be 8 + (plus) and 4 − (minus). Then it is possible to summarize the replies of any group as an average number of +'s (plusses) or −'s (minuses). Round off to the nearest whole number.

Q.14: Standard 4.

Notes on Q.5–7: 1. Score the answers to these questions as follows:

Score	Answer
3	Better;[3] more; yes; very
2	About same; all right
1	Don't know
0	Worse;[3] less; dissatisfied; no

[3] These two terms are in the wrong positions. This was later corrected, but not until some of the agencies had submitted their reports. Incorrect figures are omitted from the Tables.

This will give a range of scores from 12–0, which may be called the "Security Score."

2. Group the replies 12–10; 9–5; 4–0. Analyze these groups by Standard 4.

3. Use these three levels of Security Score to analyze the following questions: Q.3a; Q.4; Q.9.

—— Appendix D

These reports have been edited to standardize the presentation, with a consistent system of numbering and labeling column and line headings. A small amount of material has been omitted because it was not available for all the surveys, or because the variations in tabulation made it incomparable from country to country.[1] Other variations are noted, and cross referenced to the tables.

Each report consists of one or more of the following:

    A. An exact copy of the questionnaire as asked in that country.

    B. Excerpts from pertinent instructions to interviewers.

    C. Excerpts of notes and comments by the survey agency which accompanied their report.

    D. Notes and comments by the editors.

    E. Tables.

---

[1] Among these are the cross tabulations of countries and peoples mentioned by less than 5% of the sample on Q.8, 11, and 12; cross tabulations of combined negative adjectives and combined positive adjectives on Q.13; and cross tabulations of individual adjectives on Q.13.

AUSTRALIA

A. Copy of Questionnaire Used in Australia

OPINION RESEARCH CORPORATION

I am from Opinion Research, which is making a survey for the United Nations Educational, Scientific and Cultural Organization (Unesco), to find out what Australians think of their own and other nations. The survey is also being made in nine other countries.

1. (a) Do you believe that human nature can be changed?

Can	1
Cannot	2
Don't know	3

(b) If "Can" ASK: Do you think this is likely to happen?

Likely	1
Unlikely	2
Don't know	3

2. Do you think that our Australian characteristics are mainly born in us, or are they due to the way we are brought up?

Born in us	1
Way brought up	2
Don't know	3

3. (a) Do you believe that it will be possible for all countries to live together, at peace with each other?

Possible	1
Not possible	2
Don't know	3

(b) If "Possible" ASK: Do you think that this likely to happen?

Likely	1
Unlikely	2
Don't know	3

4. Some people say there should be a World Government, able to control the laws made by each country. Do you agree or disagree?

Agree	1
Disagree	2
Don't know	3

5. When the war ended, did you expect you would be getting along *better*, *worse* or *about the same*, as you are actually getting along at the present time?

Better	1
Worse	2
Same	3
Don't know	4

6. (a) Do you feel that, from the point of view of your (husband's) job, you are more secure, or less secure, than the average Australian?

More	1
Less	2
Same	3
Don't know	4

(b) In general, do you feel that you are sufficiently secure to be able to plan ahead?

Yes	1
No	2
Don't know	3

7. How satisfied are you with the way you are getting on now?

Very	1
All right	2
Dissatisfied	3
Don't know	4

8. Which country in the world gives the best chance of leading the kind of life you would like to lead? ....

NOTE TO INTERVIEWER
This question includes Australia, if interviewee asks you

9. If you were asked to use a name for your social class, would you say you belonged in the middle class, working class, or upper class?

Middle	1
Working	2
Upper	3
Don't know	4

NOTE TO INTERVIEWER Where "own" appears in next question, read answer to Question 9

10. (a) Do you feel that you have anything in common with (own) class people abroad?

Yes	1
No	2
Don't know	3

(b) Do you feel that you have anything in common with Aus-

Yes	1
No	2

tralians who are not (own) class?

Don't know	3

Ask (c) only if "YES" on both (a) and (b), or "NO" on both (a) and (b).

(c) Which of these two would you say that you have more in common with?

Abroad	1
Australia	2
Don't know	3

11. Which foreign people do you feel most friendly toward? ....

12. Which foreign people do you feel least friendly toward? ....

13. (a) From the list of words on this card, which seems to you to describe the American people best? Select as many as you wish and tell me the letters and the words that go with them. If you have no particular feelings one way or the other just say so.

(b) Now go over the list again and select the words you think best describe the Russian people?

(c) Now select the words that best describe Australians?

1. Hardworking
2. Intelligent
3. Practical
4. Conceited
5. Generous
6. Cruel
7. Backward
8. Brave
9. Self-controlled
10. Domineering
11. Progressive
12. Peace-loving
13. Impossible to characterize

14. Do you think our present Federal Government is too much to the right, too much to the left, or about where you would like it to be?

Too right	1	OK as is	3
Too left	2	Don't know	4

15. SEX

Man	1
Woman	2

16. AGE

21 to 29 years	1
30 to 49 years	2
50 to 59 years	3
60 and over	4

17. ECONOMIC CLASSIFICATION

Well to do	1	Artisans etc.	3
Better off	2	Lowest Income	4

18. Would you please tell me how many years of school you had? (Include University but not Technical)
........................years

19. What was the last grade or class you completed at school or University? (Tick most advanced stage reached. Matriculation means "passed exams needed to enter University")
1 State School incomplete
2 State School complete (grades 1 to 8)
3 High or Private School incomplete
4 High or Private School matriculated
5 University incomplete
6 University graduated

20. May I record your occupation? (Record housewives as such, instead of according to the Husband's occupation)
Business........................ Position........................

21. May I record your name? M........................
Postal Address: No........................
St. Suburb or Town........................
Interviewer........................ Date........................'48

B. Excerpts from Instructions to Interviewers

The same wording (drafted by Americans) is being used in all countries. Sometimes you may have to repeat questions to convey meaning of such phrases as "human nature" and "Australian characteristics."

Q.5: "At the present time" could be abbreviated to "now."

Q.6: "The average Australian" means "most Australians."

Q.7: It might help to read the answer-places, thus: ". . . getting on now; Very satisfied, All right, or Dissatisfied."

Q.10: If you have to ask Q.10c, "these two" may need elaboration, e.g., "middle-class people abroad and Australians who are not middle class."

Q.11: "Foreign people" includes U.S.A., but not England.

Q.13: "Self-controlled" means "not excitable."

Q.14: It may be necessary to read "that is, conservative" after "right," and "that is, socialistic" after "left."

C. Excerpts from Notes and Comments by Survey Agency

During the test interviews, we found that several of the questions presented considerable difficulty. Q.5, 7, and 14 were the most difficult. [Instructions above were based on these tests.]

D. Notes and Comments by the Editors

On Q.3b only those replying "Possible" in Q.3a were tabulated. These percentages are not comparable with other surveys. The sample (col. D) is the number of respondents who replied "Possible" to Q.3a.

Security Scores are not available (see note p. 123), hence cross tabulations (ll. 33, 34, 35) are omitted.

Sample on Q.1b is the number of respondents who answered "Can" to Q.1a. Percentages on Q.1b total 100% of this sample.

In the final column (Sample) in the following tables, the totals of subclasses, e.g., men plus women, are frequently less than 945, the total number of interviews. This is because there were a few questionnaires on which interviewers had neglected to check the boxes for age, sex, etc. These questionnaires could not be used in these particular cross-tabulations.

E. Tables

AUSTRALIA A

	QUESTION 1a Change human nature?			QUESTION 1b (If *Can*) Likely?[a]				QUESTION 2 National character?			SAMPLE
	(A) Can	(B) Cannot	(C) Don't know	(A) Likely	(B) Unlikely	(C) Don't know	(D) (Sample)	(A) Born in us	(B) Way brought up	(C) Don't know	
1 Total	43	51	6	57	31	12	(406)	23	74	3	945
2 Men	44	52	4	59	34	7	(244)	23	73	4	558
3 Women	42	50	8	54	28	18	(162)	22	75	3	386
4 21–29	39	56	5	54	37	9	(79)	22	76	2	203
5 30–49	42	52	6	55	32	13	(171)	22	76	2	403
6 50–65	47	46	7	61	28	11	(89)	25	68	7	189
7 Over 65	47	47	6	60	27	13	(67)	23	71	6	143
8 A–wealthy	54	38	8	71	29	—	(14)	23	73	4	26
9 B–average	45	50	5	53	30	17	(92)	26	70	4	203
10 C–below av.	42	52	6	58	33	9	(252)	22	75	3	589
11 D–very poor	39	55	6	55	20	25	(44)	25	73	2	114
12 Primary	39	53	8	56	30	14	(206)	25	72	3	519
13 Secondary	46	51	3	56	35	9	(162)	20	76	4	355
14 University	61	37	2	66	24	10	(38)	21	77	2	62
29 Leftist (tr)[b]	40	57	3					19	79	2	72
30 Rightist (tl)[c]	44	52	4					24	72	4	515
31 All right	45	48	7					23	75	2	236
32 Don't know	38	52	10					18	76	6	122
25 Upper class								47	53	—	17
26 Middle class								2?	76	3	474
27 Working class								2.	73	4	440
28 Don't know								14	79	7	14
36 Can (Q.1a)								21	75	4	406
37 Cannot								24	73	3	485
38 Don't know								26	72	2	54
39 Possible (Q.3a)								21	76	3	391
40 Impossible								23	74	3	513
41 Don't know								32	63	5	41
42 Agree (Q.4)								21	77	2	327
43 Disagree								24	72	4	552
44 Don't know								20	79	1	66

[a] Sample on Q.1b is the number of respondents who answered "Can" to Q.1a. Percentages on Q.1b total 100% of this sample.

[b] "tr" = too right.

[c] "tl" = too left.

AUSTRALIA B

	QUESTION 3a Live in peace?			QUESTION 3b (If *Possible*) Likely?[a]				QUESTION 4 World government?			SAMPLE
	(A) Pos- sible	(B) Not pos- sible	(C) Don't know	(A) Like- ly	(B) Un- likely	(C) Don't know	(D) (Sam- ple)	(A) Agree	(B) Dis- agree	(C) Don't know	
1 Total	42	54	4	36	52	12	(391)	35	58	7	945
2 Men	45	53	2	40	52	8	(249)	39	58	3	558
3 Women	37	56	7	29	51	20	(142)	29	59	12	386
4 21–29	37	59	4	25	64	11	(75)	33	56	11	203
5 30–49	42	53	5	37	51	12	(171)	39	56	5	403
6 50–65	43	54	3	38	51	11	(82)	29	65	6	189
7 Over 65	44	52	4	44	40	16	(63)	32	59	9	143
8 A–wealthy	35	65	—	33	67	—	(9)	46	54	—	26
9 B–average	39	58	3	34	57	9	(80)	36	58	6	203
10 C–below av.	41	54	5	37	51	12	(242)	35	59	6	589
11 D–very poor	45	50	5	41	41	18	(51)	32	54	14	114
12 Primary	41	54	5	38	50	12	(211)	33	59	8	519
13 Secondary	40	56	4	30	57	13	(141)	34	59	7	355
14 University	53	45	2	46	39	15	(33)	52	47	1	62
29 Leftist (tr)	57	39	4					39	47	14	72
30 Rightist (tl)	38	59	3					33	61	6	515
31 All right	47	48	5					43	51	6	236
32 Don't know	35	58	7					23	66	11	122
33 Sec. (12–10)[b]											
34 Medium (9–5)											
35 Insec. (4–0)											
36 Can (Q.1a)	51	45	4					41	53	6	406
37 Can't change	34	62	4					30	63	7	485
38 Don't know	33	58	9					26	63	11	54
45 Agree (Q.4)	54	42	4								327
46 Disagree	33	63	4								552
47 Don't know	44	47	9								66
39 Possible (Q.3a)								46	47	7	391
40 Impossible								27	67	6	513
41 Don't know								32	54	14	41

[a] On Q.3b only those replying "Possible" on Q.3a were tabulated. These percentages are not comparable with other surveys. The sample (col. D) is the number of respondents who replied "Possible" to Q.3a.

[b] Security Scores are not available (see note p. 123), hence cross tabulations (ll. 33, 34, 35) are omitted.

AUSTRALIA C

	QUESTION 5 Postwar expectation?				QUESTION 6a Job security?				QUESTION 6b Able to plan?			SAMPLE
	(A) Better	(B) Worse	(C) About same	(D) Don't know	(A) More	(B) Less	(C) About same	(D) Don't know	(A) Yes	(B) No	(C) Don't know	
1 Total	54	16	28	2	52	13	30	5	57	36	7	945
2 Men	52	17	30	1	55	13	28	4	61	33	6	558
3 Women	58	15	24	3	48	14	33	5	51	41	8	386

AUSTRALIA C continued

	Postwar expectation?				Job security?				Able to plan?			Sample
	(A)	(B)	(C)	(D)	(A)	(B)	(C)	(D)	(A)	(B)	(C)	
	Better	Worse	About same	Don't know	More	Less	About same	Don't know	Yes	No	Don't know	
4 21–29	51	15	31	3	64	6	29	1	66	29	5	203
5 30–49	55	15	28	2	54	14	27	5	57	38	5	403
6 50–65	56	18	26	—	46	14	34	6	55	39	6	189
7 Over 65	52	19	29	—	39	20	34	7	50	40	10	143
8 A–wealthy	42	15	39	4	77	8	15	—	81	19	—	26
9 B–average	58	15	26	1	63	13	20	4	66	29	5	203
10 C–below av.	55	16	28	1	51	13	33	3	56	38	6	589
11 D–very poor	45	22	31	2	34	18	37	11	42	45	13	114
12 Primary	56	15	28	1	45	15	35	5	52	41	7	519
13 Secondary	53	17	28	2	60	10	26	4	64	30	6	355
14 University	48	24	28	—	69	18	11	2	66	31	3	62
15 Profess.	39	22	37	2	79	7	12	2	78	20	2	67
16 Bus. owners	49	13	35	3	60	19	16	5	68	24	8	37
17 Ind. workers	55	21	21	3	50	12	29	9	59	36	5	42
18 Sal.—mangrs.	52	23	25	—	70	7	21	2	68	27	5	56
19 Clerks	49	14	35	2	57	6	34	3	60	34	6	116
20 Man. wkrs.	53	15	31	1	48	13	36	3	58	36	6	193
21 Farm wkrs.	42	33	25	—	33	8	59	—	75	25	—	12
22 Farm owners	66	13	20	1	53	20	21	6	62	33	5	61
23 Housewives	59	15	23	3	46	15	33	6	47	45	8	313
24 Retired, Ind.	48	15	37	—	41	33	22	4	48	41	11	27
No answer	57	14	24	5	33	10	38	19	53	33	14	21

AUSTRALIA D

	QUESTION 7 Satisfaction?.				Security Scores[a]			QUESTION 8 Best opportunity?			SAMPLE
	(A) Very	(B) All right	(C) Dis-sat.	(D) Don't know	(A) Sec. 12–10	(B) Med. 9–5	(C) Ins. 4–0	(A) Aus-tral.	(B) U.S.A.	(C) Eng.-Scot.	
1 Total	22	57	20	1				83	5	4	945
2 Men	23	57	19	1				83	6	3	558
3 Women	20	57	22	1				85	5	6	386
4 21–29	26	56	17	1				80	9	2	203
5 30–49	22	56	20	2				86	4	4	403
6 50–65	15	60	24	1				84	5	5	189
7 Over 65	24	56	19	1				79	4	8	143
8 A–wealthy	42	42	16	—				65	11	8	26
9 B–average	23	61	15	1				83	7	4	203
10 C–below av.	22	56	21	1				85	4	5	589
11 D–very poor	16	56	27	1				80	8	3	114
12 Primary	20	58	21	1							519
13 Secondary	23	55	20	2							355
14 University	23	56	21	—							62

AUSTRALIA D continued

	Satisfaction?				Security Scores[a]			Best opportunity?			Sample
	(A) Very	(B) All right	(C) Dis-sat.	(D) Don't know	(A) Sec. 12–10	(B) Med. 9–5	(C) Ins. 4–0	(A) Aus-tral.	(B) U.S.A.	(C) Eng.-Scot.	
15 Profess.	31	54	15	—							67
16 Bus. owners	27	62	11	—							37
17 Ind. workers	29	40	31	—							42
18 Sal.-mangrs.	23	57	18	2							56
19 Clerks	22	55	22	1							116
20 Man. wkrs.	22	60	17	1							193
21 Farm wkrs.	33	50	17	—							12
22 Farm owners	28	54	18	—							61
23 Housewives	18	57	23	2							313
24 Retired, Ind.	7	74	19	—							27
No answer	9	62	29	—							21
							25 Upper class	59	23	12	17
							26 Middle class	81	7	5	474
							27 Working class	87	3	3	440
							28 Don't know	79	7	—	14
Totals (Q.8)			%				**29** Leftist (tr)	83	2	4	72
							30 Rightist (tl)	81	7	6	515
Australia			83				**31** All right	88	3	3	236
United States			5				**32** Don't know	85	7	2	122
England-Scotland			4								
Russia			1								
Sweden			1								
New Zealand			1								
Canada			1								
Switzerland			1								
South Africa			1								
Anywhere British Empire			—								
South America			—								
China			—								
No answer			2								
			100								

[a] Security Scores are not available (see note p. 123).

AUSTRALIA E

	QUESTION 9 Social class?				QUESTION 10a Own class abroad?			QUESTION 10b Others at home?			SAMPLE
	(A) Mid-dle	(B) Work-ing	(C) Up-per	(D) Don't know	(A) Yes	(B) No	(C) Don't know	(A) Yes	(B) No	(C) Don't know	
1 Total	50	47	2	1	67	17	16	78	15	7	945
2 Men	48	49	2	1	73	14	13	80	15	5	558
3 Women	54	44	1	1	59	21	20	75	15	10	386
4 21–29	49	49	1	1	65	17	18	79	15	6	203
5 30–49	48	49	2	1	66	19	15	79	14	7	403
6 50–65	56	41	1	2	71	15	14	79	14	7	189
7 Over 65	50	42	6	2	66	16	18	73	16	11	143

AUSTRALIA E continued

	Social class?				Own class abroad?			Others at home?			Sample
	(A) Mid- dle	(B) Work- ing	(C) Up- per	(D) Don't know	(A) Yes	(B) No	(C) Don't know	(A) Yes	(B) No	(C) Don't know	
8 A–wealthy	65	—	31	4	77	4	19	85	8	7	26
9 B–average	83	11	4	2	73	10	17	86	8	6	203
10 C–below av.	45	54	—	1	66	19	15	78	15	7	589
11 D–very poor	16	82	—	2	60	24	16	63	28	9	114
12 Primary	40	58	1	1	62	20	18	73	18	9	519
13 Secondary	62	36	2	—	71	14	15	83	11	6	355
14 University	73	16	6	5	85	10	5	85	15	—	62
15 Profess.	68	25	4	3	85	4	11	88	9	3	67
16 Bus. owners	87	8	5	—	68	13	19	89	8	3	37
17 Ind. workers	55	45	—	—	64	22	14	81	12	7	42
18 Sal.-mangrs.	84	9	5	—	75	5	20	86	9	5	56
19 Clerks	53	46	—	1	71	15	14	83	12	5	116
20 Man. wkrs.	19	80	—	1	66	22	12	69	26	5	193
21 Farm wkrs.	8	92	—	—	58	17	25	83	8	9	12
22 Farm owners	64	31	5	—	79	10	11	89	8	3	61
23 Housewives	51	46	2	1	59	21	20	75	15	10	313
24 Retired, Ind.	67	18	11	4	67	15	18	63	26	11	27
25 Upper class					76	6	18	65	29	6	17
26 Middle class					69	14	17	87	8	5	474
27 Working class					66	21	13	70	22	8	440
28 Don't know					36	7	57	36	7	57	14

33 Sec. (12–10)[a]
34 Medium (9–5)
35 Insec. (4–0)

	QUESTION 10c More in common?				SAMPLE
	(A) Abroad	(B) Aus- tralia	(C) Don't know	(D) Not asked	
Total	6	51	6	37	945

[a] Security Scores are not available (see note p. 123).

AUSTRALIA F

	QUESTION 11 Most friendly?			QUESTION 12 Least friendly?				SAMPLE
	(A) Amer.	(B) Scand.	(C) Fr.	(A) Russ.	(B) Jap.	(C) Ger.	(D) Ital.	
1 Total	61	7	5	35	33	8	5	945
2 Men	65	8	5	40	30	5	6	558
3 Women	55	6	6	27	38	11	5	386
4 21–29	66	4	3	33	38	5	5	203
5 30–49	58	9	5	32	35	8	6	403
6 50–65	62	6	8	34	34	10	5	189
7 Over 65	59	6	6	45	23	9	5	143
8 A–wealthy	77	4	—	54	15	15	8	26
9 B–average	57	11	6	38	32	8	5	203
10 C–below av.	62	6	5	35	35	7	4	589
11 D–very poor	59	5	6	24	35	10	9	114

AUSTRALIA F continued

	Most friendly?			Least friendly?				Sample
	(A) Amer.	(B) Scand.	(C) Fr.	(A) Russ.	(B) Jap.	(C) Ger.	(D) Ital.	
25 Upper class	76	12	—	59	23	6	6	17
26 Middle class	59	8	7	40	33	7	5	474
27 Working class	62	6	4	28	35	9	6	440
28 Don't know	64	7	—	22	14	—	7	14
29 Leftist (tr)	53	3	11	23	36	14	3	72
30 Rightist (tl)	62	10	5	42	32	6	5	515
31 All right	65	4	5	29	37	8	6	236
32 Don't know	52	5	2	24	32	11	6	122

Totals (Q.11)   %

Americans	61
Scandinavians	7
French	5
Dutch	2
Russians	1
Irish	1
Germans	1
British Dominions	1
All	1
Others	8
No answer and British	12
	100

Totals (Q.12)   %

Russians	35
Japanese	33
Germans	8
Italians	5
Americans	1
Asiatics	1
Spanish	—
Dutch	—
Others	2
No answer	15
	100

AUSTRALIA Gª

	QUESTION 14 Present government?				SAMPLE
	(A) Too right	(B) Too left	(C) All right	(D) Don't know	
1 Total	8	54	25	13	945
2 Men	8	57	28	7	558
3 Women	7	52	20	21	386
4 21–29	5	52	29	14	203
5 30–49	9	54	25	12	403
6 50–65	9	55	22	14	189
7 Over 65	6	59	24	11	143
8 A–wealthy	4	69	12	15	26
9 B–average	4	75	12	9	203
10 C–below av.	9	50	28	13	589
11 D–very poor	10	37	34	19	114
12 Primary	9	47	29	15	519
13 Secondary	6	64	19	11	355
14 University	5	65	27	3	62

ª Results of Q.13 are tabulated on p. 47.

BRITAIN

A. Copy of Questionnaire Used in Britain

Survey 165A — July, 1948

THE GALLUP POLL WOULD LIKE YOUR OPINION

1. (a) Do you believe that human nature can be changed?

Can	1
Cannot	2
Don't know	3

   (b) If CAN: Do you think this is likely to happen?

Likely	4
Unlikely	5
Don't know	6

2. Do you think that our British characteristics are mainly born in us, or that they are due to the way we are brought up?

Born in us	7
Way brought up	8
Don't know	9

3. (a) Do you believe that it will be possible for all countries to live together at peace with each other?

Possible	1
Not possible	2
Don't know	3

   (b) Do you think that this is likely to happen?

Likely	4
Unlikely	5
Don't know	6

4. Some people say that there should be a world government able to control the laws made by each country. Do you agree or disagree?

Agree	7
Disagree	8
Don't know	9

5. When the war ended did you expect you would be getting along better, worse or about the same, as you actually are getting along at the present time?

Better	1
Worse	2
About the same	3
Don't know	4

6. (a) Do you feel that from the point of view of your (husband's) job you are more secure, or less secure, than the average Britisher?

More	5
Less	6
About the same	7
Don't know	8

   (b) In general do you feel that you are sufficiently secure to be able to plan ahead?

Yes	1
No	2
Don't know	3

7. How satisfied are you with the way you are getting on now?

Very	4
All right	5
Dissatisfied	6
Don't know	7

8. Which country in the world gives the best chance of leading the kind of life you would like to lead?....................

(NOTE TO INTERVIEWER: This question includes respondent's own country if he asks the question.)

9. If you were asked to use a name for your social class, would you say you belonged to the middle class, working class, or upper class?

Middle	1
Working	2
Upper	3
Don't know	4

10. (a) Do you feel that you have anything in common with (own) class people abroad?

Yes	5
No	6
Don't know	7

   (b) Do you feel that you have anything in common with British people who are not (own) class?

Yes	1
No	2
Don't know	3

   (c) Ask only if YES, YES or NO, NO on (a) and (b). Which of these two would you say have more in common with?

Abroad	4
British	5
Don't know	6

11. Which foreign people do you feel most friendly toward?...............

12. Which foreign people do you feel least friendly toward?...............

13. (a) From the list of words on this card, which seems to you to describe the American people best? Select as many as you wish and call off the letters and the words that go with them. If you have no particular feelings one way or the other, just say so.

   (b) Now go over the list again and select the words you think best describe the Russian people.

   (c) Now select the words that best describe British people.

1. Hardworking	8. Brave
2. Intelligent	9. Self-controlled
3. Practical	10. Domineering
4. Conceited	11. Progressive
5. Generous	12. Peace-loving
6. Cruel	13. Impossible to characterize
7. Backward	

14. Do you think our present Government is too much to the right, too much to the left, or about where you would like it to be?

Too right	1
Too left	2
All right	3
Don't know	4

15. If there were a General Election tomorrow, how would you vote?

Conservative	1
Labour	2
Liberal	3
Other	4
Don't know	5

16. How did you vote at the last General Election, or were you prevented?

Conservative	6
Labour	7
Liberal	8
Other	9
Didn't vote	Y

Man	1	Elementary	1	Professional (i) Higher professions workers	
		Secondary	2	(ii) Lower professions....................1	
Woman	2	Other	3	Owners of businesses and large, medium	
		University,		shops................................2	
21-29	3	incomplete	4	Workers on own account, owners of small	
		University,		shops................................3	
30-49	4	completed	5	Salaried-Managerial and top-grade clerical	
		Motor car	1	workers...............................4	
50-64	5	No motor car	2	Other clerical workers, shop assistants, per-	
65 & over	6	Pte. telephone	3	sonal service, including catering..........5	
		No pte.		Manual Workers........................6	
Av+	7	telephone	4	Farm workers, fishermen, gardeners.......7	
Av	8	Full-time		Farm owners..........................8	
		dom. help	5	Housewives (who will go into their husband's	
Av—	9	Part-time		socio-economic grouping)................9	
		dom. help	6	Retired: independent...................Z	
Group D	Y	None	7		

Occupation (Husband's if housewife):

....

Industry...

Place interviewed: Home....................1

Street....................2

Office, works...............3

Other...................4

Reporter's No. ..../............

Date.............................

PUT RING AROUND APPROPRIATE NUMBERS

D. Notes and Comments: by the Editors

The "secondary" group in Britain includes respondents with incomplete university education. The "university" group includes only graduates.

Percentages in cols. (A), (B), and (C) on Q.1b total the percentage of all respondents replying "Can" to Q.1a.

E. Tables

BRITAIN A

		QUESTION 1a Change human nature?			QUESTION 1b (If *Can*) Likely?[a]			QUESTION 2 National character?			SAMPLE
		(A) Can	(B) Can- not	(C) Don't know	(A) Like- ly	(B) Un- likely	(C) Don't know	(A) Born in us	(B) Way brought up	(C) Don't know	
1	Total	40	48	12	24	12	4	39	55	6	1,195
2	Men	44	48	8	26	14	4	37	58	5	605
3	Women	36	48	16	22	9	5	41	52	7	590
4	21–29	41	44	15	22	13	6	34	59	7	245
5	30–49	39	51	10	24	11	4	38	56	6	476
6	50–65	44	46	10	28	11	5	42	54	4	329
7	Over 65	35	51	14	20	13	2	41	53	6	145
8	A–wealthy	55	42	3	38	11	6	42	50	8	99
9	B–average	46	47	7	27	15	4	34	60	6	272
10	C–below av.	38	49	13	23	11	4	39	56	5	678
11	D–very poor	30	47	23	19	8	3	44	48	8	146
12	Primary	34	52	14	21	9	4	39	54	7	687
13	Secondary[b]	46	44	10	27	14	5	38	57	5	448
14	University[b]	67	30	3	37	22	8	32	65	3	60
29	Leftist (tr)[c]	56	33	11				31	67	2	132
30	Rightist (tl)[d]	41	51	8				40	55	5	478
31	All right	38	50	12				37	56	7	370
32	Don't know	33	47	20				45	47	8	215
25	Upper class							53	40	7	24
26	Middle class							40	55	5	418
27	Working class							37	56	7	717
28	Don't know							44	50	6	36
36	Can (Q.1a)							37	59	4	478
37	Cannot							40	55	5	574
38	Don't know							39	46	15	143
39	Possible (Q.3a)							39	56	5	561
40	Impossible							39	56	5	526
41	Don't know							39	46	15	108
45	Agree (Q.4)							40	55	5	526
46	Disagree							37	59	4	478
47	Don't know							39	49	12	191

[a] Percentages in cols. (A), (B), and (C) on Q.1b total the percentage of all respondents replying "Can" to Q.1a.

[b] The "secondary" group in Britain includes respondents with incomplete university education. The "university" group includes only graduates.

[c] "tr" = too right.

[d] "tl" = too left.

BRITAIN B

	QUESTION 3a Live in peace?			QUESTION 3b (If *Possible*) Likely?			QUESTION 4 World government?			SAMPLE
	(A) Pos- sible	(B) Not pos- sible	(C) Don't know	(A) Like- ly	(B) Un- likely	(C) Don't know	(A) Agree	(B) Dis- agree	(C) Don't know	
1 Total	47	44	9	21	53	26	44	40	16	1,195
2 Men	47	47	6	22	55	23	49	42	9	605
3 Women	47	41	12	20	51	29	38	37	25	590
4 21–29	46	43	11	22	52	26	46	39	15	245
5 30–49	49	45	6	21	56	23	45	39	16	476
6 50–65	48	42	10	22	53	25	44	40	16	329
7 Over 65	42	48	10	16	49	35	37	41	22	145
8 A–wealthy	48	47	5	22	61	17	49	43	8	99
9 B–average	50	44	6	23	52	25	50	39	11	272
10 C–below av.	47	44	9	20	54	26	42	40	18	678
11 D–very poor	43	41	16	18	48	34	40	34	26	146
12 Primary	45	45	10	19	53	28	42	37	21	687
13 Secondary[a]	50	43	7	22	54	24	44	44	12	448
14 University[a]	52	43	5	25	47	28	58	37	5	60
29 Leftist (tr)	61	37	2				62	33	5	132
30 Rightist (tl)	44	49	7				41	45	14	478
31 All right	48	40	12				46	35	19	370
32 Don't know	43	46	11				35	40	25	215
33 Sec. (12–10)	50	41	9				51	36	13	131
34 Medium (9–5)	49	43	8				45	41	14	634
35 Insec. (4–0)	43	47	10				40	39	21	430
36 Can (Q.1a)	62	33	5	32	47	21	52	36	12	478
37 Can't change	37	55	8	13	60	27	39	45	16	574
38 Don't know	41	36	23	18	46	36	32	29	39	143
42 Likely (Q.3b)	92	8	—							251
43 Unlikely	39	58	3							633
44 Don't know	28	45	27							311
45 Agree (Q.4)	60	33	7							526
46 Disagree	37	58	5							478
47 Don't know	40	40	20							191
39 Possible (Q.3a)							55	31	14	561
40 Impossible							33	52	15	526
41 Don't know							37	24	39	108

[a] See note b, Table A above.

BRITAIN C

	QUESTION 5 Postwar expectation?				QUESTION 6a Job security?				QUESTION 6b Able to plan?			SAMPLE
	(A)	(B)	(C)	(D)	(A)	(B)	(C)	(D)	(A)	(B)	(C)	
	Better	Worse	About same	Don't know	More	Less	About same	Don't know	Yes	No	Don't know	
1 Total	58	11	28	3	34	18	41	7	46	44	10	1,195
2 Men	56	12	29	3	39	19	37	5	50	41	9	605
3 Women	61	9	27	3	29	17	45	9	43	47	10	590
4 21–29	64	6	24	6	30	16	47	7	45	45	10	245
5 30–49	57	12	28	3	38	15	41	6	49	43	8	476
6 50–65	58	12	29	1	38	20	37	5	49	41	10	329
7 Over 65	53	13	30	4	21	24	41	14	34	50	16	145
8 A–wealthy	60	9	27	4	60	9	27	4	61	34	5	99
9 B–average	56	16	26	2	43	17	35	5	54	36	10	272
10 C–below av.	61	8	28	3	31	17	46	6	46	45	9	678
11 D–very poor	50	12	32	6	21	23	42	14	25	56	19	146
12 Primary	59	10	28	3	30	18	44	8	43	46	11	687
13 Secondary[a]	59	12	26	3	38	18	38	6	50	42	8	448
14 University[a]	49	10	38	3	52	18	27	3	60	35	5	60
15 Profess.	48	9	38	5	56	14	29	1	62	33	5	101
16 Bus. owners	61	20	12	7	47	24	24	5	46	46	8	41
17 Ind. workers	60	19	21	—	30	27	38	5	49	41	10	63
18 Sal.-mangrs.	49	15	33	3	52	10	35	3	70	22	8	73
19 Clerks	60	7	27	6	31	15	46	8	49	42	9	219
20 Man. wkrs.	56	12	31	1	32	16	47	5	41	48	11	271
21 Farm wkrs.	74	—	19	7	29	26	45	—	42	45	13	31
22 Farm owners	57	29	14	—	43	—	43	14	72	14	14	7
23 Housewives	66	9	23	2	30	20	42	8	40	51	9	277
24 Retired, Ind.	49	10	36	5	21	26	36	17	38	45	17	109
Not classified												3

[a] See note b, Table A above.

BRITAIN D

	QUESTION 7 Satisfaction?				Security Scores			QUESTION 8 Best opportunity?					SAMPLE
	(A)	(B)	(C)	(D)	(A)	(B)	(C)	(A)	(B)	(C)	(D)	(E)	
	Very	All right	Dissat.	Don't know	Sec. 12–10	Med. 9–5	Ins. 4–0	G. B.	U. S. A.	Austral.	N. Z.	S. Afr.	
1 Total	12	52	33	3	11	53	36	51	9	8	6	6	1,195
2 Men	13	50	34	3	14	53	33	50	10	9	7	5	605
3 Women	10	54	33	3	8	53	39	52	9	7	6	6	590
4 21–29	10	51	38	1	7	54	39	38	11	11	8	8	245
5 30–49	12	55	29	4	13	55	32	54	10	7	6	5	476
6 50–65	14	49	33	4	13	52	35	53	8	8	7	5	329
7 Over 65	9	50	38	3	8	47	45	61	5	5	5	6	145

BRITAIN D continued

	Satisfaction?				Security Scores			Best opportunity?					Sample
	(A)	(B)	(C)	(D)	(A)	(B)	(C)	(A)	(B)	(C)	(D)	(E)	
	Very	All right	Dissat.	Don't know	Sec. 12–10	Med. 9–5	Ins. 4–0	G. B.	U. S. A.	Austral.	N. Z.	S. Afr.	
8 A–wealthy	21	54	20	5	24	49	27	58	8	4	5	5	99
9 B–average	17	52	30	1	16	56	28	53	9	4	6	10	272
10 C–below av.	9	52	35	4	8	53	39	49	10	10	7	4	678
11 D–very poor	8	46	42	4	6	47	47	52	6	7	5	5	146
12 Primary	10	53	34	3	10	52	38						687
13 Secondary[a]	13	49	34	4	12	54	34						448
14 University[a]	25	50	25	—	21	59	20						60
15 Profess.	23	60	14	3									101
16 Bus. owners	22	37	41	—									41
17 Ind. workers	11	46	40	3									63
18 Sal.-mangrs.	23	55	21	1									73
19 Clerks	11	51	36	2									219
20 Man. wkrs.	9	49	36	6									271
21 Farm wkrs.	10	64	26	—									31
22 Farm owners	—	100	—	—									7
23 Housewives	9	49	38	4									277
24 Retired, Ind.	6	56	33	5									109
Not classified													3
					25 Upper class			43	17	7	—	10	24
					26 Middle class			52	9	7	8	8	418
					27 Working class			52	9	8	6	4	717
					28 Don't know			45	9	3	3	3	36
Totals (Q.8)			%		**29** Leftist (tr)			38	9	7	14	3	132
					30 Rightist (tl)			55	9	7	6	7	478
Great Britain			51		**31** All right			54	8	9	4	5	370
United States			9		**32** Don't know			48	12	8	5	7	215
Australia			8										
New Zealand			6										
South Africa			6										
Canada			4										
Miscellaneous			9										
Don't know, Any			7										
			100										

[a] See note b, Table A above.

BRITAIN E

	QUESTION 9 Social class?				QUESTION 10a Own class abroad?			QUESTION 10b Others at home?			SAMPLE
	(A) Mid-dle	(B) Work-ing	(C) Up-per	(D) Don't know	(A) Yes	(B) No	(C) Don't know	(A) Yes	(B) No	(C) Don't know	
1 Total	35	60	2	3	58	17	25	67	21	12	1,195
2 Men	35	60	2	3	66	15	19	71	21	8	605
3 Women	35	59	3	3	49	20	31	64	20	16	590

BRITAIN E continued

		Social class?				Own class abroad?			Others at home?			Sample
		(A) Mid-dle	(B) Work-ing	(C) Up-per	(D) Don't know	(A) Yes	(B) No	(C) Don't know	(A) Yes	(B) No	(C) Don't know	
4	21–29	30	67	1	2	59	14	27	72	20	8	245
5	30–49	38	57	2	3	63	15	22	68	20	12	476
6	50–65	38	56	3	3	57	18	25	67	21	12	329
7	Over 65	25	65	5	5	43	23	34	59	26	15	145
8	A–wealthy	63	9	24	4	72	8	20	85	7	8	99
9	B–average	70	25	1	4	62	16	22	81	13	6	272
10	C–below av.	22	76	—	2	57	17	26	66	21	13	678
11	D–very poor	11	84	1	4	44	22	34	41	40	19	146
12	Primary	19	79	—	2	53	17	30	59	27	14	687
13	Secondary[a]	55	37	4	4	62	16	22	78	14	8	448
14	University[a]	62	10	20	8	84	8	8	87	5	8	60
15	Profess.	64	21	10	5	79	10	11	86	9	5	101
16	Bus. owners	63	20	5	12	59	22	19	85	10	5	41
17	Ind. workers	52	43	—	5	49	24	27	68	24	8	63
18	Sal.-mangrs.	74	23	3	—	69	12	19	88	8	4	73
19	Clerks	40	58	—	2	52	17	31	70	23	7	219
20	Man. wkrs.	11	87	1	1	62	13	25	57	26	17	271
21	Farm wkrs.	10	90	—	—	58	19	23	52	35	13	31
22	Farm owners	43	57	—	—	86	—	14	72	14	14	7
23	Housewives	28	66	3	3	53	20	27	62	22	16	277
24	Retired, Ind.	34	55	6	5	45	19	36	71	16	13	109
	Not classified											3
25	Upper class					70	10	20	70	10	20	24
26	Middle class					58	18	24	81	14	5	418
27	Working class					58	16	26	60	25	15	717
28	Don't know					35	9	56	47	15	38	36
33	Sec. (12-10)	39	55	5	1							131
34	Med. (9–5)	38	57	2	3							634
35	Insec. (4–0)	29	66	1	4							430

		QUESTION 10c More in common?				SAMPLE
		(A) Abroad	(B) British	(C) Don't know	(D) Not asked	
	Total	7	34	7	52	1,195

[a] See note b, Table A above.

BRITAIN F

		QUESTION 11 Most friendly?					QUESTION 12 Least friendly?					SAMPLE
		(A) Amer.	(B) Dom. Col.	(C) Fr.	(D) Dutch, Belg.	(E) Scand.	(A) Russ.	(B) Ger.	(C) Jap.	(D) Ital.	(E) Jews	
1	Total	29	11	9	7	7	37	16	9	4	3	1,195
2	Men	26	12	8	8	7	38	14	8	4	4	605
3	Women	31	10	9	5	7	35	17	10	3	2	590

BRITAIN F continued

	Most friendly?					Least friendly?					Sample
	(A) Amer.	(B) Dom. Col.	(C) Fr.	(D) Dutch, Belg.	(E) Scand.	(A) Russ.	(B) Ger.	(C) Jap.	(D) Ital.	(E) Jews	
4 21–29	30	17	7	3	9	33	16	10	4	4	245
5 30–49	29	10	9	9	6	38	15	9	4	3	476
6 50–65	25	10	9	7	6	35	15	7	4	3	329
7 Over 65	31	10	12	6	8	41	20	9	3	3	145
8 A–wealthy	26	9	7	12	10	49	9	6	—	1	99
9 B–average	31	10	8	7	9	43	14	7	4	3	272
10 C–below av.	28	12	9	7	6	33	16	10	4	3	678
11 D–very poor	31	12	11	3	3	30	25	8	4	5	146
25 Upper class	24	3	3	20	10	63	7	—	3	3	24
26 Middle class	34	10	7	8	7	43	13	8	2	3	418
27 Working class	26	13	10	6	7	32	18	9	5	3	717
28 Don't know	15	6	6	—	3	21	13	9	—	3	36
29 Leftist (tr)	17	11	10	6	8	19	13	8	5	5	132
30 Rightist (tl)	33	11	7	4	8	48	13	8	4	2	478
31 All right	27	13	9	15	6	30	18	10	4	4	370
32 Don't know	24	8	10	—	5	35	21	10	3	2	215

Totals (Q.11)	%	*Totals* (Q.12)	%
Americans	29	Russians	37
The Dominions, Colonies	11	Germans	16
French	9	Japanese	9
Dutch, Belgians	7	Italians	4
Scandinavians	7	Jews	3
Germans	4	Americans	3
All people	4	Miscellaneous nations	3
All others	11	No particular people	10
Miscellaneous nations	2	All others	8
No particular people	6	Miscellaneous answers	1
Miscellaneous answers	1	Don't know	6
Don't know	9		
	100		100

BRITAIN Gᵃ

	QUESTION 14 Present government?				SAMPLE
	(A) Too right	(B) Too left	(C) All right	(D) Don't know	
1 Total	11	40	31	18	1,195
2 Men	13	39	33	15	605
3 Women	9	40	30	21	590
4 21–29	12	34	33	21	245
5 30–49	14	37	32	17	476
6 50–65	8	46	31	15	329
7 Over 65	7	44	28	21	145

BRITAIN G[a] continued

	Present government?				Sample
	(A) Too right	(B) Too left	(C) All right	(D) Don't know	
8 A–wealthy	8	67	14	11	99
9 B–average	10	55	20	15	272
10 C–below av.	13	33	36	18	678
11 D–very poor	8	23	42	27	146
12 Primary	10	31	39	20	687
13 Secondary	11	51	22	16	448
14 University	17	53	18	12	60

[a] Results of Q.13 are tabulated on p. 47.

FRANCE

A. Copy of Questionnaire Used in France

1 a) Croyez-vous que la nature humaine peut être améliorée?
Oui 1
Non 2
? 3

1 b) Pensez-vous qu'il est probable que cela arrive un jour?
Probable 1
Improbable 2
? 3

2. On parle couramment des défauts et des quali-tés des Fraïnçais. A votre avis, est-ce que ces caractéristiques viennent surtout de la race ou surtout de l'éducation?
....
Race 1
Education 2
Autre réponse 3
? 4

3 a) Pensez-vous que l'on peut concevoir un état de paix universelle entre toutes les nations?
Oui 1
Non 2
? 3

3 b) Croyez-vous que cet état de paix universelle se réalisera un jour?
Probable 1
Improbable 2
? 3

4. Certaines personnes disent qu'il devrait y avoir un gouvernement mondial qui côntrole les lois de tous les pays. Etes-vous de cet avis?
Oui 1
Non 2
? 3

5. A la fin de la guerre, en 1945, lorsque vous pensiez à ce que pourrait être la vie trois ans après, pour vous et votre famille, pensiez-vous que la situation serait moins bonne, meilleure ou à peu près ce qu'elle est maintenant?
Commentaire:.................
....
Meilleure 1
Moins bonne 2
Même chose 3
? 4

6 a) Au point de vue de votre métier (ou celui de votre mari), estimez-vous que vous êtes plus sûr ou moins sûr du lendemain que la moyenne des Français?
Plus sûr 1
Moins sûr 2
Même chose 3
? 4

6 b) D'une manière générale, est-ce que votre avenir vous paraît assez sûr pour pouvoir faire des plans?
Oui 1
Non 2
? 3

7. Comment les choses marchent-elles pour vous. Etes-vous content ou mécontent?
Très content 1
Content 2
Mécontent 3
? 4

8. Dans quel pays du monde, à votre avis, une personne comme vous a-t-elle le plus de chances de mener la vie que vous voudriez mener?
....
(Note Pour L'Enquêteur: Cette question n'exclut pas la France.)

9. Si l'on vous demandait de dire à quel groupe social vous appartenez, est-ce que vous diriez que vous appartenez à la classe moyenne, à la classe ouvrière ou à la classe aisee?
Moyenne 1
Ouvrière 2
Aisée 3
? 4

10 a) Est-ce que vous vous sentez quelque chose de commun avec des étrangers de la même classe sociale que vous?
Oui 1
Non 2
? 3

10 b) Et avec les Français qui appartiennent à une autre classe sociale que la vôtre?
Oui 1
Non 2
? 3

(Question à poser seulement aux personnes qui ont répondu OUI à 10a et OUI à 10b ou bien NON à 10a et NON à 10b)

10 c) Avec qui vous sentez-vous le plus de points communs : l'étranger de la même classe sociale que vous ou le Français d'une classe sociale différente?
Question non posée 0
Etranger 1
Français 2
? 3

11. Quel est le peuple pour lequel vous avez le plus de sympathie?
....

12. Quel est le peuple pour lequel vous avez le moins de sympathie?
....

13 a) Dans la liste de mots que voici (MONTRER LA CARTE), quels sont ceux qui vous paraissent décrire le mieux le peuple améri-cain? (Choisissez autant de mots que vous voulez.)

13 b) Et quels sont ceux qui décrivent le mieux le peuple russe?

13 c) Et les Français?..............

	AMÉRICAIN	RUSSE	FRANÇAIS
Travailleur..................	1	1	1
Intelligent..................	2	2	2
Pratique....................	3	3	3
Vaniteux....................	4	4	4
Généreux	5	5	5
Cruel	6	6	6
Arriéré.....................	7	7	7
Courageux...................	8	8	8
Maître de soi	9	9	9
Dominateur..................	10	10	10
Ouvert au progrès...........	11	11	11
Pacifique...................	12	12	12
Impossible à caractériser......	E	E	E

14. Trouvez-vous que le gouvernement actuel est trop à droite, trop à gauche, ou comme il faut?
Trop à droit 1
Trop à gauche 2
Comme il faut 3
? 4

15 a) A votre avis, y a-t-il des nations qui cher-chent à dominer le monde?
Oui 1
Non 2
? 3

15 b) (Si «OUI») Lesquelles?..................

16 a) Quelle est la dernière école ou le dernier établissement d'enseignement que vous avez fréquenté comme élève (ou étudiant)?..................

16 b) Est-ce un établissement d'enseignement : pri-maire, primaire supérieur, secondaire, technique, supérieur?
Primaire 1
Primaire supér. 2
Secondaire 3
Technique 4
Supérieur 5
Pas d'études 6

16 c) A quel âge avez-vous quitte cet établissement?
Age:.................

17. Quel journal quotidien du matin préférez-vous?
....

Homme 1	Propriété	Non................. 0	Domestiques	Non............... 0
Femme............. 2		Oui 1		Oui 1
21 à 29 ans 1	Automobile	Non................. 0	Radio	Non............... 0
30 à 49 ans 2		Oui 1		Oui 1
50 à 65 ans 3				
66 ans et plus 4	Profession:..........			
	Salarié 1	Patron 2		

Localité:.................   Nombre d'habitants:.................
Enquêteur:.................   Date de l'enquête:.................

N. B. — *Notez avec soin les caractéristiques de la personne interrogée.*
Entourez d'un cercle, à l'encre ou au crayon de couleur, le numéro correspondant à la réponse.

B. Excerpts from Instructions to Interviewers

Interview the respondent when he is not too busy, try to interest him immediately, and give him time to reflect, repeating the questions if necessary, but without comment and without trying to help him, so you will not influence his answers.

Q.2: Certain persons may reply that French characteristics stem from both "race" and "education." In this case, re-read the question, emphasizing the word "surtout."

Q.7: "Cette question a un sens très général; elle comprend à la fois les affaires, le métier, la situation de famille de l'enquêté. On veut savoir si, d'une manière générale, il est content ou mécontent de son sort actuel."

C. Excerpts from Notes and Comments by Survey Agency

Sampling: Interviewers—94. Dates—June 21–July 3, 1948. Interviews—1,000 throughout France (except Corsica). Sampling based on census of March 8, 1936.

Structure of the sample:

Sex	Planned	Actual
Men	481	524
Women	512	476
Age		
20-29	180	293
30-49	364	359
50-64	284	207
65 and over	172	140
Not specified		1
Occupation		
Professions libérales	11	18
Industriels, commerçants, artisans, cadres	92	97
Employés, fonctionnaires	113	189
Ouvriers	192	177
Ouvriers agricoles	74	56
Agriculteurs	162	146
Ménagères	298	264
Retraités, rentiers	58	53
Socio-economic		
Aisée	(No of-	70
Moyenne plutôt aisée	ficial	267
Moyenne plutôt pauvre	statis-	389
Pauvre	tics)	177
Not specified		97
Education		
Pas d'étude		19
Primaire	(No of-	535
Primaire supérieur	ficial	165
Secondaire	statis-	140
Technique	tics)	65
Supérieur		76

Geographic		
Nord-ouest	190	193
Nord-est	265	221
Sud-ouest	158	176
Sud-est	226	198
Paris et Seine	118	119
Seine et Oise, Seine et Marne	43	93

Socio-economic classification was based on four objective criteria, as follows:

D—(Very poor): Do not own radio, automobile, or real property.
C—(Below average): Own either radio or real property.
B—(Average): Own radio and automobile, radio and real property, or all three.
A—(Wealthy): Own radio and automobile, and employ servants. May also own real property.

D. Notes and Comments by the Editors

Respondents classified by IFOP (see Education above) as "primaire" are listed in the tables (1. 12) as "primary." Those classified as "primaire supérieur," "secondaire," and "technique" are combined (1. 13) as "secondary." "Supérieur" is listed (1. 15) as "university." The "pas d'étude" group, with only nineteen respondents, was not tabulated.

All respondents were asked Q.1b, regardless of their answers on Q.1a, hence results are not strictly comparable with other countries.

The "Don't know" category (col. C) on Q.2 includes, besides "Don't know's," the "autre réponse" category which was not on the questionnaire in other countries: 14% were "Don't know's"; 6% "Other answers." With education and socio-economic status, the former decreased, the latter increased. See above instructions on Q.2 to interviewers on this point.

Security Scores are not available (see note, p. 123), hence cross tabulations (ll. 33, 34, 35) are omitted.

On Q. 11 and 12 only those peoples liked or disliked by more than 5% of respondents were tabulated. "Others," "Don't know's," etc., were omitted from the count.

FRANCE A

	QUESTION 1a Change human nature?			QUESTION 1b (If *Can*) Likely?[a]			QUESTION 2 National character?[b]			SAMPLE
	(A) Can	(B) Can-not	(C) Don't know	(A) Like-ly	(B) Un-likely	(C) Don't know	(A) Born in us	(B) Way brought up	(C) Don't know[c]	
1 Total	59	22	19	38	36	26	35	45	20	1,000
2 Men	62	23	15	40	35	25	36	44	20	524
3 Women	57	21	22	36	36	28	34	47	19	476
4 21–29	62	20	18	41	36	23	36	47	17	293
5 30–49	64	21	15	43	34	23	31	47	22	359
6 50–65	57	22	21	30	39	31	39	40	21	207
7 Over 65	48	29	23	32	37	31	37	44	19	140
8 A–wealthy[d]	70	19	11	49	30	21	37	46	17	70
9 B–average	63	22	15	41	37	22	40	45	15	267
10 C–below av.	61	20	19	38	35	27	36	44	20	389
11 D–very poor	50	22	28	36	32	32	23	49	28	177
12 Primary[e]	54	20	26	35	33	32	36	39	25	535
13 Secondary[e]	69	22	9	44	37	19	48	42	10	370
14 University	62	30	8	40	47	13	24	58	18	76
29 Leftist (tr)[f]	65	17	18				37	40	23	254
30 Rightist (tl)[g]	65	20	15				34	53	13	141
31 All right	65	22	13				38	48	14	277
32 Don't know	49	47	24				31	45	24	328
25 Upper class							29	62	9	58
26 Middle class							34	50	16	435
27 Working class							36	40	24	466
28 Don't know							39	37	24	41
36 Can (Q.1a)							33	53	14	596
37 Cannot							45	37	18	222
38 Don't know							29	31	40	182
39 Possible (Q.3a)							32	48	20	476
40 Impossible							40	45	15	414
41 Don't know							27	42	31	110
45 Agree (Q.4)							30	49	21	455
46 Disagree							39	49	12	362
47 Don't know							38	32	30	183

[a] All respondents were asked Q.1b, regardless of their answers on Q.1a, hence results are not strictly comparable with other countries.

[b] Certain persons may reply that French characteristics stem from both "race" and "education". In this case, re-read Q.2 emphasizing the word "surtout."

[c] This category includes, besides "Don't know's," the "autre reponse" category which was not on the questionnaire in other countries. 14% were "Don't know's"; 6% "Other answers"; with education and socioeconomic status, the former decreased, the latter increased. See fn. b above on this point.

[d] Socio-economic classification was based on four objective criteria, as follows: D—(Very poor): Do not own radio, automobile, or real property. C—(Below average): Own either radio or real property. B—(Average): Own radio and automobile, radio and real property, or all three. A—(Wealthy): Own radio and automobile, and employ servants. May also own real property.

[e] Respondents classified by IFOP as "primaire" are listed in the tables (l. 12) as "primary." Those classified as "primaire supérieur," "secondaire," and "technique" are combined (l. 13) as "secondary." "Supèrieur" is listed (l. 15) as "university." The "pas d'étude" group, with only nineteen respondents, was not tabulated.

[f] "tr" = too right.

[g] "tl" = too left.

FRANCE B

	QUESTION 3a Live in peace?			QUESTION 3b (If *Possible*) Likely?			QUESTION 4 World government			SAMPLE
	(A) Possible	(B) Not possible	(C) Don't know	(A) Likely	(B) Unlikely	(C) Don't know	(A) Agree	(B) Disagree	(C) Don't know	
1 Total	47	41	12	24	54	22	45	36	19	1,000
2 Men	53	39	8	28	53	19	50	36	14	524
3 Women	42	43	15	20	56	24	40	36	24	476
4 21–29	52	36	12	29	51	20	45	40	15	293
5 30–49	52	39	9	27	52	21	50	34	16	359
6 50–65	41	49	10	17	58	25	40	36	49a	207
7 Over 65	38	46	16	19	61	20	41	34	35a	140
8 A–wealthyb	56	36	8	33	46	21	43	40	17	70
9 B–average	46	43	11	24	59	17	46	39	15	267
10 C–below av.	48	42	10	24	54	22	47	36	17	389
11 D–very poor	52	33	15	26	49	25	46	28	26	177
12 Primaryc	47	41	12	24	55	21	45	33	22	535
13 Secondary	48	42	10	23	56	21	46	38	16	370
14 University	54	38	8	36	46	18	55	40	5	76
29 Leftist (tr)	67	25	8				57	29	14	254
30 Rightist (tl)	36	53	11				38	45	17	141
31 All right	47	39	14				45	36	19	277
32 Don't know	38	51	11				41	38	21	328
33 Sec. (12–10)d										
34 Medium (9–5)										
35 Insec. (4–0)										
36 Can (Q.1a)	60	33	7	52	35	13	52	35	13	596
37 Can't change	26	66	8	31	51	18	31	51	18	222
38 Don't know	32	40	28	43	21	36	43	21	36	182
42 Likely (Q.3b)	99	1	—							244
43 Unlikely	25	70	5							545
44 Don't know	46	14	40							211
45 Agree (Q.4)	69	23	8							455
46 Disagree	29	63	8							362
47 Don't know	33	43	24							183
39 Possible (Q.3a)							66	22	12	476
40 Impossible							25	56	19	414
41 Don't know							34	26	40	110

a Percentages in these two lines add to 125% and 110%, respectively. Scanning the table suggests that the "Don't know" figures are incorrect.

b See note d, Table A above.

c See note e, Table A above.

d Security Scores are not available (see note p. 123), hence cross tabulations (ll. 33, 34, 35) are omitted.

FRANCE C

	QUESTION 5 Postwar expectation?				QUESTION 6a Job security?				QUESTION 6b Able to plan?			SAMPLE
	(A) Better	(B) Worse	(C) About same	(D) Don't know	(A) More	(B) Less	(C) About same	(D) Don't know	(A) Yes	(B) No	(C) Don't know	
1 Total	81	5	10	4	17	32	42	9	14	74	12	1,000
2 Men	81	5	10	4	19	33	41	7	15	74	11	524
3 Women	81	5	10	4	14	32	43	11	13	74	13	476
4 21–29	81	5	8	6	21	25	44	10	20	69	11	293
5 30–49	81	4	11	4	19	29	45	7	15	74	11	359
6 50–65	79	5	13	3	10	36	45	9	11	75	14	207
7 Over 65	85	6	8	1	10	49	29	12	6	84	10	140
8 A–wealthy[a]	70	4	17	9	30	34	30	6	27	57	16	70
9 B–average	82	5	10	3	18	33	42	7	15	75	10	267
10 C–below av.	85	5	6	4	13	36	42	9	11	78	11	389
11 D–very poor	80	4	12	4	11	30	45	14	13	76	11	177
12 Primary[b]	83	4	10	3	14	34	43	9	11	77	12	535
13 Secondary	80	5	10	5	19	31	41	9	17	72	11	370
14 University	76	5	16	3	28	24	38	10	24	64	12	76
15 Profess.	89	6	5	—	28	28	44	—	33	61	6	18
16 Bus. owners	67	5	28	—	24	52	24	—	29	57	14	21
17 Ind. workers	81	6	5	8	16	40	37	7	15	77	8	62
18 Sal.-mangrs.	79	—	21	—	43	21	36	—	36	64	—	14
19 Clerks	79	3	12	6	20	23	45	12	19	68	13	189
20 Man. wkrs.	81	5	10	4	10	38	44	8	8	82	10	177
21 Farm wkrs.	80	5	13	2	11	41	46	2	9	82	9	56
22 Farm owners	80	5	12	3	27	22	46	5	21	66	13	146
23 Housewives	84	6	7	3	14	30	43	13	11	74	15	264
24 Retired, Ind.	85	4	9	2	11	59	19	11	4	91	5	53

[a] See note d, Table A above.

[b] See note e, Table A above.

FRANCE D

	QUESTION 7 Satisfaction?[a]				Security Scores[b]			QUESTION 8 Best opportunity?				SAMPLE
	(A) Very	(B) All right	(C) Dissat.	(D) Don't know	(A) Sec. 12–10	(B) Med. 9–5	(C) Ins. 4–0	(A) France	(B) America	(C) Switz.	(D) Russia	
1 Total	2	27	56	15				43	12	9	4	1,000
2 Men	2	28	57	13				39	14	8	6	524
3 Women	2	26	56	16				46	11	9	2	476
4 21–29	2	34	51	13				47	16	7	7	293
5 30–49	2	28	54	16				39	13	8	6	359
6 50–65	—	23	62	15				41	12	9	1	207
7 Over 65	1	21	66	12				46	6	14	—	140

FRANCE D continued

	Satisfaction?[a]				Security Scores[b]			Best opportunity?				Sample
	(A)	(B)	(C)	(D)	(A)	(B)	(C)	(A)	(B)	(C)	(D)	
	Very	All right	Dissat.	Don't know	Sec. 12–10	Med. 9–5	Ins. 4–0	France	America	Switz.	Russia	
8 A–wealthy[c]	9	40	37	14				40	20	9	—	70
9 B–average	2	27	53	18				50	13	9	1	267
10 C–below av.	1	25	61	13				38	14	9	6	389
11 D–very poor	1	20	67	12				43	8	3	10	177
12 Primary[d]	1	24	62	13								535
13 Secondary	2	32	52	14								370
14 University	3	28	46	23								76
15 Profess.	6	28	55	11								18
16 Bus. owners	10	33	38	19								21
17 Ind. workers	3	31	56	10								62
18 Sal.-mangrs.	—	43	29	28								14
19 Clerks	2	30	56	12								189
20 Man. wkrs.	1	21	67	11								177
21 Farm wkrs.	4	21	63	12								56
22 Farm owners	2	39	42	17								146
23 Housewives	1	25	56	18								264
24 Retired, Ind.	—	11	78	11								53
25 Upper class								50	12	7	—	58
26 Middle class								41	15	11	1	435
27 Working class								43	12	5	9	466
28 Don't know								37	7	29	—	41
29 Leftist (tr)								35	11	4	16	254
30 Rightist (tl)								41	23	8	—	141
31 All right								50	12	9	—	277
32 Don't know								43	10	12	—	328

Totals (Q.8) %

	%
France	43
America	12
Switzerland	9
Russia	4
Belgium	4
Great Britain	3
Canada	2
Sweden	1
Argentina	1
South America	1
Other countries	6
No answer	14
	100

[a] "Cette question a un sens très général; elle comprend à la fois les affaires, le métier, la situation de famille de l'enquête. On veut savoir si, d'une manière générale, il est content ou mécontent de son sort actuel."

[b] Security Scores are not available (see note, p. 123).

[c] See note d, Table A above.

[d] See note e, Table A above.

FRANCE E

	QUESTION 9 Social class?				QUESTION 10a Own class abroad?			QUESTION 10b Others at home?			SAMPLE
	(A) Mid-dle	(B) Work-ing	(C) Up-per	(D) Don't know	(A) Yes	(B) No	(C) Don't know	(A) Yes	(B) No	(C) Don't know	
1 Total	44	46	6	4	48	27	25	63	21	16	1,000
2 Men	40	55	3	2	55	25	20	66	23	11	524
3 Women	48	38	8	6	41	29	30	60	20	20	476
4 21–29	42	51	5	2	56	23	21	63	23	14	293
5 30–49	43	50	5	2	53	26	21	68	19	13	359
6 50–65	44	41	8	7	41	29	30	59	20	21	207
7 Over 65	46	39	7	8	34	31	35	61	22	17	140
8 A–wealthy[a]	56	3	37	4	50	24	26	68	13	19	70
9 B–average	57	34	4	5	48	32	20	70	17	13	267
10 C–below av.	37	57	2	4	50	24	26	63	24	13	389
11 D–very poor	16	78	1	5	52	20	28	51	28	21	177
12 Primary[b]	30	62	3	5	45	27	28	58	24	18	535
13 Secondary	57	31	9	3	49	28	23	69	18	13	370
14 University	75	11	9	5	75	16	9	79	17	4	76
15 Profess.	94	—	6	—	72	11	17	89	11		18
16 Bus. owners	76	—	24	—	57	24	19	81	14	5	21
17 Ind. workers	61	32	5	2	48	24	28	74	10	16	62
18 Sal.-mangrs.	71	29	—	—	79	14	7	93	7	—	14
19 Clerks	43	52	3	2	55	23	22	67	20	13	189
20 Man. wkrs.	10	88	—	2	60	19	21	58	28	14	177
21 Farm wkrs.	12	81	2	5	52	27	21	54	30	16	56
22 Farm owners	62	25	8	5	36	36	28	67	14	19	146
23 Housewives	50	33	10	7	42	30	28	60	22	18	264
24 Retired, Ind.	49	36	6	9	36	38	26	57	26	17	53
25 Upper class					47	31	22	67	17	16	58
26 Middle class					45	31	24	73	17	10	435
27 Working class					54	22	24	58	26	16	466
28 Don't know					22	22	56	32	15	53	41

33 Sec. (12–10)[c]
34 Med. (9–5)
35 Insec. (4–0)

	QUESTION 10c More in common?				SAMPLE
	(A) Abroad	(B) France	(C) Don't know	(D) Not asked	
Total	12	34	21	33	1,000

[a] See note d, Table A above.

[b] See note e, Table A above.

[c] Security Scores not available (see note, p. 123), hence cross tabulations (ll. 33, 34, 35) are omitted.

FRANCE F

	QUESTION 11 Most friendly?					QUESTION 12 Least friendly?				SAMPLE
	(A) Swiss	(B) Amer.	(C) Belg.	(D) Brit.	(E) Russ.	(A) Ger.	(B) Russ.	(C) Ital.	(D) Amer.	
1 Total	18	17	16	14	10	34	32	7	6	1,000
2 Men	15	17	15	11	15	33	30	6	9	524
3 Women	20	17	17	17	5	35	33	8	3	476
4 21–29	16	16	18	17	11	34	28	7	7	293
5 30–49	16	17	15	13	13	34	29	7	8	359
6 50–65	19	15	16	14	7	33	37	6	3	207
7 Over 65	22	19	17	14	6	32	39	7	5	140
8 A–wealthy[a]	17	34	14	17	1	23	57	4	1	70
9 B–average	19	17	21	16	6	35	34	7	5	267
10 C–below av.	18	15	14	14	11	31	30	6	8	389
11 D–very poor	8	12	15	10	20	41	17	9	9	177
25 Upper class	14	38	12	19	—	15	59	9	—	58
26 Middle class	21	19	15	20	2	32	41	5	3	435
27 Working class	13	12	18	9	19	37	20	8	10	466
28 Don't know	27	12	10	7	—	41	22	5	2	41
29 Leftist (tr)	10	11	13	7	34	35	9	2	20	254
30 Rightist (tl)	14	24	15	18	1	25	60	1	1	141
31 All right	21	21	22	20	1	35	41	7	1	277
32 Don't know	21	14	14	14	2	36	28	8	2	328

Totals (Q.11)[b]	%	*Totals* (Q.12)[b]	%
Swiss	18	Germans	34
Americans	17	Russians	32
Belgians	16	Italians	7
British	14	Americans	6
Russians	10		

[a] See note d, Table A above.

[b] On Q.11 and 12 only those peoples liked or disliked by more than 5% of respondents were tabulated. "Others," "Don't know's," etc., were omitted by the survey agency. Hence responses given here do not total 100% of respondents.

FRANCE G[a]

	QUESTION 14 Present government?				SAMPLE
	(A) Too right	(B) Too left	(C) All right	(D) Don't know	
1 Total	25	14	28	33	1,000
2 Men	32	13	29	26	524
3 Women	18	15	27	40	476
4 21–29	31	11	26	32	293
5 30–49	28	14	28	30	359
6 50–65	22	16	29	33	207
7 Over 65	13	18	26	43	140

FRANCE G[a] continued

	Present government?				Sample
	(A) Too right	(B) Too left	(C) All right	(D) Don't know	
8 A–wealthy[b]	11	37	15	37	70
9 B–average	16	14	37	33	267
10 C–below av.	29	13	25	33	389
11 D–very poor	43	5	30	22	177
12 Primary	31	12	24	33	535
13 Secondary	20	15	31	34	370
14 University	20	24	30	26	76

[a] Results of Q.13 are tabulated on p. 47.

[b] See note d, Table A above.

GERMANY

A. Copy of Questionnaire Used in Germany

STATISTISCHE MEINUNGSERFORSCHUNG Nr. M.M. 2 Datum des Interviews................... Schlüssel-Nr........................

1. (a) Glauben Sie, dass das Wesen des Menschen geändert werden kann?

   (a) Ja, kann.......... (b) Nein, kann nicht........(c) Weiss nicht..........

   (b) Falls ja: Halten Sie es für wahrscheinlich, dass das geschehen wird?

   (a) Wahrscheinlich...... (b) Unwahrscheinlich...... (c) Weiss nicht......

2. Glauben Sie, dass unsere deutsche Wesensart uns grösstenteils angeboren oder anerzogen ist?

   (a) Angeboren........... (b) Anerzogen........... (c) Weiss nicht...........

3. (a) Glauben Sie, dass es für alle Länder möglich sein wird, in Frieden zusammenzuleben?

   (a) Möglich........... (b) Unmöglich........... (c) Weiss nicht...........

   (b) Halten Sie es für wahrscheinlich, dass das geschehen wird?

   (a) Wahrscheinlich...... (b) Unwahrscheinlich...... (c) Weiss nicht......

4. Manche Leute meinen, es solle eine Weltregierung geben, die fähig ist, die Gesetze jedes Landes zu überwachen. Wären Sie damit einverstanden?

   (a) Einverstanden...... (b) Nicht einverstanden...... (c) Weiss nicht......

5. Als der Krieg zu Ende war, erwarteten Sie, dass es Ihnen besser, schlechter oder ungefähr so gehen würde, wie es zur Zeit tatsächlich der Fall ist?

   (a) Besser.................(b) Schlecter...............
   (c) Ungefähr so.................(d) Weiss nicht...............

6. (a) Haben Sie das Gefühl, dass Sie in Ihrer Stellung (durch die Stellung Ihres Mannes) gesicherter oder weniger gesichert sind als der Durchschnittsdeutsche?

   (a) Gesicherter.................(b) Weniger gesichert...............
   (c) Ungefähr gleich.................(d) Weiss nicht...............

   (b) Haben Sie das Gefühl, dass Ihre Lage im allgemeinen genügend gesichert ist, um im voraus Pläne zu machen?

   (a) Ja............... (b) Nein............... (c) Weiss nicht...............

7. Wie sind Sie mit Ihren gegenwärtigen Verhältnissen zufrieden?

   (a) Sehr zufrieden.................(c) Unzufrieden...............
   (b) Zufrieden.................(d) Weiss nicht...............

8. Welches Land der Welt bietet die beste Möglichkeit, das Leben so zu führen, wie Sie es sich wünschen?

   (Anmerkung an Fieldworker: Das eigene eingeschlossen, falls der Befragte danach fragen sollte.)

9. Wenn Sie Ihre soziale Schicht bezeichnen sollten, würden Sie sagen, dass Sie zum Mittelstand, Arbeiterstand oder zur Oberschicht gehören?

   (a) Mittelstand.................(d) Weiss nicht...............
   (b) Arbeiterstand.................(c) Oberschicht...............

10. (a) Finden Sie, dass Sie mit der entsprechenden Schicht im Ausland etwas gemein haben?

    (a) Ja............... (b) Nein............... (c) Weiss nicht...............

    (b) Finden Sie, dass Sie mit Deutschen, die zu einer anderen sozialen Schicht gehören, etwas gemein haben?

    (a) Ja............... (b) Nein............... (c) Weiss nicht...............

    (c) (Nur zu fragen, falls Antwort auf (a) und (b) ja/ja oder nein/nein).

    Mit welchen haben Sie mehr gemein?

    (a) Mit der gleichen sozialen Schicht im Ausland...............
    (b) Mit Deutschen aus anderen sozialen Schichten...............
    (c) Weiss nicht...............

11. Gegenüber welchem fremden Volk hegen Sie die freundschaftlichsten Gefühle?

12. Gegenüber welchem fremden Volk hegen Sie die geringsten freundschaftlichen Gefühle?

13. (a) Auf beiliegender Karte ist eine Reihe von Worten angegeben; welche dieser Worte bezeichnen nach Ihrer Meinung das amerikanische Volk am besten?

    (Wählen Sie so viele, wie Sie wollen und nennen Sie die dazugehörigen Buchstaben. Bitte sagen Sie, wenn Ihnen keines richtig zutreffend erscheint).

    (b) Nun sehen Sie die Karte noch einmal vor und sagen Sie uns, welche Worte das russische Volk am besten bezeichnen?

    (c) Und nun nennen Sie die für Ihre eigenen Landsleute am besten passenden Worte?

    (d) Nun für das englische Volk

    (e) Dann für das französische Volk

    (f) Und für das chinesische Volk

    1. Sehr arbeitsam
    2. Intelligent
    3. Practisch veranlast
    4. Eitel
    5. Grosszugig
    6. Grausam
    7. Rückstandig
    8. Tapfer
    9. Selbstbeherrscht
    10. Herrsch-zuchtig
    11. Fortschrittlich
    12. Friedlich

14. Finden Sie, dass unsere gegenwärtige Bundesregierung zu sehr rechts oder zu sehr links eingestellt ist, oder sind Sie mit ihrer Einstellung zufrieden?

    (a) Zu sehr rechts...................(b) Zu sehr links...............
    (c) Richtig so...................(d) Weiss nicht...............

15. Geschlecht: Männlich...............
    Weiblich...............

16. Alter (Anzahl der Jahre):...............

17. Soziale Schicht: Oberschicht...............
    Mittelstand...............
    Arbeiterschicht...............

18. Schulbildung:
    (a) Anzahl der Schuljahre...............
    (b) Schule:
    Volksschule...............
    Mittlere Reife/Abitur...............
    Hochschule/Universität...............

19. Religion:
    Katholisch...............
    Protestantisch/Evangelisch...............
    Andere...............

20. Beruf:
    (a) Berufstätige:
    (i) Höhere Berufe...............
    (ii) Niedere Berufe...............
    (b) Geschäftsinhaber, sowie Besitzer grosser und mittelgrosser Läden...............
    (c) Selbständige Handwerker, Besitzer kleinerer Läden...............
    (d) Angestellte: leitende und höhere Angestellte...............
    (e) Andere Angestellte, Verkäufer, Hausangestellte, einschl. Küchenchefs...............
    (f) Arbeiter...............
    (g) Landarbeiter, Fischer, Gärtner...............
    (h) Landwirte...............
    (i) Hausfrauen (diese kommen unter die wirtschaftlichsoziale Gruppe ihres Mannes)...............
    (j) Im Ruhestand, unabhängig.

21. Flüchtling:
    Ja...............
    Nein...............

C. Excerpts from Notes and Comments by Survey Agency (Dr. James White)

"Q.13 could be improved by getting the words valued by experts in the country being examined, and a further open-ended question asking people for qualities they thought they themselves or the people under question had, and then assessing the local value attached to the quality as mentioned."

Re "Brave": "The Englishman regards fear as a natural phenomenon, the German as a slur on his manhood."

Re "Industrious": "The ability to work hard and be industrious is the highest virtue to which Germans of most classes aspire and their strongest condemnation of other peoples is that they are lazy."

Re "Backward"; "They believe 'backwardness' the greatest fault a nation could possess."

Re "Self-Controlled": "This is not regarded as a particular virtue—it is, they think, slightly unnatural."

Re "Intelligent": "This is also felt to be inferior to 'feeling with one's blood.'"

D. Notes and Comments by the Editors

Only three socio-economic check boxes were provided on the ballot, hence it is not clear how the distinction was made between the "C" and "D" groups.

Sample on Q.1b is the number of respondents who answered "Can" to Q.1a. Percentages in cols. (A), (B), and (C) total the percentage of all respondents replying "Can" to Q.1a.

The first set of tables (A through G) are for the British Zone of Occupation in western Germany. The second set (A through G) beginning on p. 160 are for the British Sector in western Berlin. The first of these surveys took place in August, 1948; the second in October, 1949. On Q.13 for 1948 (see p. 47), the samples for West Germany and West Berlin are combined.

E. Tables

GERMANY (BRITISH ZONE OF OCCUPATION) A

	QUESTION 1a Change human nature? (A) Can	(B) Cannot	(C) Don't know	QUESTION 1b (If *Can*) Likely?[a] (A) Likely	(B) Unlikely	(C) Don't know	(D) (Sample)	QUESTION 2 National character? (A) Born in us	(B) Way brought up	(C) Don't know	SAMPLE
1 Total	54	30	16	32	15	7	(1812)	59	29	12	3,371
2 Men	58	31	11	34	18	6	(927)	56	36	8	1,605
3 Women	50	29	21	30	13	7	(885)	60	24	16	1,766
4 21–29	54	30	16	31	16	7	(440)	58	29	13	815
5 30–49	54	31	15	32	15	7	(852)	59	30	11	1,587
6 50–65	55	27	18	35	15	5	(423)	58	29	13	766
7 Over 65	48	27	25	25	17	6	(97)	61	20	19	203
8 A–wealthy	50	46	4	24	20	6	(57)	60	36	4	115
9 B–average	58	34	8	34	18	6	(950)	60	31	9	1,646
10 C–below av.[b]	51	25	24	30	13	8	(751)	58	27	15	1,476
11 D–very poor	40	23	37	24	12	4	(54)	47	21	32	134
12 Primary	53	26	21	32	14	7	(1298)	60	26	14	2,461
13 Secondary	58	37	5	32	20	6	(438)	53	38	9	760
14 University	51	48	1	27	19	5	(76)	28	21	51[c]	150
29 Leftist (tr)[d]	56	32	12					49	42	9	456
30 Rightist (tl)[e]	55	39	6					62	33	5	381
31 All right	60	31	9					61	31	8	777
32 Don't know	50	27	23					59	24	17	1,757
25 Upper class								59	34	7	116
26 Middle class								61	30	9	1,742
27 Working class								56	29	15	1,384
28 Don't know								49	21	30	129
36 Can (Q.1a)								57	36	7	1,812
37 Cannot								67	26	7	1,008
38 Don't know								45	15	40	551
39 Possible (Q.3a)								58	31	11	1,941
40 Impossible								63	28	9	1,190
41 Don't know								42	18	40	240
45 Agree (Q.4)								56	35	9	1,722
46 Disagree								64	29	7	936
47 Don't know								57	16	27	713

[a] Sample on Q.1b is the number of respondents who answered "Can" to Q.1a. Percentages in cols. (A), (B), and (C) total the percentage of all respondents replying "Can" to Q.1a.

[b] Only three socio-economic check boxes were provided on the ballot, hence it is not clear how the distinction was made between the "C" and "D" groups.

[c] There is an error in this block of figures, probably a transposition in the last line. They are given as transmitted by the survey agency.

[d] "tr" = too right.

[e] "tl" = too left.

GERMANY (BRITISH ZONE OF OCCUPATION) B

	QUESTION 3a Live in peace?			QUESTION 3b (If *Possible*) Likely?			QUESTION 4 World government?			SAMPLE
	(A) Pos-sible	(B) Not pos-sible	(C) Don't know	(A) Like-ly	(B) Un-likely	(C) Don't know	(A) Agree	(B) Dis-agree	(C) Don't know	
1 Total	58	35	7	15	62	23	46	33	21	3,371
2 Men	60	36	4	16	67	17	57	31	12	1,605
3 Women	55	35	10	15	58	27	37	34	29	1,766
4 21–29	46	45	9	11	63	26	49	30	21	815
5 30–49	58	36	6	15	64	21	43	38	19	1,587
6 50–65	67	27	6	20	60	20	51	26	23	766
7 Over 65	65	23	12	21	52	27	48	27	25	203
8 A–wealthy	60	37	3	14	75	11	62	28	10	115
9 B–average	58	38	4	15	67	18	54	30	16	1,646
10 C–below av.ᵃ	58	32	10	17	56	27	47	27	26	1,476
11 D–very poor	50	34	16	11	52	37	41	15	44	134
12 Primary	59	33	8	17	58	25	48	27	25	2,461
13 Secondary	53	43	4	11	74	15	61	28	11	760
14 University	59	34	7	11	74	15	57	34	9	150
29 Leftist (tr)	61	34	5				63	28	9	456
30 Rightist (tl)	53	43	4				52	37	11	381
31 All right	62	34	4				59	32	9	777
32 Don't know	56	35	9				44	24	32	1,757
33 Sec. (12–10)	69	29	2				59	29	12	162
34 Medium (9–5)	60	34	6				53	27	20	1,395
35 Insec. (4–0)	55	37	8				49	28	23	1,814
36 Can (Q.1a)	63	33	4	18	65	17	56	30	14	1,812
37 Can't change	50	45	5	13	66	21	52	32	16	1,008
38 Don't know	52	25	23	10	46	44	32	13	55	551
42 Likely (Q.3b)	92	8	—							518
43 Unlikely	59	39	2							2,100
44 Don't know	29	45	26							753
45 Agree (Q.4)	66	30	4							1,722
46 Disagree	48	48	4							936
47 Don't know	50	30	20							713
39 Possible (Q.3a)							58	23	19	1,941
40 Impossible							44	38	18	1,190
41 Don't know							27	14	59	240

ᵃ See note b, Table A above.

GERMANY (BRITISH ZONE OF OCCUPATION) C

	QUESTION 5 Postwar expectation?				QUESTION 6a Job security?				QUESTION 6b Able to plan?			SAMPLE
	(A) Better	(B) Worse	(C) About same	(D) Don't know	(A) More	(B) Less	(C) About same	(D) Don't know	(A) Yes	(B) No	(C) Don't know	
1 Total	47	22	27	4	24	31	37	8	14	81	5	3,371
2 Men	43	26	28	3	26	29	38	7	16	80	4	1,605
3 Women	49	18	27	6	22	33	35	10	12	82	6	1,766
4 21–29	47	21	26	6	24	29	37	10	15	80	5	815
5 30–49	46	21	30	3	25	30	38	7	14	82	4	1,587
6 50–65	48	23	24	5	24	32	36	8	16	79	5	766
7 Over 65	49	20	26	5	17	42	30	11	7	84	9	203
8 A–wealthy	44	27	25	4	30	40	23	7	26	70	4	115
9 B–average	45	24	28	3	30	28	35	7	18	78	4	1,646
10 C–below av.ª	48	20	28	4	19	30	42	9	10	84	6	1,476
11 D–very poor	58	15	19	8	2	69	15	14	2	90	8	134
12 Primary	48	20	27	5	22	31	38	9	12	82	6	2,461
13 Secondary	42	27	28	3	29	30	35	6	20	77	3	760
14 University	46	22	29	3	29	39	27	5	22	77	1	150
15 Profess.	47	24	26	3	24	40	24	12	17	76	7	205
16 Bus. Owners	49	22	27	2	29	25	39	7	19	78	3	145
17 Ind. wkrs.	39	24	34	3	42	23	31	4	25	72	3	194
18 Sal.-mangrs.	45	25	27	3	26	26	42	6	16	80	4	318
19 Clerks	44	24	27	5	28	28	38	6	17	78	5	917
20 Man. wkrs.	50	18	28	4	20	29	42	9	10	84	6	1,030
21 Farm wkrs.	42	24	25	9	12	40	35	13	9	83	8	107
22 Farm owners	37	27	30	6	28	35	30	7	17	82	1	60
23 Housewives	60	12	21	7	15	47	28	10	6	92	2	85
24 Retired, Ind.	50	19	26	5	12	48	28	12	8	86	6	35
No answer												05

ª See note b, Table A above.

GERMANY (BRITISH ZONE OF OCCUPATION) D

	QUESTION 7 Satisfaction?				Security Scores			QUESTION 8 Best opportunity?			SAMPLE
	(A) Very	(B) All right	(C) Dis-sat.	(D) Don't know	(A) Sec. 12–10	(B) Med. 9–5	(C) Ins. 4–0	(A) Ger.	(B) U.S.A.	(C) Switz.	
1 Total	2	51	44	3	5	41	54	30	25	8	3,371
2 Men	2	51	45	2	6	43	51	28	26	9	1,605
3 Women	3	51	43	3	4	40	56	32	24	8	1,766
4 21–29	3	55	40	2	5	43	52	26	29	8	815
5 30–49	3	51	43	3	6	42	52	31	25	9	1,587
6 50–65	3	46	48	3	5	40	55	31	23	8	766
7 Over 65	1	47	49	3	2	34	64	37	17	6	203
8 A–wealthy	3	45	50	2	9	42	49	23	24	14	115
9 B–average	3	55	39	3	6	46	48	30	26	10	1,646
10 C–below av.ª	2	49	46	3	3	39	58	31	25	6	1,476
11 D–very poor	—	18	78	4	—	10	90	15	25	4	134

GERMANY (BRITISH ZONE OF OCCUPATION) D continued

	Satisfaction?				Security Scores			Best opportunity?			Sample
	(A) Very	(B) All right	(C) Dis- sat.	(D) Don't know	(A) Sec. 12–10	(B) Med. 9–5	(C) Ins. 4–0	(A) Ger.	(B) U.S.A.	(C) Switz.	
12 Primary	3	50	44	3	4	40	56	32	25	7	2,461
13 Secondary	2	53	43	2	8	45	47	22	26	12	760
14 University	1	45	52	2	8	36	56	23	24	10	150
15 Profess.	4	44	50	2							205
16 Bus. owners	1	48	46	5							145
17 Ind. workers	4	55	37	4							194
18 Sal.-mangrs.	4	54	39	3							318
19 Clerks	3	60	35	2							917
20 Man. wkrs.	2	47	48	3							1,030
21 Farm wkrs.	2	44	52	2							107
22 Farm owners	3	50	43	4							60
23 Housewives	2	46	47	5							85
24 Retired, Ind.	1	38	58	3							305
No answer											5
					25 Upper class			22	23	13	116
					26 Middle Class			26	31	10	1,742
					27 Working class			25	30	6	1,384
					28 Don't know			21	22	6	129

Totals (Q.8)	%		29 Leftist (tr)	28	22	11	456
			30 Rightist (tl)	29	27	8	381
Germany	30		31 All right	31	30	9	777
United States	25		32 Don't know	21	32	7	1,757
Switzerland	8						
Denmark	2						
Sweden	2						
Canada	2						
Argentina	2						
Australia, New Zealand	2						
Great Britain	1						
Netherlands	1						
Belgium	1						
Russia	1						
South Africa	1						
Other	1						
No reply	21						
	100						

a See note b, Table A above.

GERMANY (BRITISH ZONE OF OCCUPATION) E

	QUESTION 9 Social class?				QUESTION 10a Own class abroad?			QUESTION 10b Others at home?			SAMPLE
	(A) Mid- dle	(B) Work- ing	(C) Up- per	(D) Don't know	(A) Yes	(B) No	(C) Don't know	(A) Yes	(B) No	(C) Don't know	
1 Total	52	41	3	4	30	32	38	64	16	20	3,371
2 Men	51	42	4	3	39	32	29	71	15	14	1,605
3 Women	52	40	3	5	22	31	47	58	16	26	1,766

GERMANY (BRITISH ZONE OF OCCUPATION) E continued

	Social class?				Own class abroad?			Others at home?			Sample
	(A) Middle	(B) Working	(C) Upper	(D) Don't know	(A) Yes	(B) No	(C) Don't know	(A) Yes	(B) No	(C) Don't know	
4 21–29	50	43	2	5	28	34	38	63	16	21	815
5 30–49	54	40	3	3	31	32	37	67	16	17	1,587
6 50–65	51	41	5	3	31	30	39	61	18	21	766
7 Over 65	46	38	6	10	29	28	43	54	14	32	203
8 A–wealthy	24	3	70	3	53	20	27	80	9	11	115
9 B–average	90	5	2	3	30	33	37	74	11	15	1,646
10 C–below av.ᵃ	15	82	—	3	29	32	89	54	22	24	1,476
11 D–very poor	16	67	1	16	17	25	58	32	25	43	134
12 Primary	43	53	—	4	26	33	41	58	19	23	2,461
13 Secondary	78	11	7	4	37	30	33	80	9	11	760
14 University	65	2	31	2	55	20	25	87	6	7	150
15 Profess.	64	11	18	7	45	25	27	78	8	14	205
16 Bus. owners	85	7	6	2	37	32	31	81	10	9	145
17 Ind. workers	79	6	13	2	43	28	29	77	11	12	194
18 Sal.-mangrs.	73	21	3	3	27	37	36	66	14	20	318
19 Clerks	70	25	2	3	29	32	39	71	13	16	917
20 Man. wkrs.	21	76	—	3	29	32	39	55	22	23	1,030
21 Farm wkrs.	23	75	—	2	27	25	48	51	23	26	107
22 Farm owners	60	23	8	9	27	20	53	67	12	21	60
23 Housewives	49	45	4	2	13	56	31	64	19	17	85
24 Retired, Ind.	43	42	4	11	22	29	49	49	17	34	305
No answer											5
25 Upper class					61	18	21	84	9	7	116
26 Middle class					29	35	36	74	12	14	1,742
27 Working class					31	32	37	53	23	24	1,384
28 Don't know					5	4	91	30	5	65	129
33 Sec. (12–10)	74	19	7	—							162
34 Med. (9–5)	57	37	3	3							1,395
35 Insec. (4–0)	46	46	3	5							1,814

	QUESTION 10c More in common?				SAMPLE
	(A) Abroad	(B) German	(C) Don't know	(D) Not asked	
Total	5	20	6	69	3,371

ᵃ See note b, Table A above.

GERMANY (BRITISH ZONE OF OCCUPATION) F

	QUESTION 11 Most friendly?				QUESTION 12 Least friendly?			SAMPLE
	(A) Amer.	(B) Brit.	(C) Swed.	(D) Swiss	(A) Russ.	(B) Pol.	(C) Fr.	
1 Total	23	11	7	5	50	14	4	3,371
2 Men	24	11	8	6	47	16	6	1,605
3 Women	21	11	7	5	52	13	3	1,766

GERMANY (BRITISH ZONE OF OCCUPATION) F continued

	Most friendly?				Least friendly?			Sample
	(A) Amer.	(B) Brit.	(C) Swed.	(D) Swiss	(A) Russ.	(B) Pol.	(C) Fr.	
4 21–29	25	11	7	5	54	15	4	815
5 30–49	22	11	8	6	49	15	5	1,587
6 50–65	21	12	7	5	48	14	3	766
7 Over 65	20	6	8	5	46	9	7	203
8 A–wealthy	19	16	10	9	50	13	3	115
9 B–average	21	11	9	7	52	15	5	1,646
10 C–below av.[a]	24	10	6	3	49	13	3	1,476
11 D–very poor	24	8	3	5	37	22	7	134
12 Primary	24	10	4	6	50	14	4	2,461
13 Secondary	18	14	9	9	52	15	4	760
14 University	13	11	9	11	38	14	9	150
25 Upper class	15	13	10	13	43	12	5	116
26 Middle class	23	11	9	7	53	15	4	1,742
27 Working class	24	10	5	2	47	14	4	1,384
28 Don't know	12	10	6	2	39	12	6	129
29 Leftist (tr)	22	10	7	4	41	16	5	456
30 Rightist (tl)	26	13	8	10	58	18	6	381
31 All right	29	14	9	7	56	15	6	777
32 Don't know	19	9	6	4	47	13	3	1,757

Totals (Q.11)	%	*Totals* (Q.12)	%
Americans	23	Russians	50
British	11	Polish	14
Swedish	7	French	4
Swiss	5	British	3
Dutch	3	Czechs	2
Danish	2	Italians	1
French	2	Others	3
Norwegians	1	Don't know	23
Spanish	1		——
Canadians	1		100
Others	7		
No answer	37		
	——		
	100		

[a] See note b, Table A above.

GERMANY (BRITISH ZONE OF OCCUPATION) G[a]

	QUESTION 14 Present government?				SAMPLE
	(A) Too right	(B) Too left	(C) All right	(D) Don't know	
1 Total	14	12	22	52	3,371
2 Men	20	14	30	36	1,605
3 Women	8	10	16	66	1,766
4 21–29	13	11	19	57	815
5 30–49	15	12	23	50	1,587
6 50–65	14	13	23	50	766
7 Over 65	6	11	24	59	203

GERMANY (BRITISH ZONE OF OCCUPATION) G[a] continued

	Present government?				Sample
	(A) Too right	(B) Too left	(C) All right	(D) Don't know	
8 A–wealthy	10	30	24	36	115
9 B–average	9	16	26	49	1,646
10 C–below av.[b]	18	5	21	56	1,476
11 D–very poor	18	5	10	67	134
12 Primary	15	8	22	55	2,461
13 Secondary	9	20	26	45	760
14 University	11	28	24	37	150

[a] Results of Q.13 for West Zone and Berlin are combined and given on p. 47.

[b] See note b, Table A above.

GERMANY (WEST BERLIN, 1948 AND 1949) A

QUESTION 1a
Change human nature?

	(A) Can		(B) Cannot		(C) Don't know		Sample	
	1948	1949	1948	1949	1948	1949	1948	1949
1 Total	69	73	23	22	8	5	644	430
2 Men	71	77	23	21	6	2	231	161
3 Women	67	71	23	22	10	7	413	269
4 21–29	65	61	28	35	7	4	123	74
5 30–49	70	73	24	23	6	4	272	178
6 50–65	69	81	19	14	12	5	188	134
7 Over 65	72	73	16	18	12	9	61	44
8 A–wealthy	33	75	67	25	—	–	12	4
9 B–average	71	74	26	24	3	2	319	184
10 C–below av.	68	73	18	20	14	7	306	242
11 D–very poor	57	—	—	—	43	—	7	—
12 Primary	70	73	19	21	11	6	503	324
13 Secondary	66	78	33	22	1	—	126	95
14 University	53	55	47	45	—	—	15	11
29 Leftist (tr)	80	73	15	24	5	3	20	62
30 Rightist (tl)	74	100	24	—	2	—	89	5
31 All right	68	73	28	23	4	4	306	210
32 Don't know	68	73	16	20	16	7	229	153

QUESTION 1b
(If Can) Likely?

	(A) Likely		(B) Unlikely		(C) Don't know		Sample	
	1948	1949	1948	1949	1948	1949	1948	1949
1 Total	54	60	9	7	6	6	444	316
2 Men	56	63	11	10	4	4	165	124
3 Women	53	58	7	6	7	7	279	192
4 21–29	50	41	11	9	4	11	80	45
5 30–49	56	61	9	8	5	4	191	130
6 50–65	52	71	9	4	8	6	129	109
7 Over 65	56	57	6	9	10	7	44	32

GERMANY (WEST BERLIN, 1948 AND 1949) A continued

	(If *Can*) Likely? (A) Likely 1948	1949	(B) Unlikely 1948	1949	(C) Don't know 1948	1949	Sample 1948	1949
8 A–wealthy	25	75	—	—	8	—	4	3
9 B–average	57	60	9	11	5	3	227	136
10 C–below av.	52	60	9	5	7	8	209	177
11 D–very poor	43	—	—	—	14	—	4	—
12 Primary	54	60	9	6	7	7	353	236
13 Secondary	52	61	11	14	3	3	83	74
14 University	53	46	—	9	—	—	8	6

QUESTION 2
National character?

	(A) Born in us 1948	1949	(B) Way brought up 1948	1949	(C) Don't know 1948	1949	Sample 1948	1949
1 Total	57	54	28	37	15	9	644	430
2 Men	48	47	39	44	13	9	231	161
3 Women	62	58	21	33	17	9	413	269
4 21–29	55	45	28	47	17	8	123	74
5 30–49	56	53	28	37	16	10	272	178
6 50–65	59	58	28	34	13	8	188	134
7 Over 65	57	61	25	32	18	7	61	44
8 A–wealthy	33	50	59	50	8	—	12	4
9 B–average	55	59	29	32	16	5	319	184
10 C–below av.	60	51	25	40	15	9	306	242
11 D–very poor	71	—	—	—	29	—	7	—
12 Primary	59	53	26	38	15	9	503	324
13 Secondary	51	60	32	33	17	7	126	95
14 University	47	36	40	55	13	9	15	11
25 Upper class	38	60	50	40	12	—	8	10
26 Middle class	55	57	30	34	15	9	368	211
27 Working class	60	51	25	41	15	8	253	198
28 Don't know	67	46	—	27	33	27	15	11
29 Leftist (tr)	40	58	40	37	20	5	20	62
30 Rightist (tl)	47	80	36	20	17	—	89	5
31 All right	62	51	29	40	9	9	306	210
32 Don't know	56	56	22	34	22	10	229	153
36 Can (Q.1a)	54	52	32	39	14	9	444	316
37 Cannot	71	62	20	34	9	4	146	93
38 Don't know	43	48	9	19	48	33	54	21
39 Possible (Q.3a)	58	52	28	40	14	8	440	325
40 Impossible	55	65	29	28	16	7	178	85
41 Don't know	46	50	12	25	42	25	26	20
45 Agree (Q.4)	55	52	32	40	13	8	372	285
46 Disagree	62	65	26	32	12	3	153	75
47 Don't know	56	50	15	33	29	17	119	70

GERMANY (WEST BERLIN, 1948 AND 1949) B

QUESTION 3a
Live in peace?

	(A) Possible		(B) Not possible		(C) Don't know		Sample	
	1948	*1949*	*1948*	*1949*	*1948*	*1949*	*1948*	*1949*
1 Total	68	76	28	20	4	4	644	430
2 Men	70	81	28	19	2	—	231	161
3 Women	67	73	28	20	5	7	413	269
4 21–29	61	61	37	34	2	5	123	74
5 30–49	71	78	25	19	4	3	272	178
6 50–65	69	81	25	13	6	6	188	134
7 Over 65	71	77	26	18	3	5	61	44
8 A–wealthy	67	50	33	50	—	—	12	4
9 B–average	68	74	29	23	3	3	319	184
10 C–below av.	69	77	26	17	5	6	306	242
11 D–very poor	43	—	29	—	28	—	7	—
12 Primary	69	77	26	18	5	5	503	324
13 Secondary	66	71	33	26	1	3	126	95
14 University	67	82	33	18	—	—	15	11
29 Leftist (tr)	65	79	35	21	—	—	20	62
30 Rightist (tl)	68	80	32	20	—	—	89	5
31 All right	72	76	26	21	2	3	306	210
32 Don't know	63	73	29	18	8	9	229	153
33 Sec. (12–10)	67	100	33	—	—	—	3	19
34 Medium (9–5)	63	72	33	23	4	5	132	146
35 Insec. (4–0)	69	75	27	20	4	5	509	265
36 Can (Q.1a)	73	79	25	18	2	3	444	316
37 Can't change	60	69	37	27	3	4	146	93
38 Don't know	56	52	24	19	20	29	54	21
42 Likely (Q.3b)	99	99	1	1	—	—	182	87
43 Unlikely	66	89	33	11	1	—	334	236
44 Don't know	30	27	52	54	18	19	128	107
45 Agree (Q.4)	72	80	26	17	2	3	372	285
46 Disagree	59	69	38	31	3	—	153	75
47 Don't know	69	66	20	17	11	17	119	70

QUESTION 3b
(If *Possible*) Likely?

	(A) Likely		(B) Unlikely		(C) Don't know		Sample	
	1948	*1949*	*1948*	*1949*	*1948*	*1949*	*1948*	*1949*
1 Total	28	20	52	55	20	25	644	430
2 Men	28	24	56	58	16	18	231	161
3 Women	28	18	50	53	22	29	413	269
4 21–29	15	8	63	61	22	31	123	74
5 30–49	30	20	52	58	18	22	272	178
6 50–65	37	24	42	54	21	22	188	134
7 Over 65	21	30	56	36	23	34	61	44
8 A–wealthy	17	25	75	50	8	25	12	4
9 B–average	28	23	56	36	16	21	319	184
10 C–below av.	29	18	47	54	24	28	306	242
11 D–very poor	14	—	57	—	29	—	7	—

GERMANY (WEST BERLIN, 1948 AND 1949) B continued

	(If *Possible*) Likely?							
	(A) Likely		(B) Unlikely		(C) Don't know		Sample	
	1948	1949	1948	1949	1948	1949	1948	1949
12 Primary	30	19	48	55	22	26	503	324
13 Secondary	23	23	63	53	14	24	126	95
14 University	7	36	80	55	13	9	15	11
36 Can (Q.1a)	32	23	50	54	18	23	444	316
37 Can't change	19	12	62	64	19	24	146	93
38 Don't know	24	14	35	33	41	55	54	21

QUESTION 4
World government?

	(A) Agree		(B) Disagree		(C) Don't know		Sample	
	1948	1949	1948	1949	1948	1949	1948	1949
1 Total	58	66	24	18	18	16	644	430
2 Men	65	77	27	19	8	4	231	161
3 Women	54	60	22	16	24	24	413	269
4 21–29	60	65	26	24	14	11	123	74
5 30–49	59	67	25	19	16	14	272	178
6 50–65	57	71	22	11	21	18	188	134
7 Over 65	49	52	20	18	31	30	61	44
8 A–wealthy	83	100	17	—	—	—	12	4
9 B–average	62	72	23	18	15	10	319	184
10 C–below av.	53	62	24	17	23	21	306	242
11 D–very poor	43	—	29	—	28	—	7	—
12 Primary	53	66	23	16	22	18	503	324
13 Secondary	67	66	26	24	7	10	126	95
14 University	73	82	20	9	7	9	15	11
29 Leftist (tr)	55	73	35	24	10	3	20	62
30 Rightist (tl)	63	100	25	—	12	—	89	5
31 All right	68	71	24	17	8	12	306	210
32 Don't know	42	56	23	16	35	28	229	153
33 Sec. (12–10)	67	84	33	11	—	5	3	19
34 Medium (9–5)	64	67	21	17	15	16	132	146
35 Insec. (4–0)	56	65	24	18	20	17	509	265
36 Can (Q.1a)	58	69	24	16	18	15	444	316
37 Can't change	66	66	24	22	10	12	146	93
38 Don't know	32	33	24	10	44	57	54	21
39 Possible (Q.3a)	60	70	21	16	19	14	440	325
40 Impossible	54	59	33	27	13	14	178	85
41 Don't know	35	40	15	—	50	60	26	20

GERMANY (WEST BERLIN, 1948 AND 1949) C

QUESTION 5
Postwar expectation?

	(A) Better 1948	1949	(B) Worse 1948	1949	(C) About same 1948	1949	(D) Don't know 1948	1949	Sample 1948	1949
1 Total	78	52	5	22	15	24	2	2	644	430
2 Men	78	41	5	32	15	26	2	1	231	161
3 Women	78	58	6	16	14	23	2	3	413	269
4 21–29	77	43	7	26	14	30	2	1	123	74
5 30–49	78	50	6	25	15	22	1	3	272	178
6 50–65	80	52	3	20	15	25	2	3	188	134
7 Over 65	74	68	10	12	13	18	3	2	61	44
8 A–wealthy	50	75	8	25	42	—	—	—	12	4
9 B–average	75	57	7	21	16	21	2	1	319	184
10 C–below av.	83	47	4	22	12	28	1	3	306	242
11 D–very poor	72	—	—	—	14	—	14	—	7	—
12 Primary	80	51	5	21	14	25	1	3	503	324
13 Secondary	73	56	8	22	17	20	2	2	126	95
14 University	60	45	13	27	27	28	—	—	15	11

QUESTION 6a
Job security?

	(A) More 1948	1949	(B) Less 1948	1949	(C) About same 1948	1949	(D) Don't know 1948	1949	Sample 1948	1949
1 Total	21	23	30	42	43	27	6	8	644	430
2 Men	26	26	25	38	44	29	5	7	231	161
3 Women	18	22	33	44	43	26	6	8	413	269
4 21–29	27	24	26	30	41	35	6	11	123	74
5 30–49	23	26	27	48	46	22	4	4	272	178
6 50–65	14	23	33	38	45	30	8	9	188	134
7 Over 65	18	11	43	48	29	27	10	14	61	44
8 A–wealthy	25	75	42	25	33	—	—	—	12	4
9 B–average	22	28	34	38	38	31	6	3	319	184
10 C–below av.	19	18	26	45	49	25	6	12	306	242
11 D–very poor	—	—	58	—	14	—	28	—	7	—
12 Primary	20	22	30	43	44	25	6	10	503	324
13 Secondary	24	26	32	37	37	35	7	2	126	95
14 University	20	18	33	46	47	27	—	9	15	11

QUESTION 6b
Able to plan?

	(A) Yes 1948	1949	(B) No 1948	1949	(C) Don't know 1948	1949	Sample 1948	1949
1 Total	6	13	92	86	2	1	644	430
2 Men	8	15	90	84	2	1	231	161
3 Women	5	11	93	88	2	1	413	269
4 21–29	8	27	90	72	2	1	123	74
5 30–49	5	12	94	87	1	1	272	178
6 50–65	6	9	91	89	3	2	188	134
7 Over 65	2	—	95	100	3	—	61	44

165

GERMANY (WEST BERLIN, 1948 AND 1949) C continued

	Able to plan?								
	(A) Yes		(B) No		(C) Don't know		Sample	
	1948	1949	1948	1949	1948	1949	1948	1949
8 A–wealthy	—	50	100	50	—	—	12	4
9 B–average	8	15	91	85	1	—	319	184
10 C–below av.	5	10	93	88	2	2	306	242
11 D–very poor	—	—	86	—	14	—	7	2
12 Primary	6	10	92	88	2	2	503	324
13 Secondary	6	15	93	85	1	—	126	95
14 University	13	55	87	45	—	—	15	11

GERMANY (WEST BERLIN, 1948 AND 1949) D

	QUESTION 7 Satisfaction?									
	(A) Very		(B) All right		(C) Dissatisfied		(D) Don't know		Sample	
	1948	1949	1948	1949	1948	1949	1948	1949	1948	1949
1 Total	—	4	31	48	68	47	1	1	644	430
2 Men	—	4	30	50	68	46	2	0	231	161
3 Women	—	4	31	48	68	47	1	1	413	269
4 21–29	—	5	29	46	71	49	—	—	123	74
5 30–49	—	4	30	44	69	51	1	1	272	178
6 50–65	—	4	34	56	65	39	1	1	188	134
7 Over 65	—	—	23	50	70	50	7	—	61	44
8 A–wealthy	—	—	25	50	75	50	—	—	12	4
9 B–average	—	3	31	42	68	54	1	1	319	184
10 C–below av.	—	4	31	53	68	42	1	1	306	242
11 D–very poor	—	—	14	—	72	—	14	—	7	—
12 Primary	—	4	31	52	67	43	2	1	503	324
13 Secondary	—	3	28	37	71	60	1	—	126	95
14 University	—	—	27	45	73	46	—	9	15	11

	Security Scores							
	(A) Secure (12–10)		(B) Medium (9–5)		(C) Insecure (4–0)		Sample	
	1948	1949	1948	1949	1948	1949	1948	1949
1 Total	—	4	21	34	79	62	644	430
2 Men	—	6	24	40	76	54	231	161
3 Women	—	4	20	31	80	65	413	269
4 21–29	—	7	24	39	76	54	123	74
5 30–49	—	5	21	33	79	62	272	178
6 50–65	1	4	19	37	80	59	188	134
7 Over 65	—	—	17	18	83	82	61	44
8 A–wealthy	—	—	33	50	67	50	12	4
9 B–average	—	5	22	32	78	63	319	184
10 C–below av.	1	4	18	35	81	61	306	242
11 D–very poor	—	—	—	—	100	—	7	—
12 Primary	—	4	22	34	78	62	503	324
13 Secondary	1	4	20	33	79	63	126	95
14 University	—	18	27	36	73	46	15	11

GERMANY (WEST BERLIN, 1948 AND 1949) D continued

QUESTION 8
Best opportunity?

	(A) U. S. A. 1948	1949	(B) Germany 1948	1949	(C) Switzerland 1948	1949	Sample 1948	1949
1 Total	36	34	30	34	8	7	644	430
2 Men	36	42	26	22	10	10	231	161
3 Women	36	30	32	41	7	6	413	269
4 21–29	36	42	30	29	13	11	123	74
5 30–49	37	29	29	38	7	8	272	178
6 50–65	35	36	29	34	8	6	188	134
7 Over 65	34	36	36	30	2	5	61	44
8 A–wealthy	33	25	42	25	17	—	12	4
9 B–average	35	27	27	37	9	10	319	184
10 C–below av.	38	40	31	32	7	5	306	242
11 D–very poor	14	—	72	—	—	—	7	—
25 Upper class	25	20	50	40	12	—	8	10
26 Middle class	36	30	27	37	9	10	368	211
27 Working class	37	40	31	31	7	5	253	198
28 Don't know	13	18	67	36	7	9	15	11
29 Leftist (tr)	20	36	40	36	20	2	20	62
30 Rightist (tl)	48	40	24	40	8	—	89	5
31 All right	38	38	29	32	9	8	306	210
32 Don't know	30	29	32	35	6	10	229	153

GERMANY (WEST BERLIN, 1948 AND 1949) E

QUESTION 9
Social class?

	(A) Middle 1948	1949	(B) Working 1948	1949	(C) Upper 1948	1949	(D) Don't know 1948	1949	Sample 1948	1949
1 Total	57	49	39	46	1	2	3	3	644	430
2 Men	52	42	44	55	2	2	2	1	231	161
3 Women	60	54	37	41	1	2	2	3	413	269
4 21–29	59	51	37	46	2	1	2	2	123	74
5 30–49	57	53	39	42	1	3	3	2	272	178
6 50–65	54	48	44	52	2	2	—	3	188	134
7 Over 65	62	48	33	43	—	5	5	4	61	44
8 A–wealthy	33	—	—	—	67	100	—	—	12	4
9 B–average	90	89	8	7	—	3	2	1	319	184
10 C–below av.	25	19	72	77	—	—	3	4	306	242
11 D–very poor	29	—	71	—	—	—	—	—	7	—
12 Primary	50	38	48	57	—	2	2	3	503	324
13 Secondary	85	86	10	12	3	2	2	—	126	95
14 University	80	64	—	9	20	27	—	—	15	11
33 Sec. (12–10)	33	58	67	37	—	5	—	—	3	19
34 Medium (9–5)	63	47	33	47	2	3	2	3	132	146
35 Insec. (4–0)	56	49	40	46	1	2	3	3	509	265

GERMANY (WEST BERLIN, 1948 AND 1949) E continued

	QUESTION 10a Own class abroad?								
	(A) Yes *1948*	*1949*	(B) No *1948*	*1949*	(C) Don't know *1948*	*1949*	Sample *1948*	*1949*
1 Total	49	44	17	13	34	43	644	430
2 Men	58	56	17	19	25	25	231	161
3 Women	45	37	17	8	38	55	413	269
4 21–29	42	45	24	13	34	42	123	74
5 30–49	53	46	18	14	29	40	272	178
6 50–65	52	45	13	8	35	47	188	134
7 Over 65	41	32	13	18	46	50	61	44
8 A–wealthy	67	100	8	—	25	—	12	4
9 B–average	54	46	18	17	28	37	319	184
10 C–below av.	45	42	17	9	38	49	306	242
11 D–very poor	—	—	14	—	86	—	7	—
12 Primary	46	41	18	11	36	48	503	324
13 Secondary	61	49	16	18	23	33	126	95
14 University	60	82	13	—	27	18	15	11
25 Upper class	88	80	—	—	12	20	8	10
26 Middle class	51	47	17	17	32	36	368	211
27 Working class	47	41	20	9	33	50	253	198
28 Don't know	20	—	7	—	73	100	15	11

	QUESTION 10b Others at home?								
	(A) Yes *1948*	*1949*	(B) No *1948*	*1949*	(C) Don't know *1948*	*1949*	Sample *1948*	*1949*
1 Total	67	63	16	19	17	18	644	430
2 Men	73	77	14	14	13	9	231	161
3 Women	64	55	16	22	20	23	413	269
4 21–29	73	73	16	14	11	13	123	74
5 30–49	71	64	15	22	14	14	272	178
6 50–65	64	60	14	17	22	23	188	134
7 Over 65	49	55	20	20	31	25	61	44
8 A–wealthy	83	100	—	—	17	—	12	4
9 B–average	76	76	13	16	11	8	319	184
10 C–below av.	58	53	19	21	23	26	306	242
11 D–very poor	43	—	—	—	57	—	7	—
12 Primary	63	58	17	20	20	22	503	324
13 Secondary	82	78	10	18	8	4	126	95
14 University	100	100	—	—	—	—	15	11
25 Upper class	88	80	—	10	12	10	8	10
26 Middle class	73	75	13	17	14	8	368	211
27 Working class	60	53	20	23	20	24	253	198
28 Don't know	27	—	—	—	73	100	15	11

GERMANY (WEST BERLIN, 1948 AND 1949) F

QUESTION 11
Most friendly?

	(A) British 1948	1949	(B) American 1948	1949	(C) Swedish 1948	1949	Sample 1948	1949
1 Total	33	29	31	36	4	4	644	430
2 Men	34	26	28	36	4	5	231	161
3 Women	33	32	33	37	3	3	413	269
4 21–29	37	24	24	39	3	7	123	74
5 30–49	33	29	31	30	4	4	272	178
6 50–65	31	36	34	41	4	1	188	134
7 Over 65	31	20	41	43	2	2	61	44
8 A–wealthy	25	75	8	25	—	—	12	4
9 B–average	36	35	27	27	5	5	319	184
10 C–below av.	31	24	36	44	2	2	306	242
11 D–very poor	—	—	57	—	—	—	7	—
25 Upper class	25	60	13	20	—	10	8	10
26 Middle class	34	35	30	31	5	4	368	211
27 Working class	32	22	35	43	2	2	253	198
28 Don't know	33	27	13	27	—	—	15	11
29 Leftist (tr)	35	32	10	34	5	2	20	62
30 Rightist (tl)	45	40	27	20	5	—	89	5
31 All right	34	27	33	39	4	3	306	210
32 Don't know	27	31	32	35	2	5	229	153

QUESTION 12
Least friendly?

	(A) Russians 1948	1949	(B) Polish 1948	1949	(C) French 1948	1949	(D) Others 1948	1949	(E) Don't know 1948	1949	Sample 1948	1949
1 Total	79	79	3	3	1	2	2	2	15	14	644	430
2 Men	74	77	3	3	2	2	2	1	19	17	231	161
3 Women	83	81	2	3	1	1	2	2	12	13	413	269
4 21–29	77	80	5	3	2	4	4	—	12	13	123	74
5 30–49	80	78	3	3	—	2	4	3	13	14	272	178
6 50–65	78	86	2	3	—	—	3	1	17	10	188	134
7 Over 65	84	66	—	2	—	3	—	2	16	27	61	44
8 A–wealthy	83	75	8	—	—	—	—	—	9	25	12	4
9 B–average	80	79	3	3	—	2	3	3	14	13	319	184
10 C–below av.	79	80	2	3	1	1	3	1	15	15	306	242
11 D–very poor	71	—	—	—	—	—	—	—	29	—	7	—
12 Primary	81		2		1		2		14		503	
13 Secondary	73		4		1		5		17		126	
14 University	80		7		6		—		7		15	
25 Upper class	88	70	—	—	—	—	—	10	12	20	8	10
26 Middle class	81	81	4	3	1	2	1	2	13	12	368	211
27 Working class	77	78	2	3	1	2	4	1	16	16	253	198
28 Don't know	80	82	—	—	—	—	—	—	20	18	15	11
29 Leftist (tr)	35	81	—	2	—	2	—	4	65	11	20	62
30 Rightist (tl)	88	60	4	—	—	—	1	—	7	49	89	5
31 All right	83	81	2	3	1	2	4	1	10	13	306	210
32 Don't know	75	77	3	3	1	1	2	3	19	16	229	153

GERMANY (WEST BERLIN, 1948 AND 1949) G

QUESTION 13
Words best describing?

	(A) Germans 1948	1949	(B) Americans 1948	1949	(C) Russians 1948	1949
Hardworking	20	18	8	10	3	6
Intelligent	16	15	15	14	1	1
Practical	13	13	15	14	2	2
Conceited	4	5	4	3	3	3
Generous	3	4	13	14	2	1
Cruel	—	1	1	1	25	29
Backward	—	—	—	—	24	28
Brave	15	14	4	7	4	6
Self-controlled	4	3	4	3	2	1
Domineering	2	4	2	1	7	8
Progressive	11	11	20	17	1	1
Peace-loving	11	11	11	12	4	3
Impossible to characterize and no answer	1	1	3	4	22	11

QUESTION 14
Present government?

	(A) Too right 1948	1949	(B) Too left 1948	1949	(C) All right 1948	1949	(D) Don't know 1948	1949	Sample 1948	1949
1 Total	3	14	14	1	47	49	36	36	644	430
2 Men	5	22	19	1	54	58	22	19	231	161
3 Women	2	10	11	1	44	43	43	46	413	269
4 21–29	5	12	14	—	49	54	32	34	123	74
5 30–49	3	13	15	2	51	52	31	33	272	178
6 50–65	3	15	12	1	47	45	38	39	188	134
7 Over 65	—	21	16	2	33	36	51	41	61	44
8 A–wealthy	—	25	33	25	50	—	17	50	12	4
9 B–average	3	11	16	1	52	57	29	31	319	184
10 C–below av.	3	16	11	1	43	44	43	39	306	242
11 D–very poor	—	—	14	—	29	—	57	—	7	—
12 Primary	3	15	12	1	47	46	38	38	503	324
13 Secondary	4	13	21	1	48	57	27	29	126	95
14 University	—	9	33	—	60	64	7	27	15	11

ITALY

A. Copy of Questionnaire Used in Italy

DOXA

ISTITUTO PER LE RICERCHE STATISTICHE E L'ANALISI DELL' OPINIONE PUBBLICA

SONDAGGIO 822

MILANO = piazza E. Duse, 4 — Tel. 26-01-49 — telegr.: **METRODOX = MILANO**

LUGLIO 1948

AVVERTENZE — Formare un cerchietto attorno al numero corrispondente alla risposta, oppure scrivere sulla riga punteggiata.

La DOXA, un Istituto scientifico indipendente e apolitico, affiliato all'organizzazione Gallup, studia continuamente l'opinione pubblica, interrogando migliaia di cittadini in tutte le regioni d'Italia e in tutte le classi sociali.

I risultati di questi "sondaggi statistici dell'opinione pubblica" sono riportati dai giornali di tutto il mondo.

Desidererei intervistarla su alcuni importanti problemi: non chiedo il Suo nome, ma solo la Sua opinione.

Ecco la prima domanda.

A. Da quanto tempo vive in questa città (paese)?

Dalla nascita 1
Da . . . . anni

B. È stato qualche volta all'estero? Per quanto tempo?

Mai stato all'estero. 1
Sì, per meno di una settimana in complesso. 2
Sì, da una settimana a un mese. 3
Sì, da un mese a un anno. 4
Sì, per . . . . anni

C. Dove?

1. Crede che la natura umana possa essere cambiata?

sì, può essere cambiata. 1
no, non può essere cambiata. 2
non so 3
(Se la risposta è: "PUÒ ESSERE CAMBIATA," chiedere:)

1b. Crede probabile che ciò avvenga?

probabile 1
poco probabile 2
non so 3

2. Crede Lei che le qualità di noi Italiani siano dovute principalmente alla nostra natura (al nostro carattere) o piuttosto alla educazione che abbiamo ricevuta?

alla nostra natura, carattere. 1
all' educazione ricevuta. 2
non so 3

3a. Crede *possibile* che un giorno tutti i paesi del mondo vivano in pace fra loro?

possibile. 1
impossibile. 2
non so 3

3b. Crede *probabile* che ciò avvenga?

probabile 1
poco probabile 2
non so 3

4. Qualcuno dice che ci dovrebbe essere un governo mondiale capace di controllare le leggi fatte dai vari Stati. Lei approva o disapprova questa proposta?

approvo 1
disapprovo 2
non so 3

5. Alla fine della guerra, cosa prevedeva per il Suo futuro? Che la Sua situazione personale sarebbe stata migliore o peggiore della Sua situazione presente?

la mia situazione attuale è peggiore di quella che mi
aspettavo 1
migliore 2
press'a poco quella che mi aspettavo. 3
non so. 4

6a. Lei (o Suo marito) è sicuro di non perdere il Suo posto? Con riguardo alla sicurezza del Suo posto (o di Suo marito), Le sembra di star meglio o peggio degli altri Italiani?

meglio 1
peggio 2
nè meglio nè peggio degli altri Italiani. 3
non so 4

6b. In generale Le sembra che la sicurezza del Suo posto (impiego, lavoro) (o di quello di Suo marito) sia tale da permetterLe di far piani per l'avvenire?

sì, il posto è tanto sicuro da permettermi di fare piani. 1
no, il posto non è tanto sicuro da permettermi difare piani. . . .2
non so
Commenti dell'intervistato: (Trascriverli nella forma originale, anche se sgrammaticata o dialettale)

7. È contento della Sua situazione attuale?

sì, molto contento 1
sì, contento. 2
no, non sono contento 3
non so 4

8. Secondo Lei, in quale paese vi è la maggior possibilità di fare il genere di vita al quale Lei aspirerebbe? (L'intervistato può indicare un paese qualunque, compresa l'Italia).

9. Se Le chiedessero di dire a quale classe sociale appartiene, direbbe di appartenere alla classe media, alla classe operaia o alla classe superiore?

classe media. 1
classe operaia. 2
classe superiore 3

10a. Lei ritiene di aver qualcosa in comune con le persone della classe . . . . (la classe sociale indicata dall'intervistato alla domanda 9) *degli altri paesi?*

sì 1
no. 2
non so 3

10b. Lei ritiene di avere qualcosa in comune con gli Italiani che non appartengono alla classe . . . ? (la classe sociale indicata dall'intervistato alla domanda 9)

sì 1
no. 2
non so 3
(Se l'interrogato risponde "Sì" tanto alla domanda 10a che alla 10b, oppure "no" a entrambe chiedere:)

10c. Con quale di queste due categorie Le sembra di avere più punti in comune: con stranieri della Sua stessa classe sociale o con Italiani di altre classi sociali?

ho più cose in comune con stranieri della mia classe sociale. . 1
ho più cose in comune con Italiani di altre classi sociali. 2
non so 3

11. Verso quale popolo straniero sente maggior simpatia?

12. Verso quale popolo straniero sente minor simpatia?

13a. Ecco una lista (mostrare foglietto). Quali parole, secondo Lei, descrivono meglio gli Americani? Scelga quante parole vuole, ed indichi per ogni parola anche la rispettiva lettera (A, B, C, ecc.). Se non ha alcuna particolare opinione, lo dica pure. (SCRIVERE LE LETTERE CORRISPONDENTI)

. . . .

13b. Ed ora rilegga la lista e scelga le parole che descrivono meglio i Russi.

13c. Scelga ora le parole che descrivono meglio gli Italiani.

1. Laborioso	8. Coraggioso
2. Intelligente	9. Sa controllarsi
3. Pratico	10. Prepotente
4. Vanitoso	11. Progressivo
5. Generoso	12. Pacifico
6. Crudele	Impossible caratterizzarlo
7. Arretrato	

14. Secondo Lei, l'attuale Governo è troppo a destra, troppo a sinistra, oppure press'a poco come Lei lo desidera?

troppo a destra. 1
troppo a sinistra. 2
va bene così. 3
non so 4

SESSO: Maschio. 1   Femmina. 2
ETÀ DELL'INTERVISTATO:
CLASSE SOCIALE:

A — Ricchi. 1	C — Classe medio-inf. 5
Agiati. 2	Classe inferiore 6
B — Classe medio-sup. . . .3	D — Poveri. 7
Classe media. 4	Poverissimi 8
	Non classificabili 9

ANNI DI SCUOLA compiuti complessivamente dall 'intervistato:
SCUOLA COMPIUTA:

nessuna scuola. 1   scuola medio-sup. 4
scuola elementare. 2   università 5
scuola medio-inf. 3

PROFESSIONE DELL'INTERVISTATO:

Liberi professionisti (avvocati, medici, ingegneri, ecc.), 1X; Liberi professionisti (ragionieri, maestri, periti, levatrici), 1Y; Proprietari di aziende e di negozi grandi e medi, 2; Artigiani, proprietari di piccoli negozi, 3; Impiegati con funzioni di grado elevato, 4; Altri impiegati, commessi di negozio, personale di servizio, 5; Operai, lavoratori manuali in genere, 6; Braccianti agricoli, pescatori, giardinieri, 7; Proprietari di aziende agricole (agricoltori conduttori), 8; Casal inghe, 9; Pensionati, studenti, persone senza professione, 0

Nota sulle professioni: I liberi professionisti sono divisi in una classe superiore e in una classe inferiore.

C. Excerpts from Notes and Comments by Survey Agency

Interviews were made July 14–24, 1948; 107 interviewers were employed and 1,078 usable ballots obtained.

The sample is representative with regard to sex, age, geographic distribution, and occupation. The "Retired, independent" occupational group (l. 24) appears oversampled, as several housewives were included in that class.

There is in our country a very important class of rural workers, the "mezzadri," a kind of sharecropper, who in general are much better off than farm hands. We usually classify them with farm owners, and do so in this survey.

We are confident that the cross section is fairly representative with regard to education, but an actual check is impossible, owing to lack of educational statistics in Italy.

The following questions were found most interesting: 13, 11, 12, 14, 4 (in that order). The average duration of interviews was about twenty to twenty-five minutes.

People belonging to the lower classes—especially women—did not understand fully the meaning of Q.1a and 2. But even intellectuals were puzzled.

Answers to Q.3a point to a widespread pessimism about world peace— a pessimism confirmed by other DOXA surveys, which showed that the percentage fearing a third world war within ten years is higher in Italy than in most other countries.

Q.6a puzzled most respondents, who found it difficult to make comparisons. However, the contrast between the upper and lower social classes is striking. The minimum of security is found among farm workers and manual workers. It is interesting to note that these two classes provide the bulk of the Communist Party in Italy. Other occupations in which the "Less" outnumber the "More" are clerical workers and retired.

We think that both "America" and "North America" on Q.8 mean to most people the U.S.A., therefore the table can be abridged as follows:

	%
Italy	36
U.S.A.	27
South America	8
European countries	11
Other and no answer	18
	100

The meaning of Q.10 was not clear to all respondents. Practically all interviewers reported that for the prevailing educational level such questions are too difficult.

Some of the twelve adjectives on Q.13 are used every day, and some almost never; there is an obvious bias in favor of the former. Since this occurs to different words in different languages, international comparisons will be misleading.

D. Notes and Comments by the Editors

Sample in Q.1b is the number of respondents who answered "Can" to Q.1a. Percentages on Q.1b total 100% of this sample.

E. Tables

ITALY A

	QUESTION 1a Change human nature?[a]			QUESTION 1b (If Can) Likely?[b]				QUESTION 2 National character?[a]			SAMPLE
	(A) Can	(B) Cannot	(C) Don't know	(A) Likely	(B) Unlikely	(C) Don't know	(D) (Sample)	(A) Born in us	(B) Way brought up	(C) Don't know	
1 Total	34	43	23	73	22	5	(364)	51	39	10	1,078
2 Men	33	46	21	77	17	6	(186)	53	39	8	558
3 Women	34	41	25	69	28	3	(178)	49	39	12	520
4 21–29	32	46	22	66	25	9	(89)	53	35	12	275
5 30–49	33	43	24	77	20	3	(173)	54	37	9	521
6 50–65	36	39	25	72	22	6	(83)	45	44	11	231
7 Over 65	37	47	16	68	32	—	(19)	44	51	5	51
8 A–wealthy	31	57	12	84	8	8	(24)	62	30	8	77
9 B–average	37	49	14	69	29	2	(162)	54	42	4	438
10 C–below av.	31	38	31	74	20	6	(140)	48	39	13	455
11 D–very poor	35	29	36	79	10	11	(38)	44	31	25	108
12 Primary	28	40	32	75	20	5	(170)	45	40	15	601
13 Secondary	42	42	16	70	27	3	(93)	55	39	6	221
14 University	39	52	9	71	27	2	(101)	61	37	2	256
29 Leftist (tr)[c]	37	42	21					53	39	8	318
30 Rightist (tl)[d]	43	48	9					55	43	2	58
31 All right	33	47	20					52	40	8	462
32 Don't know	28	36	36					45	26	19	240
25 Upper class								60	36	4	44
26 Middle class								55	40	5	585
27 Working class								45	38	17	449
28 Don't know								—	—	—	—
36 Can (Q.1a)								50	47	3	288
37 Cannot								59	38	3	484
38 Don't know								37	29	34	256
39 Possible (Q.3a)								52	41	7	326
40 Impossible								53	38	9	631
41 Don't know								38	35	27	121
45 Agree (Q.4)								53	40	7	607
46 Disagree								52	43	5	299
47 Don't know								41	28	31	172

[a] People belonging to the lower classes—especially women—did not understand fully the meaning of Q.1a and 2. But even intellectuals were puzzled.

[b] Sample in Q.1b is the number of respondents who answered "Can" to Q.1a. Percentages on Q.1b total 100% of this sample.

[c] "tr" = too right.

[d] "tl" = too left.

ITALY B

	QUESTION 3a			QUESTION 3b (If *Possible*) Likely?			QUESTION 4 World government?			SAMPLE
	(A) Pos- sible	(B) Not pos- sible	(C) Don't know	(A) Like- ly	(B) Un- likely	(C) Don't know	(A) Agree	(B) Dis- agree	(C) Don't know	
1 Total	30	59	11	23	45	32	56	28	16	1,078
2 Men	32	60	8	25	43	32	59	32	9	558
3 Women	29	56	15	20	48	32	53	24	23	520
4 21–29	29	61	10	20	51	29	57	27	16	275
5 30–49	30	58	12	23	45	32	54	30	16	521
6 50–65	31	55	14	22	41	37	62	23	15	231
7 Over 65	31	67	2	35	37	28	55	27	18	51
8 A–wealthy	31	59	10	26	51	23	73	20	7	77
9 B–average	29	62	9	21	49	30	56	33	11	438
10 C–below av.	33	55	12	26	42	32	55	25	20	455
11 D–very poor	27	58	15	17	42	41	52	25	23	108
12 Primary	30	56	14	22	41	37	55	24	21	601
13 Secondary	31	63	6	25	49	26	57	34	9	221
14 University	30	60	10	21	52	27	59	30	11	256
29 Leftist (tr)	31	64	5				57	31	12	318
30 Rightist (tl)	28	69	3				59	38	3	58
31 All right	33	55	12				61	26	13	462
32 Don't know	23	56	21				45	24	31	240
33 Sec. (12–10)	27	61	12				61	33	6	84
34 Medium (9–5)	30	58	12				56	28	16	605
35 Insec. (4–0)	31	59	10				56	26	18	389
36 Can (Q.1a)	38	53	9	29	47	24	61	29	10	364
37 Can't change	25	68	7	19	47	34	56	33	11	464
38 Don't know	28	49	23	20	40	40	51	16	33	250
42 Likely (Q.3b)	92	6	2							244
43 Unlikely	16	79	5							489
44 Don't know	7	67	26							345
45 Agree (Q.4)	39	51	10							607
46 Disagree	17	76	7							299
47 Don't know	22	53	25							172
39 Possible (Q.3a)							73	15	12	326
40 Impossible							49	36	15	631
41 Don't know							48	16	36	121

ITALY C

		QUESTION 5 Postwar expectation?				QUESTION 6a Job security?[a]				QUESTION 6b Able to plan?			SAMPLE
		(A)	(B)	(C)	(D)	(A)	(B)	(C)	(D)	(A)	(B)	(C)	
		Better	Worse	About same	Don't know	More	Less	About same	Don't know	Yes	No	Don't know	
1	Total	40	25	30	5	20	20	48	12	25	51	24	1,078
2	Men	46	25	26	3	20	21	48	11	27	52	21	558
3	Women	34	26	33	7	20	18	48	14	24	50	26	520
4	21–29	39	25	30	6	18	20	48	14	24	49	27	275
5	30–49	40	28	29	3	22	20	47	11	27	54	19	521
6	50–65	42	22	30	6	19	18	49	14	25	46	19	231
7	Over 65	45	20	29	5	14	26	51	9	20	55	25	51
8	A–wealthy	26	36	31	7	42	8	31	19	46	27	27	77
9	B–average	36	23	36	5	25	11	51	13	33	43	24	438
10	C–below av.	42	27	25	6	15	23	52	10	18	58	24	455
11	D–very poor	57	19	19	5	7	53	31	9	10	71	19	108
12	Primary	43	25	26	6	15	25	48	12	19	57	24	601
13	Secondary	41	23	32	4	27	15	50	8	33	47	20	221
14	University	32	29	36	3	27	12	47	14	33	41	26	256
15	Profess.	21	29	42	8	34	8	50	8	46	50	4	24
16	Bus. owners	38	23	36	3	39	5	44	12	44	33	23	39
17	Ind. workers	37	33	25	5	18	18	51	13	25	55	20	49
18	Sal.-mangrs.	29	35	29	7	18	24	53	5	35	53	12	17
19	Clerks	37	31	29	3	31	8	51	10	29	57	14	51
20	Man. wkrs.	52	27	18	3	15	31	46	8	14	71	15	185
21	Farm wkrs.	54	24	16	6	6	46	41	7	11	67	22	70
22	Farm owners[b]	37	20	36	7	22	12	50	16	40	33	27	193
23	Housewives	35	26	34	5	21	16	51	12	24	50	26	294
24	Retired, Ind.[c]	40	25	29	6	18	19	44	19	20	45	35	156

[a] Q.6a puzzled most respondents, who found it difficult to make comparisons. However, the contrast between the upper and lower social classes is striking.

[b] There is in our country a very important class of rural workers, the "mezzadri," a kind of sharecropper, who in general are much better off than farm hands. We usually classify them with farm owners, and do so also in this survey.

[c] The sample is representative with regard to sex, age, geographic distribution, and occupation. The "Retired, independent" occupational group (l. 24) appears oversampled, as several housewives were included in that class.

ITALY D

		QUESTION 7 Satisfaction?				Security Scores			QUESTION 8 Best opportunity?[a]				SAMPLE
		(A)	(B)	(C)	(D)	(A)	(B)	(C)	(A)	(B)	(C)	(D)	
		Very	All right	Dissat.	Don't know	Sec. 12–10	Med. 9–5	Ins. 4–0	Italy	America[b]	S. Amer.[c]	Switz.	
1	Total	5	45	46	4	8	56	36	36	27	8	5	1,078
2	Men	5	43	49	3	8	56	36	32	29	11	5	558
3	Women	5	47	43	5	8	56	36	41	26	5	4	520

	Satisfaction? (A)	(B)	(C)	(D)	Security Scores (A)	(B)	(C)	Best opportunity?[a] (A)	(B)	(C)	(D)	Sample
	Very	All right	Dissat.	Don't know	Sec. 12–10	Med. 9–5	Ins. 4–0	Italy	America[b]	S. Amer.[c]	Switz.	
4 21–29	5	47	44	4	7	56	37	31	32	7	6	275
5 30–49	5	45	48	2	9	54	37	36	28	8	4	521
6 50–65	5	44	44	7	6	62	32	40	24	9	6	231
7 Over 65	8	41	47	4	8	53	39	51	18	6	4	51
8 A–wealthy	18	57	22	3	14	64	22	41	28	13	5	77
9 B–average	5	54	37	4	12	63	25	42	27	6	7	438
10 C–below av.	3	42	51	4	4	54	42	32	29	9	3	455
11 D–very poor	3	16	79	2	2	33	65	31	23	8	5	108
12 Primary	4	42	49	5	5	54	41					601
13 Secondary	6	47	44	3	12	60	28					221
14 University	6	50	40	4	11	59	30					256
15 Profess.	8	38	46	8								24
16 Bus. owners	3	64	31	2								39
17 Ind. workers	10	41	43	6								49
18 Sal.-mangrs.	—	59	35	6								17
19 Clerks	4	39	55	2								51
20 Man. wkrs.	3	30	64	3								185
21 Farm wkrs.	—	34	63	3								70
22 Farm owners[d]	9	57	32	2								193
23 Housewives	5	47	43	5								294
24 Retired, Ind.[d]	5	47	42	6								156
25 Upper class								48	25	11	2	44
26 Middle class								39	28	7	6	585
27 Working class								32	27	9	3	449
28 Don't know								—	—	—	—	—
29 Leftist (tr)								29	26	8	5	318
30 Rightist (tl)								45	16	12	9	58
31 All right								42	30	8	4	462
32 Don't know								36	26	8	5	240

Totals (Q.8) %

	%
Italy	36
America	{ 17
North America	{ 10
(of which U. S.)	(8.2)
South America	8
(of which Argentina)	(4.6)
Switzerland	5
France	2
Russia	2
Great Britain	1
South Africa	1
Sweden	1
Other countries	4
No reply	13
	——
	100

[a] We think that both "America" and "North America" on Q.8 mean to most people the U. S. A., therefore the table can be abridged as follows:

	%
Italy	36
U. S. A.	27
South America	8
European countries	11
Other and no answer	18
	——
	100

[b] Includes all respondents who said "America," "North America," or "United States."
[c] Includes respondents who named a specific South American country.
[d] See notes b and c, Table C above.

ITALY E

		QUESTION 9 Social class?				QUESTION 10a Own class abroad?[a]			QUESTION 10b[a] Others at home?			SAMPLE
		(A) Mid-dle	(B) Work-ing	(C) Up-per	(D) Don't know	(A) Yes	(B) No	(C) Don't know	(A) Yes	(B) No	(C) Don't know	
1	Total	54	42	4	—	41	27	32	50	26	24	1,078
2	Men	50	47	3	—	47	27	26	58	21	21	558
3	Women	59	36	5	—	35	27	38	48	24	28	520
4	21–29	52	44	4	—	47	23	30	53	23	24	275
5	30–49	52	44	4	—	39	28	33	49	27	24	521
6	50–65	61	37	2	—	41	27	32	45	27	28	231
7	Over 65	57	31	12	—	39	29	32	55	24	21	51
8	A–wealthy	68	1	31	—	47	22	31	73	12	15	77
9	B–average	89	7	4	—	45	24	31	57	21	22	438
10	C–below av.	31	69	—	—	38	30	32	43	30	27	455
11	D–very poor	4	96	—	—	34	29	37	29	41	30	108
12	Primary	35	64	1	—	33	30	37	37	33	30	601
13	Secondary	73	24	3	—	47	21	32	61	20	19	221
14	University	84	4	12	—	56	22	22	69	15	16	256
15	Profess.	67	—	33	—	71	21	8	84	12	4	24
16	Bus. owners	82	8	10	—	49	20	31	67	15	18	39
17	Ind. workers	47	53	—	—	37	31	32	37	24	39	49
18	Sal.-mangrs.	88	12	—	—	65	18	17	71	17	12	17
19	Clerks	78	22	—	—	53	20	27	57	25	18	51
20	Man. wkrs.	11	88	1	—	42	29	29	43	34	23	185
21	Farm wkrs.[b]	9	91	—	—	30	40	30	30	37	33	70
22	Farm owners	62	34	4	—	45	22	33	50	26	24	193
23	Housewives	66	30	4	—	34	26	40	50	23	27	294
24	Retired, Ind.[b]	76	17	7	—	45	29	26	54	22	24	156
25	Upper class					59	23	18	64	16	20	44
26	Middle class					43	25	32	59	21	20	585
27	Working class					38	29	33	37	33	30	449
28	Don't know					—	—	—	—	—	—	—
33	Sec. (12–10)	73	16	11	—							84
34	Med. (9–5)	59	36	5	—							605
35	Insec. (4–0)	42	56	2	—							389

	QUESTION 10c More in common?				SAMPLE
	(A) Abroad	(B) Italy	(C) Don't know	(D) Not asked	
Total	9	24	11	56	1,078

[a] The meaning of Q.10 was not clear to all respondents. Practically all interviewers reported that for the prevailing educational level such questions are too difficult.

[b] See notes b and c, Table C above.

ITALY F

		QUESTION 11 Most friendly?				QUESTION 12 Least friendly?				SAMPLE
		(A) Amer.	(B) Fr.	(C) Swiss	(D) Russ.	(A) Russ.	(B) Ger.	(C) Brit.	(D) Yugos.	
1	Total	54	7	7	5	44	16	14	8	1,078
2	Men	52	8	6	7	41	14	17	9	558
3	Women	57	6	7	3	46	18	12	7	520
4	21–29	53	5	6	7	39	18	14	9	275
5	30–49	56	8	5	5	46	14	16	8	521
6	50–65	48	10	10	5	40	19	12	10	231
7	Over 65	61	6	4	2	57	12	6	4	51
8	A–wealthy	61	5	9	1	58	12	9	13	77
9	B–average	56	8	8	1	51	16	15	9	438
10	C–below av.	52	6	6	9	37	17	14	7	455
11	D–very poor	49	8	2	13	32	16	16	3	108
25	Upper class	55	11	9	—	43	27	7	9	44
26	Middle class	58	8	9	1	51	14	14	10	585
27	Working class	50	8	4	12	34	18	16	6	449
28	Don't know	—	—	—	—	—	—	—	—	—
29	Leftist (tr)	40	13	5	18	30	19	25	7	318
30	Rightist (tl)	47	5	7	2	59	2	12	21	58
31	All right	63	8	9	—	52	15	11	8	462
32	Don't know	57	3	8	1	43	19	7	7	240

Totals (Q.11)		%	*Totals* (Q.12)		%
Americans		54	Russians		44
French		7	Germans		16
Swiss		7	British		14
Russians		5	Yugoslavians		8
Germans		4	Americans		3
British		3	French		3
Others		10	Others		4
All		—	All		1
No people		18	No people		3
No answer		15	No answer		10
		103[a]			106[a]

[a] Some respondents gave more than one answer.

ITALY G[a]

		QUESTION 14 Present government?				SAMPLE
		(A) Too right	(B) Too left	(C) All right	(D) Don't know	
1	Total	30	5	43	22	1,078
2	Men	36	6	42	16	558
3	Women	22	5	44	29	520
4	21–29	30	6	38	26	275
5	30–49	30	5	44	21	521
6	50–65	29	5	46	20	231
7	Over 65	22	12	45	21	51

ITALY Gª continued

	Present government?				Sample
	(A) Too right	(B) Too left	(C) All right	(D) Don't know	
8 A–wealthy	13	14	60	13	77
9 B–average	22	8	51	19	438
10 C–below av.	37	2	38	23	455
11 D–very poor	41	2	19	38	108
12 Primary	31	2	39	28	601
13 Secondary	28	7	52	13	221
14 University	27	11	45	17	256

ª Results of Q.13 are tabulated on p. 47.

MEXICO

A. Copy of Questionnaire Used in Mexico

Estamos haciendo una encuesta de la opinión pública mexicana, y quisiera hacerle unas preguntas . . .

0. Dentro de seis meses, cree usted que el costo de la vida aumentará, bajará, o se mantendrá poco más o menos como ahora?
   1-AUMENTARA   2-BAJARA   3-SE MANTENDRA COMO AHORA
   0-NO SABE   (1)

1. a. Cree usted que la naturaleza humana pueda cambiarse?
   1-PUEDE   2-NO PUEDE   0-NO SABE   (2)
   b. (SI PUEDE:) Cree usted probable que esto se haga?
   1-PROBABLE   2-IMPROBABLE   0-NO SABE   (3)

2. Cree usted que nuestras características de mexicano nos vienen de nacimiento, o que se deben a la manera como nos educan de chicos?
   1-DE NACIMIENTO   2-COMO NOS EDUCAN   0-NO SABE   (4)

3. a. Cree usted que será posible que todos los países puedan vivir en paz entre ellos?
   1-POSIBLE   2-IMPOSIBLE   0-NO SABE   (5)
   b. (SI DICE QUE SERA POSIBLE, PREGUNTE:) cree usted que así suceda?
   1-SUCEDERA   2-NO SUCEDERA   0-NO SABE   (6)

4. Hay gente que dice que debiera haber un gobierno mundial que pudiera controlar las leyes que hace cada país. Está usted de acuerdo con esa gente?
   1-DE ACUERDO   2-EN DESACUERDO   0-NO SABE   (7)

5. Cuando terminó la guerra, creyó usted que le iría mejor, peor, o más o menos igual de como le está yendo actualmente?
   3-MEJOR   0-PEOR   2-MAS O MENOS IGUAL   1-NO SABE (8)

6. Desde el punto de vista de su empleo (del empleo de___), se siente usted con más confianza o menos confianza en el porvenir que la generalidad de los mexicanos?
   3-MAS CONFIANZA   0-MENOS CONFIANZA   1-NO SABE (9)
   b. En general, se siente usted con bastante confianza en el porvenir para poder hacer planes para el futuro?
   3-SI   0-NO   1-NO SABE   (10)

7. Qué tan satisfecho está usted de como le está yendo actualmente?
   3-MUY SATISFECHO   2-BASTANTE SATISFECHO
   0-NO MUY SATISFECHO   1-NO SABE   (11)

   Secty.Scre. ☐ (12)

8. Qué país del mundo ofrece las mejores oportunidades para llevar la clase de vida que a usted le gustaría llevar? (ESTA PREGUNTA INCLUYE A MEXICO, SI EL RESPONSAL DESEA ACLARAR EL PUNTO.)
   País:_____ 00-NO SABE ☐☐ (13-14)

9. Si se le pidiera que nombrara la clase social a que pertenece, diría usted que ésta es la clase media, la clase trabajadora, o la clase alta?
   1-MEDIA   2-TRABAJADORA   3-ALTA   0-NO SABE   (15)

10. a. Considera usted que tiene algo en común con la gente de clase (la propia) de otros países?
   1-SI   2-NO   0-NO SABE   (16)
   b. Considera usted que tiene algo en común con los mexicanos que no pertenecen a la clase (la propia)?
   1-SI   2-NO   0-NO SABE   (17)
   c. (PREGUNTESE UNICAMENTE SI CONTESTAN SI, SI O NO, O NO A LAS DOS PREGUNTAS ANTERIORES:) Con cuál de estas dos gentes considera usted que tiene más en común: la clase (la

propia) de otros países, o los mexicanos que no pertenecen a la clase (la propia)?
   1-EXTRANJEROS   2-MEXICANOS   0-NO SABE   (18)

11. Por los habitantes de qué país siente usted mayor simpatía?
   _____ ☐☐ 00-NO SABE   (19-20)

12. Por los habitantes de qué país siente usted menor simpatía?
   _____ ☐☐ 00-NO SABE   (21-22)

13. a. De la lista de palabras que aparece en esta tarjeta, cuáles le parece que mejor describen a los norteamericanos? Seleccione tantas como desee y dígamelas. Si no se decide por ninguna, indíquemelo.
   b. Ahora seleccione las palabras que usted crea mejor describen a los rusos.
   c. Ahora indíqueme las palabras que mejor describen a los ingleses.
   d. Ahora, cuáles describen mejor a los franceses?
   e. Y cuáles describen mejor a los chinos?
   f. Finalmente, qué palabras describen mejor a los mexicanos?
   A. Trabajadores   H. Valientes
   B. Inteligentes   I. Saben controlarse (ecuánimes)
   C. Practicos   J. Dominantes
   D. Presumidos (vanidosos) K. Progresistas
   E. Generosos   L. Amantes de la paz
   F. Crueles   M. No se pueden describir
   G. Atrasados

14. Cree usted que nuestro gobierno actual se inclina mucho hacia la derecha, mucho hacia la izquierda, o que marcha como a usted le gustaría que fuera?
   1-DERECHA   2-IZQUIERDA   3-BIEN   0-NO SABE   (29)

15. Tienen automóvil particular en su casa?
   1-SI TIENEN   2-NO TIENEN   0-SIN RESP.   (30)

16. Hay teléfono en su casa?
   1-SI HAY   2-NO HAY   0-SIN RESPUESTA   (31)

17. Y tienen radio en su casa?
   1-SI TIENEN   2-NO TIENEN   0-SIN RESPUESTA   (32)

18. Tienen sirvientes en su casa?
   1-SI TIENEN   2-NO TIENEN   0-SIN RESPUESTA   (33)

19. La casa donde usted vive, es propia o de alquiler?
   1-PROPIA   2-ALQUILER   0-SIN RESPUESTA   (34)

20. Qué ocupación tiene usted?
   OCUPACION:_____ 0-SIN RESPUESTA (35)

21. a. Recuerda usted el nombre de la última escuela en que estuvo?
   NOMBRE:_____ 0-SIN RESPUESTA
   b. Hasta que año cursó?
   1-NO FUE ESCUELA   2-CURSO PRIMARIA   3-CURSO SECUNDARIA   4-ESTUVO UNIVERSIDAD   0-SIN RESPUESTA (36)
   c. Entonces, cuántos años fue usted a la escuela?
   NUM.DE ANOS:_____ 00-SIN RESPUESTA   (37-38)

22. Tiene usted inconveniente en darme su nombre?
   NOMBRE:_____ 0-SIN RESPUESTA

EDAD:	0 — 12 a 15	1 — 16 a 19	2 — 20 a 29	3 — 30 a 39	4 — 40 a 49	5 — 50 a 59	6 — 60 o más	(39)
CALLE:			NUM.:		SEXO:	1-HOMBRE	2-MUJER	(40)
CASA SOLA:		DEPARTAMENTO NUM:			NIVEL ECONOMICO:	1-A 2-B 3-C 4-D		(41)
ENTREVISTANTE:			FECHA:		NOMBRE DE LA CIUDAD:			(42)

C. Excerpts from Notes and Comments by Survey Agency

Only adults living in cities of 10,000 or more population were interviewed. Cities of this size account for approximately one-fourth of Mexico's inhabitants. Small villages and rural areas were not covered because of lack of communication facilities. All interviewing was done during December, 1948, and January, 1949.

Interviews were conducted in the following twenty-three cities in which we had personally trained field reporters:

	Number of Interviews	Est. 1947 Population
Celaya, Guanajuato	37	27,845
Coatzacoalcos, Veracruz	5	15,620
Durango, Durango	44	42,387
Guadalajara, Jalisco	97	273,368
Guanajuato, Guanajuato	12	28,768
Iguala, Guerrero	4	15,322
Jalapa, Veracruz	20	44,937
La Paz, Baja California	5	12,754
Merida, Yucatan	31	111,503
Mexico, D.F.[a]	473	2,003,563
Monterrey, Nuevo Leon	104	241,957
Morelia, Michoacan	21	52,606
Nogales, Sonora	8	17,681
Oaxaca, Oaxaca	18	33,184
Orizaba, Veracruz	17	54,473
Puebla, Puebla	45	156,687
Queretaro, Queretaro	57	39,526
San Francisco del Oro, Chihuahua	5	13,123
Tampico, Tamaulipas	37	103,127
Tepic, Nayarit	13	21,455
Torreon, Coahuila	45	97,080
Tuxtla Gutierrez, Chiapas	9	18,322
Veracruz, Veracruz	18	81,535
Total	1,125	3,506,823

[a] For purposes of this survey, we combined with Mexico, D.F., the suburbs listed in the census as Atzcapozalco, Coyoacan, Gustavo Madero, and Villa Obregon.

These 1,125 interviews were pre-controlled so as to represent correct proportions of the adult population by sex, age, and socio-economic levels. Assignments were made by age groups for men and women separately, and by socio-economic level for both sexes together. The sample was then weighted to conform with distribution of the population in various size cities as shown by the 1947 estimates of the Mexican census.

[*All figures in the tables are based upon the weighted samples, and the samples therein are based upon the weighted total of 1,752.*]

The quotas used to pre-control the 1,125 interviews were based upon population characteristics as determined in a previously conducted independent market survey. A system of area or probability sampling, in which more than 5,000 interviews were collected, was followed in the market study. The weighting was done to balance the sample as follows:

	Basic Interviews	Weighted Sample	1947 Census Estimates
Total number	1,125	1,752	5,494,197[a]
	%	%	%
Cities 10,000 to 50,000	21.1	31.4	31.5
Cities 50,000 to 100,000	11.7	16.0	15.9
Cities 100,000 to 500,000	25.2	16.1	16.1
Cities 500,000 or over	42.0	36.5	36.5
	100.0	100.0	100.0

[a] Total population of all cities of 10,000 or more population, as of 1947, estimated by the Mexican census.

Distributions of the basic and weighted samples by sex, age, and socio-economic levels are as follows:

	Basic Interviews	Weighted Sample
Total	1,125	1,752

Sex	%	%
Men	43.9	42.9
Women	56.1	57.1

Socio-Economic	%	%
Well-to-do (AV+)	2.2	1.9
Middle class (AV)	8.5	8.4
Working class (AV—)	38.8	38.8
Very poor (Group D)	50.5	50.9
	100.0	100.0

Age: Note that the questionnaire groups ages slightly differently from the table below. However, interviewers were also instructed to report their estimate of the age of each respondent individually. These individual estimates were used in the tabulation of the age groups shown here:

Men	%	%
20 to 29	34.2	34.8
30 to 49	47.8	47.5
50 to 65	15.8	15.3
66 & over	1.6	1.9
Undetermined	.6	.5
	100.0	100.0

Women	%	%
20 to 29	33.4	33.0
30 to 49	44.8	44.4
50 to 65	18.7	19.0
66 & over	2.5	2.9
Undetermined	.6	.7
	100.0	100.0

The sample upon which the tabulations for other background factors are based may be broken down as follows:

By Age Groups
	%
20 to 29	33.8
30 to 49	45.7
50 to 65	17.4
66 and over	2.5
Undetermined	.6
	100.0

By Education
	%
Primary	58.3
Secondary	17.4
College	10.2
No schooling	9.3
Undetermined	4.8
	100.0

By Occupations
	%
Professional workers	6.0
Owners of businesses, & large or medium shops	3.0
Workers on own account, owners of small shops	19.3
Salaried—managerial and top-grade clerical workers	1.3
Other clerical workers, shop assistants, personal service including catering	17.3
Manual workers	21.6
Farm workers, fishermen, gardeners	.5
Farm owners	.4
Housewives	26.1
Retired, students, miscellaneous others	3.5
Undetermined	1.0
	100.0

By Automobile Ownership
	%
Family has passenger automobile	11.3
Family does not have passenger automobile	87.0
Undetermined	1.7
	100.0

By Telephone Ownership
	%
Family has telephone in home	16.2
Family does not have telephone in home	80.8
Undetermined	3.0
	100.0

By Radio Ownership
	%
Family has radio in home	65.6
Family does not have radio in home	33.9
Undetermined	.5
	100.0

By Home Ownership	%
Family owns (or is buying) its home	29.3
Family lives in rented house	69.4
Undetermined	1.3
	100.0

By Use of Servants in Home	%
Family has servants in home	30.8
Family does not have servants in home	68.2
Undetermined	1.0
	100.0

Total cases in weighted sample 1,752

A staff of forty-three interviewers, mostly women, was used in this survey. They received their assignments and instructions by mail. However, each of the interviewers had obtained previous experience interviewing in market and opinion surveys. Each was personally trained, during the summer of 1948, in connection with market studies in which he participated.

To open the interview, we decided to add Q.0—"During the next six months, do you think the cost of living will go up, go down, or stay about the same as now?" Our pre-testing indicated that interviewers could better establish rapport with respondents by using this question than by starting with Q.1.

D. Notes and Comments by the Editors

Percentages in cols. (A), (B), and (C) of Q.1b total the percentage of respondents replying "Can" to Q.1a.

All percentages were given to the nearest tenth of a percent by the survey agency. These have been rounded off in the tables so as to equal 100%, which conformed with the practices of other survey agencies.

The samples given here are the *weighted* samples. In the text, "significance" has been computed on the basis of 64.2% of the number of cases given in the "Sample" column. (64.2% of weighted samples gives the actual sample, 1,125.) This is a close enough approximation for the purpose. For the details of the weighting scheme, see above.

The "Primary" group (l. 12) in the tables includes those with no education, who comprise approximately 9% of the total population, or 14% of the "Primary" group.

On Q.3b only those replying "Possible" to Q.3a were tabulated. These percentages are not comparable to other surveys. Cross tabulations with other questions (ll. 42, 43, and 44) are omitted.

The "About the same" check box on Q.6a was omitted from the Mexican questionnaire. This affects the Security Score and the "security index" to a small extent. Method of computing Security Score explained on p. 123.

The word "foreign" was left out of both Q.11 and 12, with the result that "Mexicans" polled 28% on Q.11. The figures for the other peoples were consequently reduced, so are not strictly comparable to those of other countries.

It has been noted in the breakdown of the sample above that age, education, and occupation for certain respondents were not filled in by the interviewers. Questionnaires lacking a datum were omitted from that particular cross-tabulation. Hence the weighted samples for age groups total 1,741, education 1,668, and occupation 1,734—instead of 1,752.

E. Tables

MEXICO A

	QUESTION 1a Change human nature?			QUESTION 1b (If *Can*) Likely?[a]			QUESTION 2 National character?[b]			WEIGHTED SAMPLE[b]
	(A) Can	(B) Can- not	(C) Don't know	(A) Like- ly	(B) Un- likely	(C) Don't know	(A) Born in us	(B) Way brought up	(C) Don't know	
1 Total	32	55	13	26	4	2	28	64	8	1,752
2 Men	38	52	10	32	5	2	28	65	7	752
3 Women	27	57	16	22	3	2	28	64	8	1,000
4 21–29	33	56	11	29	2	2	26	70	4	592
5 30–49	31	55	14	24	4	2	31	60	9	801
6 50–65	31	54	15	26	4	1	24	66	10	305
7 Over 65	40	39	21	23	12	5	23	68	9	43
8 A–wealthy	59	41	—	53	6	—	23	68	9	34
9 B–average	37	54	9	30	5	2	25	68	7	147
10 C–below av.	38	54	8	30	5	3	31	65	4	680
11 D–very poor	26	56	18	22	3	2	27	63	10	891
12 Primary[c]	26	58	16	22	3	2	27	65	8	1,185
13 Secondary	44	49	7	34	7	2	33	64	3	304
14 University	57	40	3	49	6	2	21	70	9	179
29 Leftist (tr)[d]	33	56	11				27	63	10	365
30 Rightist (tl)[e]	36	56	8				26	70	4	403
31 All right	35	50	15				25	68	7	489
32 Don't know	25	57	18				33	58	9	495
25 Upper class							31	64	5	39
26 Middle class							30	64	6	789
27 Working class							26	65	9	888
28 Don't know							36	58	6	36
36 Can (Q.1a)							24	74	4	561
37 Cannot							30	64	6	959
38 Don't know							30	49	21	232
39 Possible (Q.3a)							26	71	3	323
40 Impossible							28	65	7	1,295
41 Don't know							34	40	26	134
45 Agree (Q.4)							29	67	4	327
46 Disagree							27	66	7	1,271
47 Don't know							36	44	20	154

[a] Percentages in cols. (A), (B), and (C) of Q.1b total the percentage of respondents replying "Can" to Q.1a.

[b] The samples given here are the *weighted* samples. In the text, "significance" has been computed on the basis of 64.2% of the number of cases given in the "Sample" col. (64.2% of weighted sample gives the actual sample, 1,125.) This is a close enough approximation for the purpose.

[c] The "Primary" group (l. 12) in the tables includes those with no education, who comprise approximately 9% of the total population, or 14% of the "Primary" group.

[d] "tr" = too right.

[e] "tl" = too left.

MEXICO B

	QUESTION 3a Live in peace?			QUESTION 3b (If *Possible*) Likely?[a]			QUESTION 4 World government			WEIGHTED SAMPLE[b]
	(A) Possible	(B) Not possible	(C) Don't know	(A) Likely	(B) Unlikely	(C) Don't know	(A) Agree	(B) Disagree	(C) Don't know	
1 Total	18	74	8	10	5	3	19	72	9	1,752
2 Men	21	73	6	13	6	2	18	74	8	752
3 Women	17	74	9	9	5	3	19	71	10	1,000
4 21–29	17	77	6	9	6	2	19	74	7	592
5 30–49	19	72	9	11	5	3	21	70	9	801
6 50–65	19	72	9	12	5	2	14	73	13	305
7 Over 65	19	67	14	9	7	2	12	79	9	43
8 A–wealthy	44	56	—	29	15	—	18	82	—	34
9 B–average	17	76	7	8	7	3	24	70	6	147
10 C–below av.	23	72	5	13	7	3	20	74	6	680
11 D–very poor	15	75	10	8	4	2	17	71	12	891
12 Primary[c]	16	75	9	10	—	—	16	74	10	1,185
13 Secondary	19	78	3	9	8	3	22	74	14	304
14 University	33	66	1	10	2	6	19	78	3	179
29 Leftist (tr)	20	77	3				16	77	7	365
30 Rightist (tl)	17	78	5				20	76	4	403
31 All right	20	72	8				21	70	10	489
32 Don't know	17	70	13				18	69	13	495
33 Sec. (12–10)[d]	29	64	7				21	73	6	238
34 Medium (9–5)	19	75	6				22	70	8	871
35 Insec. (4–0)	14	77	9				14	76	10	643
36 Can (Q.1a)	34	63	4				23	71	6	561
37 Can't change	12	81	7				17	77	6	959
38 Don't know	8	71	21				15	60	25	232
42 Likely (Q.3b)[a]										
43 Unlikely										
44 Don't know										
45 Agree (Q.4)	30	64	6							327
46 Disagree	16	79	5							1,271
47 Don't know	14	56	30							154
39 Possible (Q.3a)							30	63	7	323
40 Impossible							16	77	7	1,295
41 Don't know							15	51	34	134

[a] On Q.3b only those replying "Possible" to Q.3a were tabulated. These percentages are not comparable to other surveys. Cross tabulations with other questions (ll. 42, 43, and 44) are omitted.

[b] See note b, Table A above.

[c] See note c, Table A above.

[d] The "About the same" check box on Q.6a was omitted from the Mexican questionnaire. This affects the Security Score and the "security index" to a small extent. Method of computing Security Score explained on p. 123.

MEXICO C

		QUESTION 5 Postwar expectation?				QUESTION 6a Job security?[a]				QUESTION 6b Able to plan?			WEIGHTED SAMPLE[b]
		(A) Better	(B) Worse	(C) About same	(D) Don't know	(A) More	(B) Less	(C) About same	(D) Don't know	(A) Yes	(B) No	(C) Don't know	
1	Total	41	33	24	2	54	36		10	54	31	15	1,752
2	Men	40	34	26	1	56	36		9	57	30	13	752
3	Women	41	34	23	2	53	36		11	51	32	17	1,000
4	21–29	41	31	27	1	62	27		11	65	24	11	592
5	30–49	42	34	23	1	52	38		10	49	35	16	801
6	50–65	36	36	26	2	48	41		11	48	30	22	305
7	Over 65	49	39	7	5	23	68		9	23	49	28	43
8	A–wealthy	23	24	53	—	77	23		—	85	15	—	34
9	B–average	52	22	25	1	68	22		10	69	16	15	147
10	C–below av.	43	32	24	1	63	29		8	59	30	11	680
11	D–very poor	38	37	23	2	44	44		12	45	35	20	891
12	Primary[e]	42	36	21	1	48	41		11	48	34	18	1,185
13	Secondary	39	29	31	1	66	27		7	65	28	7	304
14	University	43	27	29	1	77	15		8	79	15	6	179
15	Profess.	41	31	28	—	80	14		6	76	22	2	106
16	Bus. owners	35	52	13	—	59	31		10	62	21	17	52
17	Ind. workers	43	33	21	3	50	42		8	56	29	15	338
18	Sal.-mangrs.	52	22	17	9	74	26		—	78	13	9	23
19	Clerks	34	35	31	—	62	30		8	62	29	9	303
20	Man. wkrs.	37	36	25	2	46	39		15	43	38	19	379
21	Farm wkrs.	38	37	25	—	38	25		37	—	75	25	8
22	Farm owners	14	43	43	—	100	—		—	72	14	14	7
23	Housewives	46	32	21	1	53	38		9	50	34	16	457
24	Retired, Ind.	47	25	28	—	41	26		33	44	13	43	61

[a] The "About the same" check box on Q.6a was omitted from the Mexican questionnaire. This affects the Security Score and the "security index" to a small extent. Method of computing Security Score explained on p. 123.

[b] See note b, Table A above.

[e] See note c, Table A above.

MEXICO D

		QUESTION 7 Satisfaction?				Security Scores[a]			QUESTION 8 Best opportunity?			WEIGHTED SAMPLE[b]
		(A) Very	(B) All right	(C) Dis-sat.	(D) Don't know	(A) Sec. 12–10	(B) Med. 9–5	(C) Ins. 4–0	(A) Mex.	(B) U.S.A.	(C) Arg.	
1	Total	20	18	61	1	13	50	37	45	31	3	1,752
2	Men	19	18	62	1	14	50	36	44	33	4	752
3	Women	20	19	60	1	13	50	37	47	30	1	1,000
4	21–29	19	22	58	1	16	56	28	43	36	3	592
5	30–49	22	16	61	1	13	47	40	43	33	2	801
6	50–65	17	18	64	1	12	48	40	53	21	4	305
7	Over 65	14	21	61	4	7	28	65	58	16	—	43

MEXICO D continued

	Satisfaction?				Security Scores[a]			Best opportunity?			Weighted Sample[b]
	(A) Very	(B) All right	(C) Dis-sat.	(D) Don't know	(A) Sec. 12–10	(B) Med. 9–5	(C) Ins. 4–0	(A) Mex.	(B) U.S.A.	(C) Arg.	
8 A–wealthy	27	35	38	—	41	45	15	47	24	21	34
9 B–average	24	32	44	—	23	52	25	40	39	4	147
10 C–below av.	23	18	58	1	15	54	31	41	41	3	680
11 D–very poor	16	17	66	1	10	47	43	50	23	1	891
12 Primary[c]	19	15	65	1	11	47	42				1,185
13 Secondary	20	24	55	1	16	56	28				304
14 University	24	29	47	—	27	56	17				179
15 Profess.	24	25	50	1							106
16 Bus. owners	11	31	58	—							52
17 Ind. workers	19	13	67	1							338
18 Sal.-mangrs.	4	39	57	—							23
19 Clerks	26	16	55	3							303
20 Man. wkrs.	15	19	65	1							379
21 Farm wkrs.	25	—	75	—							8
22 Farm owners	29	43	28	—							7
23 Housewives	22	20	58	—							457
24 Retired, Ind.	15	29	56	—							61
25 Upper class								57	28	5	39
26 Middle class								42	39	4	789
27 Working class								48	25	1	888
28 Don't know								33	22	—	36
29 Leftist (tr)								45	38	4	365
30 Rightist (tl)								44	34	2	403
31 All right								42	34	3	489
32 Don't know								50	22	2	495

Totals (Q.8) %

Mexico	45
United States	31
Argentina	3
Spain	1
All other countries	3
No answer	17
	100

[a] The "About the same" check box on Q.6a was omitted from the Mexican questionnaire. This affects the Security Score and the "security index" to a small extent. Method of computing Security Score explained on p. 123.

[b] See note b, Table A above.

[c] See note c, Table A above.

MEXICO E[a]

	QUESTION 9 Social class?				QUESTION 10a Own class abroad?			QUESTION 10b Others at home?			WEIGHTED SAMPLE[b]
	(A) Mid-dle	(B) Work-ing	(C) Up-per	(D) Don't know	(A) Yes	(B) No	(C) Don't know	(A) Yes	(B) No	(C) Don't know	
1 Total	45	51	2	2	40	37	23	56	27	17	1,752
2 Men	42	54	3	1	47	33	20	56	29	15	752
3 Women	48	48	2	2	35	39	26	56	25	19	1,000
4 21–29	47	49	3	1	38	40	22	56	28	16	592
5 30–49	46	50	2	2	43	32	25	57	24	19	801
6 50–65	40	52	4	4	36	40	24	52	31	17	305
7 Over 65	30	65	—	5	33	53	14	65	21	14	43

MEXICO E[a] continued

	Social class?				Own class abroad?			Others at home?			Weighted
	(A) Middle	(B) Working	(C) Upper	(D) Don't know	(A) Yes	(B) No	(C) Don't know	(A) Yes	(B) No	(C) Don't know	Sample[b]
8 A–wealthy	26	6	68	—	68	6	6	94	6	—	34
9 B–average	76	13	10	1	61	26	13	73	18	9	147
10 C–below av.	73	26	—	1	46	36	18	65	25	10	680
11 D–very poor	20	77	—	3	30	40	30	45	30	25	891
12 Primary[c]	34	63	1	2	31	42	27	49	30	21	1,185
13 Secondary	70	23	6	1	55	27	18	72	21	7	304
14 University	80	12	7	1	73	21	6	82	14	4	179
15 Profess.	79	16	4	1	68	18	14	76	20	4	106
16 Bus. owners	60	23	17	—	63	33	4	75	19	6	52
17 Ind. workers	39	60	—	1	39	41	20	55	29	16	338
18 Sal.-mangrs.	69	22	9	—	78	18	4	74	22	4	23
19 Clerks	50	49	—	1	41	39	20	56	34	10	303
20 Man. wkrs.	25	71	2	2	29	35	36	45	24	31	379
21 Farm wkrs.	—	63	—	37	13	—	87	25	37	38	8
22 Farm owners	43	14	43	—	57	43	—	71	29	—	7
23 Housewives	51	44	2	3	36	40	24	58	25	17	457
24 Retired, Ind.	52	38	5	5	54	30	16	69	16	15	61
25 Upper class					77	18	5	90	5	5	39
26 Middle class					49	34	17	68	22	10	789
27 Working class					31	41	28	46	32	22	888
28 Don't know					22	8	70	11	11	78	36
33 Sec. (10–12)[d]	60	35	5	—							238
34 Med. (9–5)	49	27	3	1							871
35 Insec. (4–0)	34	61	1	4							643

[a] Results of Q.10c not available.
[b] See note b, Table A above.
[c] See note e, Table A above.
[d] See note d, Table B above.

MEXICO F

	QUESTION 11 Most friendly?[a]			QUESTION 12 Least friendly?[a]				WEIGHTED SAMPLE[b]
	(A) Amer.	(B) Sp.	(C) Arg	(A) Russ.	(B) Amer.	(C) China	(D) Jap.	
1 Total	28	10	4	24	10	10	7	1,752
2 Men	26	9	6	28	13	8	6	752
3 Women	29	12	2	21	8	11	8	1,000
4 21–29	30	10	5	23	13	10	7	592
5 30–49	29	10	4	25	9	10	8	801
6 50–65	24	14	2	24	7	12	6	305
7 Over 65	21	14	2	30	5	—	2	43
8 A–wealthy	32	27	6	47	6	—	—	34
9 B–average	33	8	5	34	6	3	8	147
10 C–below av.	34	12	5	27	10	10	7	680
11 D–very poor	22	9	3	19	11	11	7	891
25 Upper class	28	15	5	36	13	—	5	39
26 Middle class	33	13	5	30	9	10	7	789
27 Working class	23	8	3	19	11	10	8	888
28 Don't know	19	—	—	6	6	11	—	36

MEXICO F continued

	Most friendly?a			Least friendly?a				Weighted Sampleb
	(A) Amer.	(B) Sp.	(C) Arg.	(A) Russ.	(B) Amer.	(C) China	(D) Jap.	
29 Leftist (tr)	34	12	6	30	13	12	9	365
30 Rightist (tl)	23	13	5	31	12	9	5	403
31 All right	27	9	3	18	8	13	10	489
32 Don't know	29	9	2	19	8	6	5	495

Totals (Q.11)	%	*Totals* (Q.12)	%
(Mexicans)ᶠ	28	Russians	24
Americans	28	Americans	10
Spanish	10	Chinese	10
Argentines	4	Japanese	7
Others	14	Others	17
No answer	16	No answer	32
	100		100

a The word "foreign" was left out of both Q.11 and 12, with the result that "Mexicans" polled 28% on Q.11. The figures for the other peoples were consequently reduced, so are not strictly comparable to those of other countries.

b See note b, Table A above.

MEXICO Gª

	QUESTION 14 Present government?				WEIGHTED SAMPLEb
	(A) Too right	(B) Too left	(C) All right	(D) Don't know	
1 Total	21	23	28	28	1,752
2 Men	25	24	30	21	752
3 Women	18	22	26	34	1,000
4 21–29	25	27	25	23	592
5 30–49	20	20	31	29	801
6 50–65	17	22	28	33	305
7 Over 65	10	37	23	30	43
8 A–wealthy	41	18	35	6	34
9 B–average	26	33	16	25	147
10 C–below av.	20	24	32	24	680
11 D–very poor	20	21	26	33	891
12 Primaryᶜ	20	23	27	30	768
13 Secondary	19	29	30	22	304
14 University	31	21	32	16	179

a Results of Q.13 are not available.

b See note b, Table A above.

c See note c, Table A above.

THE NETHERLANDS

A. Copy of Questionnaire Used in the Netherlands

N.B. *Ondervraagde nooit op het formulier laten kijken of meelezen. Antwoorden accuraat weergeven. Stel de vragen letterlijk als hieronder aangegeven, antwoorden aangeven door cirkeltjes om codecijfers. Schrijven op stippellijnen, nooit in de kaders!!*

BEANTW. DOOR:	Enq. zelf 1
	kennis 2
	Onbek. 3

1a. (7) Gelooft U dat de menselijke natuur, de aard van de mensen, veranderd kan worden?
- Kan ver 1
- Niet 2
- G.oord 3

1b. (8) (Alleen indien antwoord KAN veranderd bij vraag 1a): Denkt U dat er veel kans op is, dat dat gebeurt?
- Veel kans 4
- Niet 5
- G.oord 6

2. (9) Wat denkt U: zijn de typische eigenschappen van ons, Nederlanders, in hoofdzaak aangeboren of komen zij voort uit de manier waarop we zijn grootgebracht?
- Aangeboren 7
- Groot gebr 8
- G.oord 9

3a. (10) Denkt U dat het mogelijk zal zijn dat alle landen in vrede met elkaar leven?
- Mogelijk 1
- Niet 2
- G.oord 3

3b. (11) Denkt U dat er veel kans op is dat dit zal gebeuren?
- Veel kans 4
- Niet 5
- G.oord 6

4. (12) Er wordt wel gezegd, dat er een wereldregering moest zijn, die de wetten van ieder land kan controleren. Bent U het daarmee eens of niet?
- Eens 7
- Oneens 8
- G.oord 9

5. (13) Toen in 1945 de oorlog eindigde, verwachtte U toen dat U beter, slechter of ongeveer net zo vooruit zoudt komen als U in werkelijkheid op 't ogenblik vooruit komt?
- Beter 1
- Slechter 2
- Net zo 3
- G.oord 4

6a. Wat is Uw indruk: Hebt U, wat Uw baan betreft (de baan van Uw man) meer of minder bestaanszekerheid dan de gemiddelde Nederlander?
- Meer 5
- Minder 6
- Ong. hetzelfde 7
- G.oord 8

6b. (15) Hebt U wat dat betreft voldoende zekerheid om plannen voor de toekomst te maken of niet?
- Wel 9
- Niet 11
- G.oord 0

7. (16) Nu een vraag over Uw tevredenheid met de manier waarop U op 't ogenblik vooruitkomt. Bent U daar zeer tevreden, (gewoon) tevreden of ontevreden over?
- Zeer tevr 1
- Gew. tevr 2
- Ontevr 3
- G.oord 4

8. (17) Wat denkt U: in welk land zou men de beste kans hebben om te leven zoals U het graag wilt?
In..
(Indien de ondervraagde dit mocht vragen: Nederland kan hier ook genoemd worden)

9. (18) Indien U zichzelf in een van de volgende drie klassen zoudt moeten indelen, tot welke zoudt U dan zeggen, dat U behoort: tot de middenklasse, de werkende klasse of de hoogste klasse?
- Middenkl 5
- Werkende kl. 6
- Hoogste kl. 7
- G.oord 8

10a. (19) Hebt U het gevoel dat U iets gemeen hebt met de mensen van de werkende klasse/ middenklasse/hoogste klasse (noem hier de door ondervraagde zelf aangegeven klasse, zie vraag 9) in het buitenland?
- Wel 1
- Niet 2
- G.oord 3

10b. (20) En hebt U het gevoel dat U iets gemeen hebt met de Nederlanders, die niet tot de . . . . . klasse (noem klasse ondervraagde, zie vraag 9) behoren?
- Wel 4
- Niet 5
- G.oord 6

10c. (21) (Alleen stellen indien Wel/Wel of Neen/ Neen op vragen 10a en 10b): Met welke van de twee, de mensen van Uw eigen klasse in het buitenland of de Nederlanders van een andere klasse, hebt U naar Uw idee het meeste gemeen?
- Buitenl 7
- Nederl 8
- G.oord 9

11. (22) Tegenover welk volk in 't buitenland staat U het vriendelijkst?
....
....

12. (23) En tegenover welk volk het minst vriendelijk?
....
....

(Kaartje tonen)

13a. (24) Wilt U op deze kaart kijken welke woorden naar Uw idee het beste het Amerikaanse volk beschrijven? Zoek er zoveel uit als U wilt en noem mij de letters, die bij de woorden staan die U uitkiest. Zegt U het gerust wanneer U er eigenlijk geen idee over heeft.

13b. (25) Wilt U nu nog eens op de kaart kijken en de woorden uitzoeken, die naar Uw idee het beste het Russische volk beschrijven?

13c. (26) En zoekt U nu de woorden uit, die het beste ons Nederlanders beschrijven.

	Am.	Rus.	Ned.			Am.	Rus.	Ned.
A Hardw.	1	1	1		H Dapper	8	8	8
B Verstand.	2	2	2		I Beheerst	9	9	9
C Practisch	3	3	3		J Heersz.	0	0	0
D Verwaand	4	4	4		K Vooruitstr.	11	11	11
E Vrijgevig	5	5	5		L Vredel.	12	12	12
F Wreed	6	6	6		M Niet aan te			
G Achterlijk	7	7	7		geven	R	R	R

(Antwoorden op 13a, 13b, en 13c aan te geven door onder het betreffende land de cijfers te omringen die horen bij de genoemde letters)

14. (27) Wat denkt U: is onze Regering te veel rechts, te veel links of zo ongeveer als U haar graag hebt?
- Te rechts 1
- Te links 2
- Ong.goed 3
- G.oord 4

Nog enige vragen over Uzelf om na te gaan of de antwoorden die wij verzamelen werkelijk uit alle groepen van het publiek komen.

Wat is Uw beroep? (Indien zelf geen beroep):
Wat is het beroep van de kostwinner?
(Voor gehuwde vrouwen): Van Uw man?

Man	12
Vrouw	11
(29)	

21 t/m 29 jaar	1
30 t/m 49 jaar	2
50 t/m 65 jaar	3
(30) 66 en ouder	4

(34)

(35)

....

(Zo volledig mogelijk noteren en hieronder beroepsgroep aangeven)

Vrije beroepen (als arts, notaris, advocaat 1

Fabrieksdirecteuren, eigenaren grote winkelzaken e.d. 2

Eigenaren van kleine winkels, kleinere zelfstandigen 3

Gesalarieerde leidende functies in handel en industrie, hogere ambten...... 4

Kantoorbedienden, ambtenaren en overige salaristrekkenden 5

Arbeiders in industrie en ambacht, ... 6

Landarbeiders, vissers en tuinlieden...... 7

Zelfstandige boeren 8

Gepensionneerden, rentiers 9
(28)

Welgesteld.................5	
Beter Gesitueerd (Middenklasse)..........6	
Minder gesitueerd (Volkskl.B.)..........7	
Laagste inkomens (Volkskl.A.)..........8	
(31)	

Op welke onderwijs-instelling hebt U Uw laatste schooljaar doorgebracht?
- Lagere school 0
- Vervolg-, middelbaar-, Gymnas. en vak-onderwijs............11
- (32) Univers. en Hogeschool............12

Op welke leeftijd kwam U van school af (incl. Univers.)?

10 t/m 14 jaar....1		19 t/m 22 jaar....3	
15 t/m 18 jaar....2		23 jaar en ouder...4	
(33)			

Dit interview is overeenkomstig de NIPO instructies verricht door:
Enquêteur no. ....
in de Gemeente ....
op (datum)........................1948

Het was op een:		En het interview vond plaats:
Maandag 1		
Dinsdag 2		voor 1 uur.......8
Woensdag 3		's middags 9
Donderd 4		na 6 uur.........0
Vrijdag.........5		
Zaterdag.........6		
Zondag.........7		

C. Excerpts from Notes and Comments by Survey Agency

Total population figures are based on official statistics of the Central Bureau of Statistics, The Hague (C.B.S.). Sex: figures of 1947. Age: figures of 1942. Size of towns and provinces: figures of July, 1948 for people twenty-three years and older. (Twenty-three is the voting age).

Socio-economic figures are based on income tax figures of families, not of persons. The division between AV— and Group D is an arbitrary one, based on polling.

No official statistics on education are available. Figures are based on polling during the last year.

No official, reliable statistics on occupation are available. The last Dutch census was in 1930.

Structure of the Sample	Unesco Survey Figures	Total Population Figures
Sex		
	%	%
Men	48	49
Women	52	51
Age		
21-29	26	25
30-49	47	45
50-65	20	20
66 & over	7	10
Socio-economic (AV+)	7	6
(AV)	28	24
(AV—)	34	35
(D)	31	35
Education		
Primary	59	57
Secondary	38	40
University	3	3
Towns		
100,000 inhabitants & more	46	44
20,000-100,000	22	25
Less than 20,000	46	44
Provinces		
Groningen	4	5
Friesland	5	5
Drente	3	3
Overijssel	8	7
Gelderland	10	11
Utrecht	6	6
N. Holland	20	19
Z. Holland	24	24
Zeeland	3	3
N. Brabant	11	11
Limburg	6	6

There is little difference between Unesco and total population figures because we stratify our regular surveys, and so this Unesco survey, as to provinces and size of town in the office; as to sex, age, and socio-economic status in our instructions to interviewers. We do not give figures or instructions to our interviewers in respect to education. The Unesco sample is a little too "well-to-do" (see socio-economic status figures).

We sent out 1,100 questionnaires. We got back less than 1,000 and used 942 good ones as basis for the figures given in this report. The "effective return coefficient" in this survey (viz., 942/1,100 = 0.86) is normal in our surveying.

Number of active interviewers in this Unesco survey: ninety-six. Average interviews per interviewer 9.8.

D. Notes and Comments by the Editors

Sample on Q.1b is the total number of respondents. Interviewers were instructed to ask this question only of those who answered "Can" to Q.1a. However, since the total of cols. (A) and (B) on Q.1b exceeds the percentage in col. (A) on Q.1a in certain breakdowns, it is apparent that a few interviewers did not comply. Hence, while the figures are broadly comparable to those of other countries, these comparisons should be made with reservations.

"Housewives" as a category was omitted from the Dutch questionnaire. Apparently they were classed under the occupation of their husbands.

E. Tables

THE NETHERLANDS A

	QUESTION 1a Change human nature?			QUESTION 1b (If *Can*) Likely?[a]			QUESTION 2 National character?			SAMPLE
	(A) Can	(B) Cannot	(C) Don't know	(A) Likely	(B) Unlikely	(C) Don't know	(A) Born in us	(B) Way brought up	(C) Don't know	
1 Total	44	43	13	14	31	55	44	43	13	942
2 Men	45	45	10	15	31	54	48	42	10	449
3 Women	43	41	16	13	31	56	40	44	16	493
4 21–29	43	43	14	12	31	57	40	47	13	246
5 30–49	45	41	14	17	31	52	45	44	11	445
6 50–65	43	43	14	10	33	57	46	37	17	187
7 Over 65	36	55	9	11	23	66	47	39	14	64
8 A–wealthy	42	55	3	15	35	50	45	52	3	62
9 B–average	50	45	5	14	38	48	48	45	7	267
10 C–below av.	43	44	13	14	30	56	43	45	12	325
11 D–very poor	38	38	24	14	24	62	41	38	21	288

THE NETHERLANDS A continued

	Change human nature?			(If *Can*) Likely?[a]			National character?			Sample
	(A) Can	(B) Cannot	(C) Don't know	(A) Likely	(B) Unlikely	(C) Don't know	(A) Born in us	(B) Way brought up	(C) Don't know	
12 Primary	40	41	19	14	26	60	42	41	17	553
13 Secondary	50	44	6	14	39	47	48	45	7	360
14 University	34	62	4	10	35	55	38	62	—	29
29 Leftist (tr)[b]	46	39	15				27	40	13	173
30 Rightist (tl)[c]	46	48	6				52	42	6	228
31 All right	43	45	12				42	46	12	356
32 Don't know	39	37	24				34	43	23	185
25 Upper class							52	40	8	37
26 Middle class							46	49	5	308
27 Working class							43	40	17	560
28 Don't know							32	49	19	37
36 Can (Q.1a)							43	50	7	410
37 Cannot							51	40	9	405
38 Don't know							23	32	45	127
39 Possible (Q.3a)							47	44	9	430
40 Impossible							44	44	12	461
41 Don't know							22	25	53	51
45 Agree (Q.4)							46	46	8	435
46 Disagree							46	45	9	298
47 Don't know							37	35	28	209

[a] Sample on Q.1b is the total number of respondents. Interviewers were instructed to ask this question only of those who answered "Can" to Q.1a. However, since the total of cols. (A) and (B) on Q.1b exceeds the percentage in col. (A) on Q.1a in certain breakdowns, it is apparent that a few interviewers did not comply. Hence, while the figures are broadly comparable to those of other countries, these comparisons should be made with reservations.

[b] "tr" = too right.

[c] "tl" = too left.

THE NETHERLANDS B

	QUESTION 3a Live in peace?			QUESTION 3b (If *Possible*) Likely?			QUESTION 4 World government?			SAMPLE
	(A) Possible	(B) Not possible	(C) Don't know	(A) Likely	(B) Unlikely	(C) Don't know	(A) Agree	(B) Disagree	(C) Don't know	
1 Total	46	49	5	7	69	24	46	32	22	942
2 Men	50	47	3	9	68	23	50	35	15	449
3 Women	42	51	7	5	70	25	43	29	28	493
4 21–29	44	49	7	6	68	26	44	32	24	246
5 30–49	45	50	5	8	71	21	46	31	23	445
6 50–65	45	51	4	6	65	29	46	34	20	187
7 Over 65	62	33	5	8	69	23	53	25	22	64
8 A–wealthy	48	50	2	3	79	18	61	26	13	62
9 B–average	50	45	5	6	70	24	50	36	14	267
10 C–below av.	44	51	5	7	70	23	43	35	22	325
11 D–very poor	43	50	7	9	65	26	43	25	32	288

THE NETHERLANDS B continued

		Live in peace?			(If *Possible*) Likely?			World government?			Sample
		(A) Possible	(B) Not possible	(C) Don't know	(A) Likely	(B) Unlikely	(C) Don't know	(A) Agree	(B) Disagree	(C) Don't know	
12	Primary	41	52	7	6	66	28	42	29	29	553
13	Secondary	52	44	4	8	73	19	51	35	14	360
14	University	45	55	—	—	69	31	66	31	3	29
29	Leftist (tr)	56	39	5				51	31	18	173
30	Rightist (tl)	40	56	4				43	43	14	228
31	All right	50	45	5				54	25	21	356
32	Don't know	35	56	9				30	30	40	185
33	Sec. (12–10)	52	43	5				51	34	15	111
34	Medium (9–5)	48	48	4				49	30	21	432
35	Insec. (4–0)	41	52	7				42	33	25	399
36	Can (Q.1a)	55	42	3	11	70	19	54	32	14	410
37	Can't change	39	59	2	3	73	24	44	36	20	405
38	Don't know	37	38	25	6	51	43	28	17	55	127
42	Likely (Q.3b)	86	14	—							65
43	Unlikely	54	45	1							648
44	Don't know	11	71	18							229
45	Agree (Q.4)	59	38	3							435
46	Disagree	30	68	2							298
47	Don't know	40	45	15							209
39	Possible (Q.3a)							59	21	20	430
40	Impossible							36	44	20	461
41	Don't know							29	10	61	51

THE NETHERLANDS C

		QUESTION 5 Postwar expectation?				QUESTION 6a Job security?				QUESTION 6b Able to plan?			SAMPLE
		(A) Better	(B) Worse	(C) About same	(D) Don't know	(A) More	(B) Less	(C) About same	(D) Don't know	(A) Yes	(B) No	(C) Don't know	
1	Total	56	12	26	6	24	22	45	9	36	42	22	942
2	Men	55	12	30	3	24	24	46	6	38	43	19	449
3	Women	58	12	22	8	24	21	44	11	33	42	25	493
4	21–29	59	9	24	8	24	24	43	9	40	39	21	246
5	30–49	56	15	24	5	25	21	46	8	37	43	20	445
6	50–65	58	9	28	5	23	24	47	6	32	47	21	187
7	Over 65	47	11	37	5	17	21	42	20	20	42	38	64
8	A–wealthy	42	24	31	3	50	10	30	10	61	16	23	62
9	B–average	51	13	30	6	40	13	38	9	52	30	18	267
10	C–below av.	59	11	25	5	18	21	54	7	34	46	20	325
11	D–very poor	62	9	22	7	9	36	45	10	16	56	28	288
12	Primary	59	12	24	5	15	29	47	9	24	50	26	553
13	Secondary	54	13	28	5	34	15	44	7	50	33	17	360
14	University	31	10	49	10	59	7	14	20	79	7	14	29

THE NETHERLANDS C continued

	Postwar expectation?				Job security?				Able to plan?			Sample
	(A) Better	(B) Worse	(C) About same	(D) Don't know	(A) More	(B) Less	(C) About same	(D) Don't know	(A) Yes	(B) No	(C) Don't know	
15 Profess.	44	22	34	—	51	10	27	12	61	20	19	41
16 Bus. owners	30	37	26	7	48	15	26	11	56	22	22	27
17 Ind. workers	56	15	22	7	19	25	50	6	35	48	17	107
18 Sal.-mangrs.	53	11	34	2	51	9	34	6	66	17	17	47
19 Clerks	52	10	32	6	36	14	42	8	48	33	19	235
20 Man. wkrs.	66	8	23	3	11	30	53	6	24	54	22	239
21 Farm wkrs.	64	7	18	11	7	36	46	11	16	54	30	106
22 Farm owners	58	11	26	5	20	22	49	9	28	46	26	74
23 Housewives[a]	—	—	—	—	—	—	—	—	—	—	—	—
24 Retired, Ind.	47	20	26	7	21	23	36	20	30	41	29	66

[a] "Housewives" as a category was omitted from the Dutch questionnaire. Apparently they were classed under the occupation of their husbands.

THE NETHERLANDS D

	QUESTION 7 Satisfaction?				Security Scores			QUESTION 8 Best opportunity?				SAMPLE
	(A) Very	(B) All right	(C) Dissat.	(D) Don't know	(A) Sec. 12-10	(B) Med. 9-5	(C) Ins. 4-0	(A) Neth.	(B) America	(C) S. Afr.	(D) Canada	
1 Total	8	54	34	4	12	46	42	31	21	8	6	942
2 Men	8	53	36	3	13	45	42	29	23	8	7	449
3 Women	8	56	32	4	11	47	42	32	19	7	5	493
4 21–29	10	55	29	6	13	49	38	39	24	5	7	246
5 30–49	8	55	35	2	13	44	43	28	22	9	6	445
6 50–65	5	54	37	4	7	46	47	32	18	10	7	187
7 Over 65	10	50	34	6	9	47	44	52	9	5	5	64
8 A-wealthy	26	50	21	3	37	42	21	40	27	8	3	62
9 B-average	12	62	24	2	19	53	28	33	24	8	5	267
10 C-below av.	6	56	34	4	9	48	43	31	18	7	5	325
11 D-very poor	3	47	45	5	2	38	60	26	20	7	10	288
12 Primary	4	53	39	4	6	44	50					553
13 Secondary	13	58	26	3	18	50	32					360
14 University	27	52	14	7	45	38	17					29
15 Profess.	27	46	22	5								41
16 Bus. owners	29	41	26	4								27
17 Ind. workers	8	52	37	3								107
18 Sal.-mangrs.	15	70	15	—								47
19 Clerks	8	64	23	5								235
20 Man. wkrs.	3	50	43	4								239
21 Farm wkrs.	8	48	41	3								106
22 Farm owners	7	57	34	2								74
23 Housewives[a]	—	—	—	8								—
24 Retired, Ind.	6	47	39	8								66

THE NETHERLANDS D continued

	Satisfaction?				Security Scores			Best opportunity?				Sample
	(A)	(B)	(C)	(D)	(A)	(B)	(C)	(A)	(B)	(C)	(D)	
	Very	All right	Dissat.	Don't know	Sec. 12–10	Med. 9–5	Ins. 4–0	Neth.	America	S. Afr.	Canada	
25 Upper class					30	32	5				3	37
26 Middle class					24	34	8				5	308
27 Working class					19	29	8				8	560
28 Don't know					22	30	5				—	37
29 Leftist (tr)					14	19	7				5	173
30 Rightist (tl)					25	35	9				8	228
31 All right					24	35	7				6	356
32 Don't know					15	29	8				6	185

Totals (Q.8)	%
Netherlands	31
America	21
South Africa	8
Canada	6
South America	3
Russia	2
Netherlands Indies	2
Belgium	1
All other European countries	5
All other countries	4
Nowhere	3
Don't know	17
	103[b]

a See note a, Table C above.

b Some respondents gave more than one answer.

THE NETHERLANDS E

	QUESTION 9 Social class?				QUESTION 10a Own class abroad?			QUESTION 10b Others at home?			SAMPLE
	(A) Middle	(B) Working	(C) Upper	(D) Don't know	(A) Yes	(B) No	(C) Don't know	(A) Yes	(B) No	(C) Don't know	
1 Total	33	60	4	3	61	13	26	56	23	21	942
2 Men	33	60	4	3	66	13	21	57	25	18	449
3 Women	32	60	4	4	58	12	30	54	21	25	493
4 21–29	29	64	2	5	61	13	26	54	27	19	246
5 30–49	34	59	4	3	64	12	24	58	21	21	445
6 50–65	34	58	5	3	59	13	28	53	23	24	187
7 Over 65	34	53	5	8	59	13	28	53	20	27	64
8 A–wealthy	40	5	53	2	73	13	14	77	13	10	62
9 B–average	79	17	1	3	60	15	25	72	15	13	267
10 C–below av.	20	75	—	5	63	11	26	52	25	23	325
11 D–very poor	3	92	1	4	59	11	30	39	31	30	288
12 Primary	17	78	1	4	59	11	30	46	28	26	553
13 Secondary	56	35	5	4	65	14	21	69	16	15	360
14 University	41	4	48	7	69	14	17	79	14	7	29

THE NETHERLANDS E continued

		Social class?			Own class abroad?			Others at home?			Sample
		(A) Mid- dle	(B) Work- ing	(C) Up- per	(D) Don't know	(A) Yes	(B) No	(C) Don't know	(A) Yes	(B) No	(C) Don't know	
15	Profess.	56	10	34	—	73	17	10	86	7	7	41
16	Bus. owners	59	4	33	4	63	22	15	89	4	7	27
17	Ind. workers	56	39	1	4	65	15	20	62	24	14	107
18	Sal.-mangrs.	72	15	13	—	68	15	17	85	9	6	47
19	Clerks	47	48	1	4	58	13	29	62	19	19	235
20	Man. wkrs.	4	93	—	3	66	9	25	42	32	26	239
21	Farm wkrs.	11	84	—	5	48	16	36	31	30	39	106
22	Farm owners	23	71	3	3	65	9	26	55	23	22	74
23	Housewives[a]	—	—	—	—	—	—	—	—	—	—	—
24	Retired, Ind.	39	45	5	11	56	12	32	58	18	24	66
25	Upper class					76	11	13	81	14	5	37
26	Middle class					61	15	24	73	14	13	308
27	Working class					62	12	26	45	30	25	560
28	Don't know					32	11	57	41	8	51	37
33	Sec. (12–10)	60	24	13	3							111
34	Med. (9–5)	35	56	4	5							432
35	Insec. (4–0)	22	73	2	3							399

	QUESTION 10c More in common?				SAMPLE
	(A) Abroad	(B) Dutch	(C) Don't know	(D) Not asked	
Total	9	24	12	55	942

[a] See note a, Table C above.

THE NETHERLANDS F

		QUESTION 11 Most friendly?				QUESTION 12 Least friendly?		SAMPLE
		(A) Amer.	(B) Brit.	(C) Belg.	(D) Can.	(A) Russ.	(B) Ger.	
1	Total	28	12	11	9	39	36	942
2	Men	28	10	12	9	40	35	449
3	Women	27	13	10	8	38	37	493
4	21–29	30	11	6	11	45	30	246
5	30–49	28	13	13	7	39	38	445
6	50–65	29	11	12	9	36	37	187
7	Over 65	13	8	13	13	34	39	64
8	A–wealthy	31	18	11	3	55	27	62
9	B–average	32	10	12	8	45	34	267
10	C–below av.	27	14	10	9	36	39	325
11	D–very poor	24	9	10	10	35	38	288
25	Upper class	38	11	11	3	54	22	37
26	Middle class	31	12	13	6	45	32	308
27	Working class	25	11	10	11	35	40	560
28	Don't know	33	16	8	8	38	33	37

THE NETHERLANDS F continued

	Most friendly?				Least friendly?		Sample
	(A) Amer.	(B) Brit.	(C) Belg.	(D) Can.	(A) Russ.	(B) Ger.	
29 Leftist (tr)	19	12	9	6	27	38	173
30 Rightist (tl)	37	11	9	11	50	40	228
31 All right	29	13	15	9	46	33	356
32 Don't know	21	10	7	8	24	36	185

Totals (Q.11)	%	*Totals* (Q.12)	%
Americans	28	Russians	39
British	12	Germans	36
Belgians	11	British	4
Canadians	9	Americans	2
Scandinavians	6	Japanese	2
French	4	Jews (Israel)	—
Russians	3	Spanish	—
Germans	2	Other E. Europeans	1
Other W. Europeans	4	Other W. Europeans	1
Other E. Europeans	—	Others	1
Others	4	No people	1
Don't know	22	Don't know	16
	105[a]		105[a]

[a] Some respondents gave more than one answer.

THE NETHERLANDS G[a]

	QUESTION 14 Present government?				SAMPLE
	(A) Too right	(B) Too left	(C) All right	(D) Don't know	
1 Total	18	24	38	20	942
2 Men	23	24	40	13	449
3 Women	14	24	36	26	493
4 21–29	21	21	37	21	246
5 30–49	19	26	35	20	445
6 50–65	14	23	44	19	187
7 Over 65	13	31	42	14	64
8 A–wealthy	8	45	31	16	62
9 B–average	13	32	41	14	267
10 C–below av.	19	21	40	20	325
11 D–very poor	25	15	34	26	288
12 Primary	19	20	39	22	553
13 Secondary	17	30	36	17	360
14 University	17	28	45	10	29

[a] Results of Q.13 are tabulated on p. 47.

NORWAY

A. Copy of Questionnaire Used in Norway

NORSK GALLUP INSTITUTT A/S   AKERSGT, 49 III OSLO   2/4/48

1a Tror De at menneskenaturen kan forandres?   1 Kan forandres
   2 Kan ikke forandres   x Vet ikke

1b (Hvis kan forandres — spm. 1a) Tror De det er sannsynlig at
   den kommer til å forandres?   1 Sannsynlig   2 Usannsynlig
   x Vet ikke

2 Mener De at våre norske karakteregenskaper for størstedelen er
   medfødt, eller skyldes de den oppdragelse vi får?   1 Medfødt
   2 Skyldes oppdragelse   x Vet ikke

3a Mener De det er mulig at alle land vil kunne leve sammen i
   fred?   1 Mulig   2 Umulig   x Vet ikke

3b Anser De det for sannsynlig at alle land kommer til å leve
   sammen i fred?   1 Sannsynlig   2 Usannsynlig   x Vet ikke

4 Enkelte mennesker hevder at det burde finnes en verdensregje-
   ring som kunne kontrollere de enkelte lands lover. Er De enig
   eller uenig i dette?   1 Enig   2 Uenig   x Vet ikke

5 Da krigen sluttet, ventet De at De skulle få bedre, dårligere
   eller omtrent de samme kår som De har nå?   3 Bedre
   0 Dårligere   2 Omtrent samme som nå   1 Vet ikke

6a Når De tar i betraktning Deres stilling (hvis gift kvinne — Deres
   manns stilling), føler De Dem mer eller mindre trygg enn
   gjennomsnittet her i Norge?   3 Mer trygg   0 Mindre trygg
   2 Omtrent som gjennomsnittet   1 Vet ikke

6b Føler De Dem stort sett trygg nok til å kunne legge planer for
   framtiden?   3 Ja   0 Nei   1 Vet ikke

7 Hvor tilfreds er De med den måten De klarer Dem på nå?
   3 Meget tilfreds   2 Noenlunne (ganske) tilfreds   0 Utilfreds
   1 Vet ikke

8 Hvilket land i verden gir best muligheter for å føre denslags
   liv som De helst ville føre?
   ....
   (Til intervjueren: Dette spørsmålet omfatter Norge, i tilfelle den
   intervjuede spør om det.)

9 Hvis man ba Dem om å benytte et navn for Deres sosiale
   klasse, ville De a si at De tilhørte middelstanden, arbeiderklassen eller den høyere sosiale klasse?   1 Middelstanden
   2 Arbeiderklassen   3 Høyere sosiale klasse

10a Føler De at De har noe til felles med folk av ...... i utlandet?
   1 Ja   2 Nei   x Vet ikke
   (Til intervjueren: Tilføy på den prikkede linje den sosiale klasse
   vedk. nevnte på spm. 9. Svares vet ikke, si: "Deres sosiale
   klasse")

10b Føler De at De har noe til felles med nordmenn som ikke
   tilhører...........?   1 Ja   2 Nei   x Vet ikke
   (Til intervjueren: Tilføy på den prikkede linje den sosiale klasse
   vedk. nevnte på spm. 9. Svares vet ikke, si: "Deres sosiale
   klasse")

10c (Stilles bare hvis vedk. enten har svart ja både på spm. 10a og
   10b, eller nei både på 10a og 10b)
   Hvilken av disse to grupper vil De si at De har mest til felles
   med, ... i utlandet og andre klasser enn i
   Norge?   1 Utlendinger i ....   2 Nordmenn som ikke
   tilhører ....   x Vet ikke
   (Til intervjueren: Tilføy på de prikkede linjer den sosiale klasse
   vedk. nevnte på spm. 9. Svares vet ikke, si: "Deres sosiale
   klasse")

11 Hvilket fremmed folk nærer De de vennligste følelser overfor?

12 Hvilket fremmed folk nærer De de minst vennlige følelser
   overfor?

13a (Vis kort) Hvilke ord på denne listen synes De best beskriver
   det amerikanske folk? Nevn så mange av ordene som De synes
   passer. Hvis De ikke har noen særlige følelser hverken i den
   ene eller den annen retning, bare si det.

13b Gå gjennom listen igjen og velg ut de ordene som De synes
   best beskriver det russiske folk.

13c Velg så ut de ordene som best beskriver det norske folk.

	AMER	RUSS	NORS
Arbeidsomme	A+	A+	A+
Intelligente	B+	B+	B+
Praktiske	C+	C+	C+
Innbilske	D÷	D÷	D÷
Gavmilde	E÷	E÷	E÷
Grusomme	F÷	F÷	F÷
De står tilbake	G÷	G÷	G÷
Tapre	H+	H+	H+
De viser selvbeherskelse	I+	I+	I+
Herskesyke	J÷	J÷	J÷
Framskrittsvennlige	K+	K+	K+
Fredselskende	L+	L+	L+
Kan ikke karakterisere	M	M	M

14 Synes De at vår nåværende regjering er for konservativ, for
   radikal eller omtrent slik som De ønsker den?   1 For konservativ   2 For radikal   3 Som ønsket   x Vet ikke

15 1 Mann   2 Kvinne

16 Hvor gammel var De siste fødselsdag?
   ....år
   (Til intervjueren: Hvis vedk. nekter å
   svare, anslå alderen og sett "anslags-
   vis" ved svaret)

17a Deres nøyaktige yrke? (livsstilling)

17b Bedriftens art:

17c Er De gift?   1 Gift   2 Ugift   3 Enke,
   enkemann (fraskilt, separert)

17d (Hvis gift) Ektefellens nøyaktige Yrke:

17e Bedriftens art: ....

17f (Hvis ugift) Forsørger De Dem selv eller
   blir De forsørget?   1 Selvforsørgende
   2 Blir forsørget

17g (Hvis forsørget) Forsørgerens yrke?

17h Bedriftens art:

17i Arbeider husstandens hovedperson for
   egen regning eller er han (hun) ansatt
   i annens tjeneste?   1 Egen regning
   2 Annens tjeneste

17j (Hvis egen regning) Hvor mange mennesker beskjeftiger bedriften (eieren
   medregnet)?
   .... personer eieren medregnet

17k Hvor meget omtrent er Deres (Hvis gift
   — og Deres ektefelles samlede) skatt-
   bare arsinntekt? kr.
   (Til intervjueren: Hvis vedk. ikke vil
   svare, anslå inntekten og skriv "ansla-
   gsvis" ved svaret)

18a Hvor mange år har De gått på skole
   (universitet og høyskole medregnet)?
   .... år

18b Hvilke skoler har De gjennomgått?
   1 Folkeskole   2 Realskole (middelskole)
   2 Gymnas   2 Handelsskole (fagskole)
   3 Universitet, høyskole

19 1 Oslo, Bergen, Trondheim   2 Andre
   byer   3 Land

20 1 Østlandet   2 Sørlandet   3 Vestlandet
   4 Trøndelag   5 Nord-Norge
   Intervjuedes navn:

   Intervjuedes nøyaktige adresse:

   Intervjuer: ....

   Dato: ....

C. Excerpts from Notes and Comments by Survey Agency

Sixty interviewers were employed in the survey. The whole of Norway was covered except Finmark, which is the northernmost county. (Less than 2% of the total population.) In this county interviewing has not yet been organized because conditions are still far from normal after the war. Strict quota-sampling was used in the survey.

Occupation of Respondents (by industry)

Agriculture, forestry, gardening	310
Fishery, whaling	71
Industry, handicraft	281
Trade, banking, insurance	105
Transport, telephone, telegraph, mail	102
Free professions, public service	57
Property, pension, relief	90
Domestic servants	14

Residence of Respondents

Eastern Norway	490
Southern Norway	61
Western Norway	254
Trendelag	109
Northern Norway (less Finmark)	115

Primary education (7 years) is compulsory for all Norwegian children between seven and fourteen. The number in the sample (568) is the total who have this education only.

On Q.9 only 1% say they belong in the upper class, a finding which is certainly due to the fact that there is no very distinct upper class in Norway. About 7% of the respondents are "well-to-do" according to the Gallup classification. 12% of these themselves even say they belong in the working class. Part of the explanation may be that they vote with the "Labor Party." Some people of other parties also dislike that the Social Democrats apply the name "Labor Party," maintaining that they all "work." The two labor parties had just under 50% of the total vote at the last election. In the "very poor" group 31% term themselves "middle" class. They are independent fishermen, small farmers, apprentices, pensioners, etc., with very low incomes, but who will not say they are "workmen." On the other hand, many of the manual workers term themselves "middle" class, no doubt because their incomes are comparatively high at present. Thus it may safely be said that class distinctions are not very definite in Norway now.

D. Notes and Comments by the Editors

Sample on Q.1b is the number of respondents who answered "Can" on Q.1a. Percentages in cols. (A), (B), and (C) total the percentage of all respondents replying "Can" to Q.1a.

The original figures from the survey on Q.2 totaled more than 100% because those who said "Both" were included in both the first two categories.

Since the Norwegian survey was the only one in which this practice was followed, the figures were adjusted as follows: The excess over 100% was subtracted from each category to give the figures in cols. (A) and (B), then added to the "Don't know's" to give the figures in col. (C).

E. Tables

NORWAY A

	QUESTION 1a Change human nature? (A) Can	(B) Cannot	(C) Don't know	QUESTION 1b (If *Can*) Likely?[a] (A) Likely	(B) Unlikely	(C) Don't know	(D) (Sample)	QUESTION 2 National character?[b] (A) Born in us	(B) Way brought up	(C) Don't know	SAMPLE
1 Total	56	31	13	41	9	6	(573)	23	57	20	1,030
2 Men	56	34	10	43	8	5	(277)	24	62	14	497
3 Women	56	28	16	40	9	7	(296)	23	54	23	533
4 21–29	50	33	17	37	9	4	(141)	18	62	20	282
5 30–49	59	31	10	43	9	7	(237)	28	57	15	403
6 50–65	57	31	12	44	8	5	(120)	21	59	20	209
7 Over 65	55	27	18	43	10	2	(75)	26	49	25	136
8 A–wealthy	57	39	4	46	6	5	(39)	25	66	9	69
9 B–average	58	32	10	41	12	5	(87)	23	60	17	150
10 C–below av.	57	30	13	43	9	5	(323)	24	58	18	568
11 D–very poor	51	30	19	37	7	7	(124)	21	52	27	243
12 Primary	54	28	18	42	7	5	(307)	25	51	24	568
13 Secondary	57	34	9	40	11	6	(250)	22	64	14	436
14 University	62	38	—	46	8	8	(16)	31	43	26	26
29 Leftist (tr)[c]	60	30	10					14	69	17	131
30 Rightist (tl)[d]	54	38	8					27	61	12	240
31 All right	53	32	15					29	53	18	274
32 Don't know	57	25	18					21	54	25	385
25 Upper class								11	67	22	9
26 Middle class								25	61	14	445
27 Working class								22	58	20	465
28 Don't know								23	38	39	111
36 Can (Q.1a)								21	63	16	573
37 Cannot								30	56	14	317
38 Don't know								22	37	41	140
39 Possible (Q.3a)								20	63	17	444
40 Impossible								25	51	24	538
41 Don't know								17	64	19	48
45 Agree (Q.4)								27	64	9	493
46 Disagree								27	59	14	360
47 Don't know								20	48	32	177

a Sample on Q.1b is the number of respondents who answered "Can" on Q.1a. Percentages in cols. (A), (B), and (C) total the percentage of all respondents replying "Can" to Q.1a.

b The original figures from the survey on Q.2 totaled more than 100% because those who said "Both" were included in both the first two categories. Since the Norwegian survey was the only one in which this practice was followed, the figures were adjusted as follows: The excess over 100% was subtracted from each category to give the figures in cols. (A) and (B), then added to the "Don't know's" to give the figures in col. (C).

c "tr" = too right.

d "tl" = too left.

NORWAY B

	QUESTION 3a Live in peace?			QUESTION 3b (If *Possible*) Likely?			QUESTION 4 World government?			SAMPLE
	(A) Pos-sible	(B) Not pos-sible	(C) Don't know	(A) Like-ly	(B) Un-likely	(C) Don't know	(A) Agree	(B) Dis-agree	(C) Don't know	
1 Total	43	52	5	12	82	6	48	35	17	1,030
2 Men	44	53	3	13	84	3	58	31	11	497
3 Women	42	52	6	11	81	8	38	38	24	533
4 21–29	37	57	6	8	85	7	50	30	20	282
5 30–49	45	50	5	14	81	5	47	37	16	403
6 50–65	49	48	3	12	83	5	46	35	19	209
7 Over 65	41	54	5	13	80	7	49	37	14	136
8 A–wealthy	51	43	6	12	84	4	62	30	8	69
9 B–average	45	53	2	13	85	2	51	39	10	150
10 C–below av.	44	53	3	11	83	6	48	35	17	568
11 D–very poor	39	53	8	13	76	11	40	33	27	243
12 Primary	44	51	5	13	79	8	42	36	22	568
13 Secondary	43	53	4	10	86	4	54	33	13	436
14 University	31	69	—	8	92	—	65	31	4	26
29 Leftist (tr)	44	51	5				57	37	6	131
30 Rightist (tl)	43	53	4				49	44	7	240
31 All right	46	50	4				56	28	16	274
32 Don't know	41	54	5				38	34	28	385
33 Sec. (12–10)	46	53	1				46	43	11	123
34 Medium (9–5)	41	54	5				48	33	19	632
35 Insec. (4–0)	46	48	6				47	35	18	275
36 Can (Q.1a)	47	49	4	14	80	6	47	37	16	573
37 Can't change	37	60	3	9	88	3	50	35	15	317
38 Don't know	42	51	7	9	81	10	46	24	30	140
42 Likely (Q.3b)	88	1	11							122
43 Unlikely	36	62	2							849
44 Don't know	54	8	38							59
45 Agree (Q.4)	48	48	4							493
46 Disagree	39	58	3							360
47 Don't know	37	52	11							177
39 Possible (Q.3a)							53	32	15	444
40 Impossible							44	39	17	538
41 Don't know							38	21	41	48

NORWAY C

	QUESTION 5 Postwar expectation?				QUESTION 6a Job security?				QUESTION 6b Able to plan?			SAMPLE
	(A) Better	(B) Worse	(C) About same	(D) Don't know	(A) More	(B) Less	(C) About same	(D) Don't know	(A) Yes	(B) No	(C) Don't know	
1 Total	53	14	30	3	22	15	48	15	47	38	15	1,030
2 Men	45	17	36	2	23	16	47	14	53	35	12	497
3 Women	60	11	25	4	21	14	49	16	41	40	19	533
4 21–29	54	11	32	3	20	13	50	17	57	32	11	282
5 30–49	52	13	32	3	24	17	45	14	47	39	14	403
6 50–65	57	16	25	2	23	15	49	13	42	39	19	209
7 Over 65	45	21	29	5	18	13	51	18	30	43	27	136
8 A–wealthy	57	10	30	3	28	17	49	6	45	41	14	69
9 B–average	49	16	35	—	32	16	42	10	57	35	8	150
10 C–below av.	48	15	32	5	22	14	47	17	49	40	11	568
11 D–very poor	62	11	23	4	12	15	54	19	35	33	32	243
12 Primary	55	13	29	3	18	16	50	16	37	42	21	568
13 Secondary	51	15	31	3	25	14	46	15	57	33	10	436
14 University	27	23	50	—	46	15	31	8	77	15	8	26
15 Profess.	28	30	40	2	24	12	56	8	68	28	4	50
16 Bus. owners	39	7	46	8	4	18	68	10	39	46	15	28
17 Ind. workers	58	22	16	4	14	28	38	20	38	50	12	50
18 Sal.-mangrs.	48	8	40	4	48	16	12	24	68	28	4	25
19 Clerks	58	12	27	3	21	14	50	15	52	32	16	211
20 Man. wkrs.	52	13	34	1	29	18	45	8	47	38	15	184
21 Farm wkrs.	57	15	27	1	9	11	62	18	45	28	27	82
22 Farm owners	36	20	40	4	18	11	53	18	55	35	10	96
23 Housewives	61	9	27	3	23	15	45	17	39	45	16	264
24 Retired, Ind.	45	20	30	5	25	10	53	12	28	40	32	40

NORWAY D

	QUESTION 7 Satisfaction?				Security Scores			QUESTION 8 Best opportunity?		SAMPLE
	(A) Very	(B) All right	(C) Dis-sat.	(D) Don't know	(A) Sec. 12–10	(B) Med. 9–5	(C) Ins. 4–0	(A) Nor-way	(B) U.S.A.	
1 Total	21	67	10	2	12	62	26	50	21	1,030
2 Men	19	68	12	1	15	63	22	47	23	497
3 Women	23	65	8	4	9	61	30	53	19	533
4 21–29	18	68	12	2	11	65	24	48	18	282
5 30–49	20	66	12	2	13	58	29	48	23	403
6 50–65	26	65	6	3	12	62	26	54	22	209
7 Over 65	22	71	7	—	11	63	26	59	17	136
8 A–wealthy	49	41	10	—	18	58	24	49	33	69
9 B–average	31	60	7	2	20	62	18	57	21	150
10 C–below av.	19	71	8	2	11	63	26	52	19	568
11 D–very poor	12	67	16	5	7	58	35	43	21	243
12 Primary	16	70	12	2	9	60	31	52	18	568
13 Secondary	28	63	7	2	15	63	22	48	25	436
14 University	27	65	8	—	35	58	7	54	23	26

NORWAY D continued

		Satisfaction?				Security Scores			Best opportunity?		Sample
		(A) Very	(B) All right	(C) Dis- sat.	(D) Don't know	(A) Sec. 12–10	(B) Med. 9–5	(C) Ins. 4–0	(A) Nor- way	(B) U.S.A.	
15	Profess.	34	60	2	4						50
16	Bus. owners	43	50	7	—						28
17	Ind. workers	34	52	12	2						50
18	Sal.-mangrs.	40	56	4	—						25
19	Clerks	25	62	11	2						211
20	Man. wkrs.	20	68	11	1						184
21	Farm wkrs.	5	73	22	—						82
22	Farm owners	9	79	9	3						96
23	Housewives	20	69	6	5						264
24	Retired, Ind.	20	70	10	—						40
						25 Upper class			67	33	9
						26 Middle class			52	26	445
						27 Working class			52	18	465
						28 Don't know			39	12	111
Totals (Q.8)			%			**29** Leftist (tr)			40	25	131
						30 Rightist (tl)			49	26	240
	Norway		50			**31** All right			57	19	274
	United States		21			**32** Don't know			50	18	385
	Sweden		2								
	Australia		1								
	South America		1								
	Russia		1								
	Switzerland		1								
	South Africa		1								
	Other		2								
	Don't know		21								
			101[a]								

[a] Some respondents gave more than one answer.

NORWAY E

		QUESTION 9 Social class?				QUESTION 10a Own class abroad?			QUESTION 10b Others at home?			SAMPLE
		(A) Mid- dle	(B) Work- ing	(C) Up- per	(D) Don't know	(A) Yes	(B) No	(C) Don't know	(A) Yes	(B) No	(C) Don't know	
1	Total	43	45	1	11	41	22	37	64	13	23	1,030
2	Men	40	50	—	10	50	19	31	66	14	20	497
3	Women	46	41	2	11	31	24	45	62	12	26	533
4	21–29	39	50	—	11	34	25	41	61	13	26	282
5	30–49	44	45	1	10	45	21	34	67	13	20	403
6	50–65	54	37	1	8	44	16	40	68	13	19	209
7	Over 65	34	50	1	15	35	26	39	53	13	34	136
8	A–wealthy	77	12	6	5	41	22	37	75	12	13	69
9	B–average	64	25	2	9	47	24	29	77	9	14	150
10	C–below av.	39	52	—	9	43	21	36	63	12	25	568
11	D–very poor	31	52	—	17	30	22	48	54	17	29	243
12	Primary	33	55	—	12	33	26	41	56	16	28	568
13	Secondary	55	34	1	10	49	17	34	74	9	17	436
14	University	65	12	8	15	58	8	34	81	4	15	26

NORWAY E continued

	Social class?				Own class abroad?			Others at home?			Sample
	(A) Mid-dle	(B) Work-ing	(C) Up-per	(D) Don't know	(A) Yes	(B) No	(C) Don't know	(A) Yes	(B) No	(C) Don't know	
15 Profess.	56	24	8	12	52	24	24	76	6	18	50
16 Bus. owners	75	18	—	7	25	29	46	75	11	14	28
17 Ind. workers	50	32	4	14	36	28	36	64	16	20	50
18 Sal.-mangrs.	84	12	—	4	68	8	24	96	4	—	25
19 Clerks	44	44	—	12	38	19	43	67	13	20	211
20 Man. wkrs.	27	67	—	6	58	17	25	60	17	23	184
21 Farm wkrs.	23	62	—	15	35	22	43	55	13	32	82
22 Farm owners	47	43	2	8	49	18	33	63	16	21	96
23 Housewives	50	40	—	10	30	26	44	64	11	25	264
24 Retired, Ind.	35	40	—	25	23	33	44	48	10	42	40
25 Upper class					56	44	—	89	11	—	9
26 Middle class					47	19	34	72	13	15	445
27 Working class					42	27	31	66	15	19	465
28 Don't know					7	9	84	19	4	77	111
33 Sec. (12–10)	51	32	4	13							123
34 Med. (9–5)	45	44	—	11							632
35 Insec. (4–0)	35	54	—	11							275

	QUESTION 10c More in common?				SAMPLE
	(A) Abroad	(B) Norway	(C) Don't know	(D) Not asked	
Total	7	22	11	60	1,030

NORWAY F

	QUESTION 11 Most friendly?				QUESTION 12 Least friendly?		SAMPLE
	(A) Amer.	(B) Dan.	(C) Swed.	(D) Brit.	(A) Russ.	(B) Ger.	
1 Total	22	20	12	12	28	22	1,030
2 Men	22	21	10	14	27	20	497
3 Women	22	19	14	10	28	25	533
4 21–29	19	24	15	11	28	25	282
5 30–49	22	21	12	9	30	21	403
6 50–65	22	17	9	18	27	19	209
7 Over 65	24	13	12	13	24	18	136
8 A–wealthy	23	30	1	28	33	17	69
9 B–average	19	30	8	9	33	21	150
10 C–below av.	32	18	13	13	25	23	568
11 D–very poor	22	15	15	10	29	20	243
25 Upper class	—	22	11	33	56	22	9
26 Middle class	22	26	11	15	33	18	445
27 Working class	21	16	13	9	23	24	465
28 Don't know	22	13	14	10	27	21	111
29 Leftist (tr)	27	16	11	5	26	24	131
30 Rightist (tl)	25	22	14	16	47	20	240
31 All right	19	22	10	13	19	26	274
32 Don't know	19	19	13	11	23	18	385

NORWAY F continued

Totals (Q.11)	%	Totals (Q.12)	%
Americans	22	Russians	28
Danish	20	Germans	22
Swedish	12	Swedish	2
British	12	British	1
Finns	2	Americans	1
Russians	2	Japanese	1
Icelanders	1	Spanish	1
Germans	1	Italians	1
Others	6	Others	4
None, none in particular	7	None, none in particular	13
Don't know	19	Don't know	29
	——		——
	103[a]		103[a]

[a] Some respondents gave more than one answer.

NORWAY G[a]

	QUESTION 14 Present government?				SAMPLE
	(A) Too right	(B) Too left	(C) All right	(D) Don't know	
1 Total	13	23	27	37	1,030
2 Men	15	25	35	25	497
3 Women	10	22	19	49	533
4 21–29	19	16	26	39	282
5 30–49	12	25	27	36	403
6 50–65	10	30	24	36	209
7 Over 65	7	23	32	38	136
8 A–wealthy	9	45	13	33	69
9 B–average	9	42	24	25	150
10 C–below av.	15	17	32	36	568
11 D–very poor	11	20	21	48	243
12 Primary	14	17	26	43	568
13 Secondary	12	31	26	31	436
14 University	—	31	54	15	26

[a] Results of Q.13 are tabulated on p. 47.

UNITED STATES

A. Copy of Questionnaire Used in the United States of America

OPINION SURVEY

Benson & Benson
B-222 9-21-48

1a. Do you believe that human nature can be changed?
☐ Yes, Can   ☐ No, Cannot   ☐ Don't Know
IF YES, ask b:
b. Do you think this is likely to happen?
☐ Yes, Likely   ☐ No, Unlikely   ☐ Don't Know

2. Do you think that our American characteristics are mainly born in us, or are they due to the way we are brought up?
☐ Born In Us   ☐ Way Brought Up   ☐ Don't Know

3a. Do you believe it will be possible for all countries to live together at peace with each other?
☐ Yes, Possible   ☐ No, Not Possible   ☐ Don't Know
b. Do you think that this is likely to happen?
☐ Yes, Likely   ☐ No, Unlikely   ☐ Don't Know

4. Some people say that there should be a world government able to control the laws made by each country. Do you agree or disagree?
☐ Agree   ☐ Disagree   ☐ Don't Know

5. When the war ended, did you expect you would be getting along better, worse or about the same, as you actually are getting along at the present time?
³☐ Better   ⁰☐ Worse   ²☐ About Same   ¹☐ Don't Know

6a. Do you feel that from the point of view of your (husband's) job you are more secure, or less secure, than the average American?
³☐ More   ⁰☐ Less   ²☐ About Same   ¹☐ Don't Know
b. In general do you feel that you are sufficiently secure to be able to plan ahead?
³☐ Yes   ⁰☐ No   ¹☐ Don't Know

7. How satisfied are you with the way you are getting on now?
³☐ Very   ²☐ All Right   ⁰☐ Dissatisfied   ¹☐ Don't Know

8. Which country in the world gives the best chance of leading the kind of life you would like to lead?......................
....
INTERVIEWER: This question includes respondent's own country.

9. If you were asked to use a name for your social class, would you say you belonged in the middle class, working class, or upper class?
☐ Middle   ☐ Working   ☐ Upper   ☐ Don't Know

10a. Do you feel that you have anything in common with your class of people abroad?
☐ Yes   ☐ No   ☐ Don't Know
b. Do you feel that you have anything in common with American people who are not of your class?
☐ Yes   ☐ No   ☐ Don't Know
INTERVIEWER: If respondent has answered YES to BOTH 10a and 10b, or NO to BOTH 10a and 10b, ask c; otherwise skip to 11.
c. Which of these two would you say that you have more in common with?
☐ Own Class Abroad
☐ Americans, Not of Own Class   ☐ Don't Know

11. Which foreign people do you feel most friendly toward?
....

12. Which foreign people do you feel least friendly toward?
....

(HAND RESPONDENT CARD)
13a. From the list of words on this card, which seem to you to describe the British people best? Select as many as you wish and

call off the letters and the words that go with them. If you have no particular feelings one way or the other, just say so.
INTERVIEWER: Record answers below in column headed "BRITISH," then ask 13b.
b. Now go over the list again and select the words you think best describe the Russian people.
INTERVIEWER: Record answers below in column headed "RUSSIAN," then ask 13c.
c. Now select the words that best describe Americans.
INTERVIEWER: Record answers below in column headed "AMERICAN."

	13a. BRITISH	13b. RUSSIAN	13c. AMERICAN
A. HARDWORKING	¹☐	¹☐	¹☐
B. INTELLIGENT	²☐	²☐	²☐
C. PRACTICAL	³☐	³☐	³☐
D. CONCEITED	⁴☐	⁴☐	⁴☐
E. GENEROUS	⁵☐	⁵☐	⁵☐
F. CRUEL	⁶☐	⁶☐	⁶☐
G. BACKWARD	⁷☐	⁷☐	⁷☐
H. BRAVE	⁸☐	⁸☐	⁸☐
I. SELF-CONTROLLED	⁹☐	⁹☐	⁹☐
J. DOMINEERING	⁰☐	⁰☐	⁰☐
K. PROGRESSIVE	ˣ☐	ˣ☐	ˣ☐
L. PEACE-LOVING	ʸ☐	ʸ☐	ʸ☐
NO PARTICULAR FEELINGS	☐	☐	☐

14. Do you think our present Government is too much to the right, too much to the left, or about where you would like it to be?
☐ Too Right   ☐ Too Left   ☐ All Right   ☐ Don't Know

And now, just a few questions to help me keep track of the cross section I'm getting:
15. What is your age?.....................

16a. Is there a telephone in your home?
☐ Yes   ☐ No
IF YES, ask:
b. Is the telephone listed either under your name or the name of a member of your immediate family?
☐ Yes   ☐ No

17. What is the last grade or class you completed in school?
¹☐ No schooling
²☐ Grammar school (grades 1 through 6)
³☐ Grammar school (7th or 8th grade)
⁴☐ High school, incomplete (9th, 10th or 11th grade)
⁵☐ High school, graduated (12th grade)
⁶☐ College, incomplete
⁷☐ College, graduated
What type of College?.................

18a. Are you employed, looking for work, retired, a student, or a housewife?
☐ Employed (ask b and c)   ☐ Looking for work (ask b and c)
b. What is your occupation? (Record SPECIFIC occupation, do NOT write in type of industry or name of company worked for)
....
c. Do you have your own business, or do you work for someone else?
☐ Own Business   ☐ Work for Someone Else
☐ Retired (ask d and e)   ☐ Student (ask d and e)
☐ Housewife (ask d and e)
d. What is the occupation of the head of the house (or the former occupation if the head of the house is retired)?
....
e. Is the head of your house in business for himself, or does he work for someone.else?
☐ Own Business   ☐ Work for Someone Else

ASK ONLY IF RESPONDENT OR HEAD OF THE HOUSE OWNS A STORE:
18f. Would you say your store is a large, medium, or small store?   ☐ Large   ☐ Medium   ☐ Small

PLEASE COMPLETE ALL VITAL INFORMATION BEFORE LEAVING RESPONDENT

Classify Respondent as:	Check for farmer interview ONLY:	Check whether:
¹☐ W ³☐ AV ⁵☐ OAA	☐ Farm Resident Interviewed { ☐ On Farm ☐ In Town }	¹☐ Man ¹☐ Wh
²☐ AV* ⁴☐ P ⁶☐ OR		²☐ Woman ²☐ CI

STREET................   CITY...........   INTERVIEWER.............   DATE OF INTERVIEW.......

C. Excerpts from Notes and Comments by Survey Agency

Interviewing was done by eighty-nine field interviewers during the last week in September and the first week in October, 1948.

The sample was a political cross section balanced for city-size, sex, age, education, occupation, and race. No area of the country was excluded from the survey. Interviews were obtained in the following areas in correct proportion to their voting populations:

New England (Me., Vt., N.H., Mass., Conn., R.I.)
Middle Atlantic (N.Y., Pa., N.J., Del., Md., W.Va.)
East North Central (Ohio, Ind., Ill., Mich.)
West North Central (N.D., S.D., Minn., Wis., Neb., Kan., Mo., Iowa)
South (Va., Ky., Tenn., N.C., S.C., Miss., Ala., Ga., Fla., La., Ark., Okla., Texas)
Mountain (Mont., Idaho, Wyo., Col., Utah, Nev., Ariz., N.M.)
Pacific (Wash., Ore., Calif.)

Undoubtedly the wording of Q.5 resulted in some confusion which would explain seeming irregularities to be found in the table of breakdowns on this question. Respondents with less education evidently thought they were to compare their present circumstances with their *circumstances* at the end of the war, rather than with their *expectations* at the end of the war.

Almost 20% of the interviewers had some difficulty with Q.11 and 12. Despite the fact that the word "people" was used in the question, some respondents appear to have answered in terms of "government" rather than "people." This problem presented itself again with regard to Q.13b, where some respondents used adjectives descriptive of the government of the U.S.S.R., although there were indications that feelings toward the Russian people were less negative or at least less informed.

20% of the interviewers mentioned that they had had varying degrees of difficulty with Q.14. Many Americans appear to be unfamiliar with the ideas "Too left" and "Too right," or their counterparts "Liberal" and "Conservative." Therefore, possibly the "All right" and certainly the "Don't know" responses to this question are higher than might ordinarily be expected.

The sample on Q.1b is the number of respondents who answered "Can" on Q.1a. Percentages in cols. (A), (B), and (C) total the percentage of all respondents replying "Can" to Q.1a.

Since twenty-three respondents' ages were not recorded, the sample in the age breakdowns totals 992 instead of 1,015.

On Q.3b only those replying "Possible" on Q.3a were tabulated. These percentages are not comparable with other surveys. Sample (col. D) is number of respondents who replied "Possible" to Q.3a.

Since seven respondents' occupations were not recorded, the samples in these breakdowns total 1,008 instead of 1,015.

E. Tables

UNITED STATES OF AMERICA A

	QUESTION 1a Change human nature?			QUESTION 1b (If *Can*) Likely?[a]				QUESTION 2 National character?			SAMPLE
	(A) Can	(B) Cannot	(C) Don't know	(A) Likely	(B) Unlikely	(C) Don't know	(D) (Sample)	(A) Born in us	(B) Way brought up	(C) Don't know	
1 Total	50	40	10	27	19	4	(508)	15	79	6	1,015
2 Men	50	41	9	25	21	4	(261)	15	80	5	517
3 Women	50	38	12	28	16	6	(247)	14	79	7	498
4 21–29	51	39	10	27	21	3	(112)	12	86	2	220
5 30–49	47	42	11	24	18	5	(190)	12	82	6	403
6 50–65	53	37	10	31	15	7	(142)	21	73	6	265
7 Over 65	51	41	8	26	21	4	(53)	15	75	10	104
8 A–wealthy	54	42	4	23	27	4	(38)	15	85	—	71
9 B–average	50	40	10	25	20	5	(264)	11	83	6	527
10 C–below av.	49	41	10	27	16	6	(166)	19	74	7	337
11 D–very poor	50	35	15	32	14	4	(40)	18	71	11	80
12 Primary	47	36	17	27	13	7	(187)	22	68	10	400
13 Secondary	51	43	6	25	21	5	(226)	12	85	3	440
14 University	54	41	5	27	25	2	(95)	7	90	3	175
29 Leftist (tr)[b]	55	40	5					9	85	6	116
30 Rightist (tl)[c]	53	41	6					15	82	3	325
31 All right	49	41	10					17	78	5	374
32 Don't know	44	35	21					13	74	13	200
25 Upper class								12	88	—	42
26 Middle class								12	84	4	421
27 Working class								17	76	7	521
28 Don't know								23	48	29	31
36 Can (Q.1a)								13	84	3	508
37 Cannot								16	77	7	404
38 Don't know								18	65	17	103
39 Possible (Q.3a)								14	81	5	501
40 Impossible								15	80	5	454
41 Don't know								18	60	22	60
45 Agree (Q.4)								13	82	5	424
46 Disagree								16	80	4	473
47 Don't know								17	64	19	118

[a] The sample on Q.1b is the number of respondents who answered "Can" on Q.1a. Percentages in cols. (A), (B), and (C) total the percentage of all respondents replying "Can" to Q.1a.

[b] "tr" = too right.

[c] "tl" = too left.

UNITED STATES OF AMERICA B

	QUESTION 3a Live in peace?			QUESTION 3b (If *Possible*) Likely?ᵃ				QUESTION 4 World government?			SAMPLE
	(A) Possible	(B) Not possible	(C) Don't know	(A) Likely	(B) Unlikely	(C) Don't know	(D) (Sample)	(A) Agree	(B) Disagree	(C) Don't know	
1 Total	49	45	6	17	28	4	(501)	42	46	12	1,015
2 Men	50	45	5	17	31	2	(261)	43	49	8	517
3 Women	48	45	7	16	25	7	(240)	41	44	15	498
4 21–29	49	45	6	17	27	5	(108)	48	42	10	220
5 30–49	48	47	5	13	31	4	(192)	42	46	12	403
6 50–65	54	40	6	20	28	6	(142)	40	50	10	265
7 Over 65	46	45	9	21	21	4	(48)	34	52	14	104
8 A–wealthy	55	39	6	10	38	7	(39)	40	56	4	71
9 B–average	48	46	6	17	28	3	(254)	43	48	9	527
10 C–below av.	51	43	6	18	27	6	(171)	41	44	15	337
11 D–very poor	46	45	9	18	22	6	(37)	39	39	22	80
12 Primary	49	43	8	20	22	7	(195)	38	45	17	400
13 Secondary	47	48	5	15	29	3	(206)	42	49	9	440
14 University	57	41	2	16	37	4	(100)	50	45	5	175
29 Leftist (tr)	59	38	3					53	40	7	116
30 Rightist (tl)	45	52	3					37	56	7	325
31 All right	52	44	4					43	47	10	374
32 Don't know	47	38	15					41	34	25	200
33 Sec. (12–10)	51	46	3					48	49	3	181
34 Medium (9–5)	49	46	5					43	46	11	537
35 Insec. (4–0)	49	41	10					36	46	18	297
36 Can (Q.1a)	56	40	4					44	47	9	508
37 Can't change	42	52	6					43	48	9	404
38 Don't know	46	37	17					28	41	31	103
45 Agree (Q.4)	58	39	3								424
46 Disagree	43	52	5								473
47 Don't know	44	35	21								118
39 Possible (Q.3a)								49	41	10	501
40 Impossible								36	55	9	454
41 Don't know								22	37	41	60

ᵃOn Q.3b only those replying "Possible" on Q.3a were tabulated. These percentages are not comparable with other surveys. Sample (col. D) is number of respondents who replied "Possible" to Q.3a.

UNITED STATES OF AMERICA C

	QUESTION 5 Postwar expectation?ᵃ				QUESTION 6a Job security?				QUESTION 6b Able to plan?			SAMPLE
	(A) Better	(B) Worse	(C) About same	(D) Don't know	(A) More	(B) Less	(C) About same	(D) Don't know	(A) Yes	(B) No	(C) Don't know	
1 Total	40	11	47	2	36	17	41	6	51	41	8	1,015
2 Men	36	13	49	2	37	15	42	6	56	39	5	517
3 Women	45	9	44	2	35	18	41	6	46	43	11	498

UNITED STATES OF AMERICA C continued

	Postwar expectation?[a]				Job security?				Able to plan?			Sample
	(A)	(B)	(C)	(D)	(A)	(B)	(C)	(D)	(A)	(B)	(C)	
	Better	Worse	About same	Don't know	More	Less	About same	Don't know	Yes	No	Don't know	
4 21–29	46	7	46	1	37	15	45	3	57	37	6	220
5 30–49	41	9	48	2	40	16	39	5	53	40	7	403
6 50–65	35	14	49	2	34	18	44	4	48	45	7	265
7 Over 65	40	15	42	3	26	21	37	16	40	45	15	104
8 A–wealthy	31	13	56	—	71	4	25	—	76	24	—	71
9 B–average	39	10	49	2	43	13	40	4	59	34	7	527
10 C–below av.	43	10	45	2	26	20	47	7	42	49	9	337
11 D–very poor	40	20	35	5	10	38	37	15	16	68	16	80
12 Primary	41	14	42	3	22	25	44	9	36	52	12	400
13 Secondary	39	9	50	2	39	14	43	4	55	39	6	440
14 University	39	8	51	2	62	6	30	2	75	22	3	175
15 Profess.	37	2	57	4	65	6	29	—	71	25	4	52
16 Bus. owners	29	20	51	—	53	13	31	3	69	29	2	55
17 Ind. workers	49	12	39	—	37	26	35	2	49	42	9	43
18 Sal.–mangrs.	38	6	53	3	47	3	47	3	78	22	—	32
19 Clerks	45	7	46	2	37	15	45	3	56	36	8	155
20 Man. wkrs.	36	12	50	2	28	18	47	7	42	53	5	170
21 Farm wkrs.	22	6	72	—	22	11	56	11	55	39	6	18
22 Farm owners	30	14	54	2	42	7	48	3	63	32	5	59
23 Housewives	44	9	45	2	36	19	39	6	47	42	11	337
24 Retired, Ind.	38	21	40	1	18	21	42	19	31	51	18	71
Students	44	6	44	6	31	19	50	—	69	31	—	16

[a] Undoubtedly the wording of Q.5 resulted in some confusion which would explain seeming irregularities to be found in the table of breakdowns on this question. Respondents with less education evidently thought they were to compare their present circumstances with their *circumstances* at the end of the war, rather than with their *expectations* at the end of the war.

UNITED STATES OF AMERICA D

	QUESTION 7 Satisfaction?				Security Scores			QUESTION 8 Best opportunity?	SAMPLE
	(A)	(B)	(C)	(D)	(A)	(B)	(C)	(A)	
	Very	All right	Dis-sat.	Don't know	Sec. 12–10	Med. 9–5	Ins. 4–0	U. S. A.	
1 Total	15	57	26	2	18	53	29	96	1,015
2 Men	18	56	25	1	21	53	26	95	517
3 Women	12	57	28	3	14	53	33	96	498
4 21–29	15	59	24	2	16	59	25	96	220
5 30–49	15	55	29	1	20	50	30	94	403
6 50–65	14	60	25	1	16	54	30	98	265
7 Over 65	22	47	28	3	15	48	37	97	104
8 A–wealthy	37	49	14	—	42	49	9	97	71
9 B–average	17	57	24	2	22	54	24	96	527
10 C–below av.	10	59	30	1	10	55	35	95	337
11 D–very poor	6	50	41	3	4	39	57	92	80
12 Primary	11	54	32	3	9	51	40		400
13 Secondary	18	58	23	1	19	56	25		440
14 University	20	59	21	—	35	49	16		175

UNITED STATES OF AMERICA D continued

		Satisfaction?				Security Scores			Best opportunity?	Sample
		(A) Very	(B) All right	(C) Dis- sat.	(D) Don't know	(A) Sec. 12–10	(B) Med. 9–5	(C) Ins. 4–0	(A) U. S. A.	
15	Profess.	23	51	26	—					52
16	Bus. owners	31	47	20	2					55
17	Ind. workers	19	51	28	2					43
18	Sal.-mangrs.	19	59	22	—					32
19	Clerks	11	61	24	4					155
20	Man. wkrs.	13	55	31	1					170
21	Farm wkrs.	17	44	39	—					18
22	Farm owners	22	66	12	—					59
23	Housewives	13	59	26	2					337
24	Retired, Ind.	14	56	28	2					71
	Students	19	50	31	—					16
25	Upper class								100	42
26	Middle class								97	421
27	Working class								95	521
28	Don't know								84	31

Totals (Q.8)	%				
		29	Leftist (tr)	93	116
		30	Rightist (tl)	97	325
United States	96	31	All right	95	374
Miscellaneous	3	32	Don't know	96	200
Don't know	1				
	—				
	100				

UNITED STATES OF AMERICA E

		QUESTION 9 Social class?				QUESTION 10a Own class abroad?			QUESTION 10b Others at home?			SAMPLE
		(A) Mid- dle	(B) Work- ing	(C) Up- per	(D) Don't know	(A) Yes	(B) No	(C) Don't know	(A) Yes	(B) No	(C) Don't know	
1	Total	42	51	4	3	42	40	18	77	15	8	1,015
2	Men	45	48	5	2	44	41	15	80	13	7	517
3	Women	38	55	3	4	40	40	20	74	17	9	498
4	21–29	39	58	2	1	51	32	17	82	13	5	220
5	30–49	41	53	3	3	40	41	19	80	12	8	403
6	50–65	41	50	6	3	42	44	14	70	21	9	265
7	Over 65	51	35	6	8	31	49	20	67	18	15	104
8	A–wealthy	55	10	35	—	62	23	15	94	4	2	71
9	B–average	53	43	2	2	48	36	16	81	12	7	527
10	C–below av.	24	73	1	2	32	49	19	73	19	8	337
11	D–very poor	28	55	1	16	26	49	25	45	34	21	80
12	Primary	24	70	1	5	31	49	20	61	25	14	400
13	Secondary	48	46	4	2	43	39	18	83	12	5	440
14	University	66	20	13	1	68	22	10	98	2	—	175

UNITED STATES OF AMERICA E continued

	Social class?				Own class abroad?			Others at home?			Sample
	(A) Mid-dle	(B) Work-ing	(C) Up-per	(D) Don't know	(A) Yes	(B) No	(C) Don't know	(A) Yes	(B) No	(C) Don't know	
15 Profess.	70	13	13	4	78	13	9	94	6	—	52
16 Bus. owners	62	27	11	—	47	36	17	87	7	6	55
17 Ind. workers	44	54	2	—	35	51	14	77	9	14	43
18 Sal.-mangrs.	59	22	19	—	50	28	22	94	3	3	32
19 Clerks	39	57	1	3	56	25	19	76	15	9	155
20 Man. wkrs.	21	78	—	1	37	48	15	75	19	6	170
21 Farm wkrs.	17	83	—	—	17	61	22	78	11	11	18
22 Farm owners	61	34	5	—	34	49	17	75	12	13	59
23 Housewives	38	54	4	4	34	46	20	75	18	7	337
24 Retired, Ind.	58	27	4	11	45	39	16	62	23	15	71
Students	50	38	6	6	81	13	6	100	—	—	16
25 Upper class					57	33	10	81	14	5	42
26 Middle class					51	35	14	87	8	5	421
27 Working class					34	47	19	70	22	8	521
28 Don't know					29	16	55	42	16	42	31
33 Sec. (12–10)	56	33	11	—							181
34 Med. (9–5)	42	53	3	2							537
35 Insec. (4–0)	31	60	2	7							297

	QUESTION 10c More in common?				SAMPLE
	(A) Abroad	(B) U. S. A.	(C) Don't know	(D) Not asked	
Total	7	32	9	52	1,015

UNITED STATES OF AMERICA F

	QUESTION 11 Most friendly?[a]				QUESTION 12 Least friendly?[a]			SAMPLE
	(A) Brit.	(B) Fr.	(C) Scand.	(D) Can.	(A) Russ.	(B) Ger.	(C) Jap.	
1 Total	31	8	6	5	51	11	11	1,015
2 Men	31	9	6	7	56	8	8	517
3 Women	31	8	5	3	45	15	14	498
4 21–29	33	8	5	4	42	14	16	220
5 30–49	30	7	6	6	56	9	9	403
6 50–65	31	9	7	5	49	15	11	265
7 Over 65	31	13	4	5	54	8	8	104
8 A–wealthy	56	3	8	6	59	13	10	71
9 B–average	31	8	7	5	53	10	10	527
10 C–below av.	26	10	4	5	47	13	12	337
11 D–very poor	27	12	3	3	46	11	9	80

UNITED STATES OF AMERICA F continued

	Most friendly?[a]				Least friendly?[a]			Sample
	(A) Brit.	(B) Fr.	(C) Scand.	(D) Can.	(A) Russ.	(B) Ger.	(C) Jap.	
25 Upper class	62	5	9	—	67	5	—	42
26 Middle class	37	9	6	4	58	11	10	421
27 Working class	26	8	5	6	45	12	13	521
28 Don't know	13	10	—	—	32	10	10	31
29 Leftist (tr)	26	16	3	6	40	8	9	116
30 Rightist (tl)	38	7	6	5	58	9	12	325
31 All right	32	7	7	5	51	14	10	374
32 Don't know	21	9	5	4	44	13	11	200

Totals (Q.11)		%	*Totals* (Q.12)		%
British		31	Russians		51
French		8	Germans		11
Scandinavians		6	Japanese		11
Canadians		5	Others		10
Germans		5	No answer		21
Italians		4			—
Others		20			104[b]
No answer		24			
		—			
		103[b]			

[a] Almost 20% of the interviewers had some difficulty with Q.11 and 12. Despite the fact that the word "people" was used in the question, some respondents appear to have answered in terms of "government" rather than "people."

[b] Some respondents gave more than one answer.

UNITED STATES OF AMERICA G[a]

	QUESTION 14 Present government?[b]				SAMPLE
	(A) Too right	(B) Too left	(C) All right	(D) Don't know	
1 Total	11	32	37	20	1,015
2 Men	13	36	37	14	517
3 Women	9	28	37	26	498
4 21–29	14	25	39	22	220
5 30–49	11	32	39	18	403
6 50–65	9	38	34	19	265
7 Over 65	16	33	31	20	104
8 A–wealthy	11	49	33	7	71
9 B–average	10	34	40	16	527
10 C–below av.	14	27	35	24	337
11 D–very poor	15	23	26	36	80
12 Primary	11	26	37	26	400
13 Secondary	10	36	37	17	440
14 University	18	34	37	11	175

[a] Results of Q.13 are tabulated on p. 47.

[b] 20% of the interviewers mentioned that they had had varying degrees of difficulty with Q.14. Many Americans appear to be unfamiliar with the ideas "Too left" and "Too right," or their counterparts "Liberal" and "Conservative." Therefore, possibly the "All right" and certainly the "Don't know" responses to this question are higher than might ordinarily be expected.

——Index